FORTY
NIGHTS

CHRIS THRALL

SERF
BOOKS

Forty Nights

Published in Great Britain by Serf Books Ltd in 2019.

www.serfbooks.com

ISBN: 978-0-9935439-2-0

Design by www.golden-rivet.co.uk

1 3 5 7 9 10 8 6 4 2

Author's note

Friends, this is a story about life and not one of regret. The journey you are about to read is part of *my* experience of substance use and addiction. Circumstances ultimately went in my favour, but they don't for everyone and a percentage of people die or suffer permanent mental or physical damage as result of recreational drug use (including alcohol) gone wrong or from long-term dependence. As such, I neither condone nor condemn the use of substances. But if you're struggling with addiction, remember you're never alone. Believe in yourself and don't forget to smile at the morning sun.

For my family

Eating Smoke

The jumbo jet stood alone on the tarmac at Kai Tak, its engines warmed and wing and tail lights flashing expectantly. Struggling off the bus, carrying my military bergen, a bag of old books, two briefcases and a guitar, I could see the strained smiles of the Virgin Atlantic flight attendants as they waited patiently to greet me. I made up my mind to tell them, the pilot *and* Richard Branson I was sorry for being late, but before doing so there was one last thing I had to do ...

I stopped halfway up the steps, turning for a final look out over the apron to see Hong Kong, scintillant and celestial in the distance. It was *my* Hong Kong, my *beautiful* Hong Kong, and I had to say goodbye before getting on the plane.

On that warm clear evening, a wave of beloved memories washed over me as I recalled the wonderful people I'd met and the extraordinary experiences we'd shared. I didn't spare a thought for any of the challenges I'd faced – the drugs, the triads, the weird cult-like conspiracy or the puppet theatre – and certainly didn't bear malice towards the beautiful people of Hong Kong, who would forever hold a special place in my heart.

I just gazed at the awe-inspiring shimmering-in-the-dark neon-highlighted sky-scraping fucking wonderment, the incredibleness of which had been my extraordinary home for thirteen months, and as I turned to walk up the last few steps, I knew I would return to the Fragrant Harbour as soon as I could.

Hello Heathrow

'**A**lright, Dad?'

My old man continued to stare right through me and scan the passengers spilling into Arrivals at London Heathrow.

'Dad, it's *me!*' I waved a hand in front of his face.

'Oh ... *Chris.*'

That look spoke volumes.

Dad's eyes flicked nervously to the guitar, a source of further disconcertion for him. Our family didn't play instruments.

After an awkward handshake, I followed him to the car park. He shoved his ticket into the payment machine, flustered and muttering something about 'effing technology' and its unsuitability for his generation. We loaded my stinking luggage and the offending guitar into the back of his Renault Laguna and left the airport in the direction of Devon.

'So what happened?' Dad asked, as the sky opened up drenching London's ugly urban sprawl.

'Well ...'

And so began one of those conversations you should never enter into with anyone – unless they're exceptionally broadminded, slightly mental or terribly bored.

It was the 24th of June 1996. I'd just landed on the Virgin Atlantic flight from Hong Kong, thirteen months since leaving the Royal Marines Commandos to run a successful business in the Orient. However, what with the drugs, the knife-wielding triads and a mysterious puppet master who operated Hong Kong with a secret set of pulleys, cables and motors, like the ghost house at a fair, my attempt at becoming the next Richard Branson hadn't *exactly* gone to plan. In fact, as my dad's credit card statement showed, Mr Branson was the only one in pocket.

Serving in the Royal Marines had been a real result, especially as

I'd signed up for a bet while living in my car. Following eight months of gruelling training to earn the coveted green beret, I'd served in the Northern Ireland Conflict, completed Arctic-warfare training, earned my parachutist's wings and sailed around the world as part of a twelve-man high-security detachment on the aircraft carrier HMS *Invincible*.

Sadly, the latter part of my seven years' service was not so glamorous or adrenaline-filled. Posted to Plymouth's Stonehouse Barracks, I found myself on endless guard duty, standing on the main gate armed with an SA80 rifle in all weathers, listening to an aging civilian security guard's plans to gloss his skirting boards at the weekend or replace the floor mats in his Sierra.

My heart told me it was time for a change of scenery, swapping life in a green suit for the anonymous grey of Civvy Street. But fellow marines would say, 'Nah, *don't* go outside, mate! There's *nothing* out there.'

I knew what they meant. Having opted for the world's toughest infantry course and role of highly trained killer, we'd passed on college, apprenticeships and Origami with Geography, making the prospect of Civvy Street's uncharted tarmac more daunting than dodging IRA bullets or playing hopscotch in a Middle Eastern minefield.

You shouldn't stay in a job because you're afraid to try something new, I'd rationalise. *There has to be a way ...*

And then that way came.

After serving my eighteen-month notice, I flew to Hong Kong to oversee the Asia-Pacific expansion of the Max *Tech* Group, a successful network-marketing operation I'd built in my spare time. However, not long after my arrival in the British colony, misfortune struck. Our parent company, Quorum International, collapsed, leaving me no choice but to walk away from three years of hard work. Before I knew it, I was homeless, addicted to crystal meth and working as a nightclub doorman for the 14K, the triad brotherhood who control Wan Chai District.

Having hocked my treasured Rolex, I rented a top-floor flat in one of Wan Chai's filthy weather-beaten tenements, only it turned out to be an anti-terrorism-training house for the Special Air Service – hence the blood splatter on the walls. I also uncovered the Foreign Triad, a secretive expat clique running 'errands' for the 14K. These sneaky misfits were partly responsible for my mock execution.

As if I didn't have enough on my plate, I happened upon a bizarre global conspiracy communicated through instructions on food packets, labels on blankets and telepathic eyes – and all this in addition to cats on strings, the old boy who slept on the stairs and a roof-dwelling psycho with a bag of dog shit nailed to his door.

Suffice to say, I experienced my fair share of trauma and ended up somewhat confused – and I don't think the drugs had helped matters. When I found myself shinning along a wire cable between two skyscrapers to see the fat lady sing, I had a wake-up call. That's where my papa and his credit card came in ...

'So I'm in the market in Wan Chai, Dad.'

My old man fixated on the road, knuckles whitening on the steering wheel.

'And I pick up a blanket and – *fuck!* – it's got this label sewn into it: *Waste.* Well, I knew what it meant, Dad, you know? It was one of those diseased blankets the North American settlers gave to the native Indians to wipe them out. But what the hell was it doing in Hong Kong? Do you know what I'm saying, Dad? I don't know if it was to do with the triads or this weird global conspiracy.'

Dad pulled into a layby somewhere around Stonehenge – although it could have been a pyramid in Egypt for all I cared because I missed Hong Kong's mad metropolis. He rummaged in the door compartment and took out a mobile phone. This was a surprise. Before leaving for the Orient, a little over a year ago, I was the only person I knew who owned such a device. Stranger still, my old man didn't exactly cope with technology.

'For my business,' he said, looking flustered.

Dad ran a small but successful carpet company in Helmstone on the edge of Dartmoor, the village we were heading for.

'Oh, right.'

He called my stepmother. 'Ellen, it's me.

'Yes, he's here now.' Dad glanced nervously to his left. 'He's lost *so* much weight I didn't even *recognise* him. And he *hasn't* stopped talking and he *isn't* making any sense.'

Huh? I felt hurt my old man was having this conversation in my presence and hadn't taken in a word I'd said in the last ... *two* hours.

As Dad checked over his shoulder before rejoining the carriageway, I noticed his hands. They'd aged so much since I last saw him, knuckles swollen, skin sallow and veiny. I wondered if this was because of me, perhaps stress from the recent phone calls. I'd spoken in hushed code as no doubt the conspirators had been listening in.

I wasn't sure if Dad was serious – about the incessant talking – so I continued to fill him in on my strange experiences, such as DJing in the biggest nightclub in Southern China and selling advertising space in a phone book that didn't exist. Before I knew it, we'd reached the Devon countryside, its lush green fields fringed by deciduous trees.

Postcards from the Edge

'Welcome home, old chap.' Dad pushed open the door of Brook Cottage.

I hadn't wanted to budge from the car.

'*Strewth!*' He manhandled my bergen up the single step. 'How do you manage to *lift* this thing?'

My old man always said this when I arrived at his place with a house on my back. The Royal Marines have a well-earned reputation for their ability to carry heavy loads over rough terrain, 'yomping', so it was his way of paying a compliment to my former career.

'Thanks, Dad,' I muttered.

I didn't mention that this *wasn't* my home – and not because I owned a house in nearby Plymouth. *Heung Gong* was my home, the 'Fragrant Harbour', to use the Pearl in the Orient's Chinese name, and just as soon as I finished the little wrap of crystal meth, or 'ice', hidden in the lining of my Caterpillar boot, I'd get a job and start saving for a flight back there.

'Listen, old chap.' Dad squeezed my shoulder. 'Take it easy for a few weeks. You've been through a lot.'

'*No!*' I was horrified. 'I'm out looking for work tomorrow, Dad. I'll be back in Hong Kong in a couple of months.'

'*Hong Kong?*' He shot me a puzzled look.

'Yeah!' I hopped up to sit on his chest freezer.

'B-b-but *why* do you want to go back there?'

For some strange reason, he appeared shocked.

'Dad, it's my home. Where all my mates are. There's nothing here for me in England. *Nothing.*'

'But after what *happened?*' His bafflement turned to frustration. 'The *phone calls.* We were worried.'

'*Why?*'

My father burst into tears – something I'd never seen him do –

and lunged across the Axminster carpet to hug me. 'Because,' he sobbed, 'I thought I was going to lose my boy.'

Wow! This was all getting confusing. Our family didn't do hugs. Well, I remember receiving one as a child, but it was only after my old man had returned from the pub with a few pints inside him.

'I spoke with my policeman friend.' Dad sniffed. 'He worked in Hong Kong for twenty years. He called his old colleagues to see if they knew you.'

'And?'

'They said *everyone* in Hong Kong knew you.'

Hmmh ... This figured. I'd had a fair few run-ins with the cops over there, like the time I slipped into oblivion in a hotel room after nine days without sleep. Of course everyone in Hong Kong knew me. I'd been at the centre of a massive conspiracy most of them were in on.

Hefting my bergen and books, I went up to the spare room to snort a line of ice off the bedside table. I was beginning to flag after my last hit, twenty hours ago, but this stuff picked me up like a rocket ship to Nirvana, replenishing my energy and restoring a sense of razor-sharp control.

My dealer in Hong Kong had told me German chemists first synthesized crystal meth during the Second World War to increase troops' endurance. He said some legendary athletes injected ice before competition and it was the drug of choice for armed criminals. Apparently, it could send people bananas, but I was glad that never happened to me.

Dad and Ellen went to bed a little after 11pm. I happened to be standing in the kitchen looking at the knick-knacks cluttering their Welsh dresser when everything *suddenly* made sense and I understood the meaning of life and my purpose in it.

... go on ... check it out ... the clues are there ...

Yeah, I see it!

With my newfound insight that these random ornaments – a small silver yachting trophy in the form of a sailboat, a pewter napkin holder, a postcard from Greece – held all the answers, I pulled them off the shelves and sat on the floor to investigate further.

... the ship comes in ...

Huh?

... when the napkin ring rings ... the ship comes in ...

Ah, very clever!

... postcards from the edge ...

Oh, I see.

I started to bring the postcards in from the edge – of the scenario, I mean, as the rest of the room had zoned out.

... Greece the wheels of industry ...

Hah! Grease the wheels of the shipping industry.

... when the napkin rings ...

Of course!

Obviously, the ring represented the *siren* in Plymouth's Devonport Dockyard.

I see it now. When the napkin – or siren – rings, the ship comes in for maintenance, greasing the wheels of industry!

Well, I really thought I was getting somewhere. It all seemed to link in with the global conspiracy. The signs were there – the ship, the napkin, the postcard – to help solve the puzzle. I just had to put the pieces together.

... sowing the seeds of love ...

Ah, the seeds!

No sooner had I got to grips with lubricating the maritime industry than the bloody *seeds* entered the game. A keen gardener, Dad had left a packet emblazoned with bright green runner beans on the dresser's top shelf.

I went to grab it, but the *Grow Your Own Vegetables* guide distracted me, so I sank back to the floor to absorb the book's contents. The backcover said it all.

There is nothing more satisfying than growing your own produce ...

Whoa! Yet another reference to the global conspiracy, its members' 'satisfaction at growing their own produce' a metaphor for spreading the underground network around the world.

... check out the tomato ...

I flipped the book and fixated on the shiny red berry decorating its cover. *I see it! The tomato represents the planet. It's subliminal and symbolic, a subtle communication between the conspirators in this international cult.*

I'd come across this cryptic symbolism in Hong Kong, the cult's way of transmitting their secretive agenda in plain sight of an oblivious public – unless a member of said public cracked the cipher, thus gaining entry into this bizarre double world. Perhaps the tomato represented the Big Apple, my favourite nightclub in Hong Kong, a clever way to let the UK network know that people in Asia were in on this thing.

So is my dad involved?

My old man had owned this book for twenty years. Maybe he'd known about the global cult all along. Perhaps he was a *member!*

... apple of my eye ...

Huh?

I continued to glean the book's esoteric information, desperate to make sense of it all.

> *Whether you are a first-timer or an old hand, this book will show you everything you need to know ...*

'Everything' I need to know. If I could break the code contained in this 'guidebook', I would finally expose the mysterious organisation enveloping my life for the last six months.

> *... including growing your own herbs ...*

Hah, we all know which 'herbs' this refers to! My thoughts flicked to the Foreign Triad, whose members frequented the Wan Chai nightclub I'd worked in as a doorman. The 14K, a pure-blooded-Chinese triad society, ran Club Nemo, but it was no secret that foreigners smuggled jewels, pimped girls and dealt drugs for them. This expat gang even had their own initiation tattoo and used secret hand signs and other covert methods of communication. The 'herbs' clue was an obvious reference to the marijuana the foreign triads sold. It was confusing, though, as I was never quite sure if the Foreign Triad and the global conspiracy were connected – or possibly the same outfit.

... looking after your investment ...

Of course. This made sense because if you've gone to the trouble of nurturing a global criminal empire, you're going to want to protect your efforts.

... and dealing with pests.

Whoa! It wasn't difficult to work out who the green-fingered goons meant by pests – interfering reprobates like me. Well, they could all piss off to their cabbage patch. Only cowards belong to gangs.

Ben

'Chris! *What* are you doing?'

My G-Shock said 4.10am. I looked up to see my old man wrapped in his dressing gown, frowning at me and my answer-giving paraphernalia – actually, *his* paraphernalia. I didn't reply. Surely, it was obvious what I was doing.

Ellen appeared and scowled. 'Just get *rid* of him, Edward!' She burst into tears.

They went back upstairs, so I retired to my room. With meth pulsing through my veins, I had no chance of sleeping, but a lie down wouldn't go amiss. When Dad and Ellen got up for work, I gave them some space, but the hushed voices told me their topic of conversation.

I spent the time flicking through photo albums I had stored at my dad's, smiling as wonderful memories washed over me. Dan grinning after his section had come under machine-gun fire while manning an observation post in Belfast during the troubles. My teammate, Jock Campbell, posing with a huge bruise on his milky-white chest, courtesy of an IRA sniper in the Ardoyne. I say 'milky-white' chest because we had no time for luxuries such as sunbathing throughout that long hot summer.

Sailing around the world aboard HMS *Invincible,* and a drunken 'Johno' Johnson holding up a pair of pants he'd pinched from a working girl in Istanbul. A shot of the aircraft carrier at anchor in Barbados, where I got stoned with Doc at a beachside cabana and he'd thrown up over the bar. Visiting the famous casinos in Macao, riding horses to the Great Pyramids, surviving in the Norwegian Artic, naked bungee in Canada, racing hired cars through the streets of Sicily. Hell, I'd done some stuff as a kid.

And yet back at square one in the bedroom I had as a teenager, what did I have to show for it? Other than a few fading photographs and a crooked nose, I had a big fat *nothing.*

Helmstone nestled on the edge of the Dartmoor National Park, a rugged landscape dotted with craggy tors, abandoned tin mines and treacherous peat bog. Shaggy wild ponies and wandering sheep kept the swaying grasses at bay, and babbling brooks teeming with small brown trout formed rivers Tavy and Plym, which eventually emptied into Plymouth Sound.

Another waterway leading off the moor was Sir Francis Drake's leat, its granite-slab construction overseen by the 'Queen's Pirate' in 1581 to supply the blossoming port of Plymouth with fresh water. A section of the leat ran alongside my dad's garden and when the council had put it up for sale, he bought it to add a unique piece of history to the property.

I walked up the country lane towards Helmstone's small shopping precinct. Unbeknown to many in the parish, beneath my feet lay a mile of railway tunnel, long since decommissioned following the days of steam. We'd stumbled upon it as kids, an ominous ivy-clad maw hidden by creepers in the forest, water seeping through dank and crumbling brickwork to drip into the pitch black. Eeriness aside, it proved a fascinating insight into a bygone age.

I cut across the large roundabout marking Helmstone's centre, recalling sepia photographs depicting a barren track junction back in the day. I was heading for Dad's carpet company, situated in a small business park at the far end of a World War II airfield. This explained why the row of shops was only one-storey high. The Royal Air Force had removed the upper floors to allow a greater clearance for Spitfire pilots taking off to defend the skies above Plymouth during the Blitz and bomber crews flying sorties over Europe.

It was a beautiful English summer day, but ambling along an overgrown runway, passing patches of golden bracken and gorse scrub, cute little ponies and dirty white sheep, I couldn't get Hong Kong out of my mind. I loved the place with a passion beyond words, more than I ever could England. With its unique language, culture and people, *Heung Gong* was a part of me, my true home, and I missed it terribly.

... the constant exhilaration of hectic streets and flashing neon signs ... the smell of steaming noodle shops and exotic food stands ... the yammer of Cantonese voices, a cacophony of traffic noise and the roar of 747s coming in low over the skyscrapers on the Kowloon peninsula ... spectacular views over dragonous mountains, quaint fishing villages and an emerald-green harbour crisscrossed by a multitude of enterprising craft ... dancing all night with the Filipinas and working as a doorman, practicing kung fu in the park at 7am ...

My family was simply happy I was back, as if my safe arrival in the UK meant the drugs were behind me and the old Chris had returned. From my perspective, they *were* behind me and I *would* soon return – to Hong Kong, where I belonged. Something told me if I didn't book a flight sharpish there'd be a problem, one far greater than the gauntlet of triad hardmen I had recently run.

My brother stood outside Helmstone Carpets unloading rolls of Treadaire from the company's Astra van. Ben was a welder by trade but had been helping Dad out to earn some extra cash.

'Working hard, mate?' I grinned.

Ben smiled although noticeably nervous, our long-overdue hug making me realise how selfish I'd been by not keeping in touch. One day, I would tell my little bro how when shinning along a flimsy cable in Wan Chai, seventy metres above the ground and risking a grisly demise, loving him so much brought me to my senses. The last time we saw each other I was four stone of muscle heavier, with seventeen-inch biceps looking a little ridiculous on my five-foot-eight frame. I certainly wasn't the gaunt impersonator stood in front of him now. Perhaps this explained the shock in his likewise turquoise eyes.

Dad's office adjoined his smart carpet showroom, full of pattern books neatly arranged on mahogany display racks. He was sitting at his desk chatting to Ellen, who worked part-time as the company's secretary. Entering the room, I heard him say, 'I just saw Pete. He's off down to Cornwall surfing for a week –'

Pete was my second cousin, an intelligent, friendly and mild-mannered chap who had left his job as a Crown prosecutor a few years ago to travel the world. I'd found this fascinating because the Costa del Sol was the destination of choice for Brits, but only those affluent and audacious enough to leave the country on an aeroplane. Pete's postcards ... *India ... Africa ... South America ... Indonesia ... Fiji ...* filled me with wanderlust and seeing the seven continents was one of my goals.

'Oh ... hi, Chris.' Dad smiled, his eyes flicking to Ellen.

'Hi ...' she muttered, not looking up from her electronic typewriter.

Ellen was twenty years younger than my father and by no means a bad person. In truth, the damaged little boy inside me loved her like a mother – especially as my own had rejected me in favour of a secret smoker with a Vauxhall Viva and poor mental health. Yet it's fair to say both Dad and Ellen carried unresolved issues into their marriage, a continuation of the turmoil my siblings and I had endured all our lives.

My real mum chucked me out of the car, following a disagreement on the way to school. I slept rough and bunked at a friend's place until one sunny morning my dad pulled up and suggested I move in with him. On our first evening together, he said, 'Make yourself at home, son,' and years of trauma lifted from my shoulders like the world's heaviest bergen. We got on like best mates, playing squash once a week and having a manly pint afterwards. For the first time in my life, it felt like a proper father-and-son relationship, like we really loved one another, and I'd never felt so happy.

Then one day I came home from school to find the house full of strange ornaments – many of them in raffia, which should ring alarm bells in any situation. Dad had met the twenty-three-year-old Ellen up the pub and she'd moved in right away. Six months later, Ellen smirked over my old man's shoulder as he threw my possessions into the street, yelling, 'You'll *never* amount to anything!' So I gritted my teeth through thirty-two weeks of commando training to prove them wrong.

'So you're off to Missus Swayne in Torpoint.' Dad handed Benny a briefcase and tape measure. 'Tell her we've got the Sunset Dream in stock, but if she wants the Walton Weave, I can order it in for Thursday.'

I was impressed and proud of my brother. He appeared to be doing a stellar job.

'And why don't you take Chris with you?' Dad added.

'Okay ...' Ben looked uncertain but nodded to the van.

Spending time with Benny felt good. Six years my junior, he was easy going, uncomplicated and streetwise, which meant I could be open with him about my Oriental adventure.

Torpoint sat across the River Tamar, the border between Devon and Cornwall. To get there involved taking a car ferry from Plymouth. Before that, though, we needed to run the blockade of Denborough Down, aka 'Alzheimer's Alley'. Helmstone was prime real estate for the blue-rinse brigade and their platinum playboys. There were more colonels entrenched in the village than the Battle of the Somme. These silver psychopaths threw caution to the wind on this super-fast stretch of A-road, winding their Nissan Micras up to the devil-may-care speed of 21 mph while searching the horizon for a tractor or steamroller *or* someone who'd actually *died* behind the wheel to race behind.

To make matters worse, a lot of the yokels still hadn't sussed the accelerator pedal. With less freewill than a Pavlovian pooch, they simply tagged onto the back of the retirement roadblock, resulting in convoys to make the Rubber Duck proud.

Overtaking the pootling pensioners on this stubborn stretch of highway had become a family crusade. Dad held the record, losing his rag to leave fourteen cars in his wake – although one time on a family holiday to Cornwall, he passed twenty-three by driving down the pavement.

As Ben glided the van around the local bridge champion's Mini

Clubman and the Golden Girls going pedal-to-the-metal in a Citroen CV6, I could tell there was something on his mind.

'We were worried about you ...' he muttered, clenching the steering wheel and glancing nervously in the rear-view mirror.

'I was alright, mate.'

My brother probably wanted me to acknowledge the stress I'd subjected everyone to, but I felt defensive, as if they expected me to apologise. My family didn't care about the weird cult I'd encountered, my work as a doorman or the DJ job in China. None of them had even asked me why the Max*Tech* Group failed. They weren't interested in Vance, my wonderful Chinese business partner, how the food tasted or the difficulties I faced learning the language. Their sole concern was the *drugs,* and it pissed me off. A million factors contributed to things going tits-up in Asia, but they didn't want to hear about them. Didn't my family realise that for a messed-up kiddy like me something had to give eventually? Did they hear me complaining or blaming anyone?

Sure, I'd come back from Hong Kong a little worse for wear, but *not* with my tail between my legs. Drugs, triads and handstands on skyscrapers were simply the way things panned out. I'd played the hand life dealt me. What was I supposed to do – swap my Hong Kong experience for a daily dose of *EastEnders* and a pair of carpet slippers? No, I'd followed my destiny and, yeah, drugs played a part and I'd fallen on my arse. That's how life goes, so get over yourselves.

The rusting tub plying the half-mile of murky brown channel was still a long way off, so Benny joined the handful of vehicles queuing in the first of four lanes.

Spotting a food van, 'Fancy a cuppa, bro?' I asked.

'Please, Chris.' Ben pulled some coins from his pocket.

As I made my way over to Baz's Burgers, Barry was chewing the fat with a customer, sausages and onions sizzling on the griddle. Although out of earshot, I knew they were discussing my cousin Pete's surf trip, and so approaching the counter, 'Yeah, he's gone down to Cornwall for a few days,' I told Baz. 'Staying in his caravan.'

Barry and his customer looked at me *slightly* askew as if I'd said something strange, making me wonder if we were bowling in the same alley.

'There you go, mate.' I handed Ben a Snickers bar.

Now it was my brother's turn to look confused. 'Where's the tea?'

'Tea?' I cocked my head. 'What you on about?'

The roll-on-roll-off lowered its bow ramp and the bank of red traffic lights changed to green. Ben drove on board, following the car in front into the far left lane as directed by the fare collector. We didn't have to pay to cross into Cornwall, only when leaving, the butt of a longstanding Devonian joke.

'Shall we sit on the upper, mate?'

'No!' Ben snapped.

For some reason, he didn't think it was a good idea, but I was already out of the car.

Sitting on the old barge's slatted wooden benches reminded me of crossing the busy Victoria Harbour on the iconic Star ferries. The skyline looked somewhat different, though. Hong Kong has to be the most vibrant city on Earth, its shiny steel-and-glass skyscrapers projecting the image of a bustling commercial hub, one steeped in exoticism and Anglo-Sino history. We, on the other hand, were heading for the anonymity of Torpoint, a town not known for its skyscrapers, exoticism ... or much else.

To our right, Plymouth's Devonport Dockyard hugged the estuary's shoreline. Hulking grey warships moored along the wharf made for an impressive sight – unlike the decommissioned nuclear submarines floating side by side like fat black pellets. Rumour had it the hunter-killer's nuclear reactors needed a thousand years to cool down before the Ministry of Defence could scrap the decaying leviathans. If only Whitehall had listened to Frankie Goes to Hollywood, they would have saved the British taxpayer a fortune and local mackerel wouldn't have three eyes and twelve tails.

We located Mrs Swayne's property and I watched as my brother measured her living room floor like a pro, just as I'd seen Dad do countless times during my childhood. 'And don't worry, Missus Swayne,' said Ben, 'our fitters will hoover up the mess.'

'Oh, *no!*' she replied, a face like a bent spanner. 'I'll do that myself.'

I smiled. When folks have a new carpet laid, they can't wait to vacuum it.

Back in Plymouth, I asked Ben if he minded a detour. What with the weird goings-on in Hong Kong, I needed a friend, someone I trusted to be truthful about the global conspiracy. We headed for Simon's place.

My relationship with Simon was simple. I'd met my mate in a dance club, the Warehouse, four years ago and thought the world of him. Privately educated and always in trouble, Simon saw something in me many of our acquaintances didn't, appreciating my random sense of humour and out-of-the-box take on life.

Ben parked in Stoke, a mile from the city centre and the historic Plymouth Hoe where Sir Francis famously insisted on finishing his game of bowls before sailing out to frazzle the Spanish Armada. Stoke wasn't a bad area as Plymouth goes, with long meandering boulevards, hundred-year-old town pubs and grand terraces that used to accommodate the dockyard's management – until globalisation emasculated the workforce and shoved everyone into call centres.

Simon rented the middle floor of one such three-storey townhouse. I made my way up the garden path, through chest-high grass uncut since my last visit. Simon didn't do gardening – possibly due to the demotivating effect of chain-smoking hashish – and other than selling party prescriptions to a colourful cast of characters, most of whom spent their days drinking coffee in his flat, he didn't do a lot else. He didn't even make the coffee – his guests did that.

I rang the bell expecting Simon to throw open the sash window and shout, 'Hey, Chrissy!' and chuck me his keys, but some random bloke opened the door. 'Yes, mate?'

'I was looking for Simon.'

'He's moved. Bottom flat.'

I walked back down the short flight of steps and rang the bell for the ground floor. I could tell it was Simon's place because a small card inserted into the bell push read 'Simon's Place' in black biro, with an arty star added to extend a real welcome should the Three Wise Men turn up. No answer, so I peered through the window into the gloomy interior.

A chill came over me ...

I sensed conspiracy ...

Why wasn't he home?

Simon was always in – unless he'd manged to manipulate some fool into chauffeuring him around Plymouth to pick up drugs. *Is this something to do with the global cult?* I wondered. Had they warned my mate I was back in Plymouth, an outsider, and told him not to open the door under any circumstances?

I should have felt disappointed, but having been through a year of this shit I no longer gave a toss. Others' rejection of me had become par for the course and in the interest of self-preservation I simply accepted it. Who ever said life was fair?

I hopped back into the passenger seat. 'He's not in,' I told Ben, wondering for a brief moment if he was in on this. Maybe our dad told him to keep me away from drug dealers. 'Can we try Elsie's?'

Elsie lived with her little boy, a mixed-race lad called Massey, in an aging block of flats surrounded by five other monsters in Plymouth's most deprived area. The communal entrance had a coded lock but some fuckhead had smashed in the jamb. I pushed the door open and began climbing the shiny concrete stairs eight floors to the top, making sure not to touch the iron bannister's sticky handrail. What with the stench rising from dumpsters in the basement, tarnished lavender walls and discarded hypodermics, the place fell short of Chungking Mansions' piss-stinking landings ...

but not by much.

Elsie and I had a special bond, having met in a nightclub through a marine buddy of mine. When my wisdom teeth began boring into the sides of my head, Elsie had driven me to hospital for my operation. She visited me in recovery and came to collect me. My girlfriend at the time didn't even ring the ward to see how I was.

Elsie wasn't in, either. I peeked through the door's small obscured-glass pane to see her place dark and spooky as Simon's had been. The creepy feeling came over me. Was someone, or some *ones,* preventing me seeing my friends?

I had to let *Elsie* know that *I* knew the devious cult's members were attempting to control the situation. I reached inside my black bomber jacket and pulled out a sunglasses case containing a cool pair of shades I'd found in a strange stash of junk in my tenement in Wan Chai. Their rectangular rose-tinted lenses had helped me decipher the cult's cryptic symbolism in books and magazines. Elsie's favourite colour was purple – she was a bit of a Goth – and the glasses had a maroon lens cloth, a close enough match. She'd realise it was from me and that I was in desperate need, so I shoved it through the letterbox.

Nothing Wrong with Me

'**G**ive us a drive, Ben?'

We were halfway home and almost past the blight of industrial parks, car dealerships and fast-food chains encroaching on Dartmoor's idyllic landscape.

'*No.*'

Ben negotiated a roundabout, staring intently at the oncoming traffic to avoid making eye contact.

'*Come on!*'

Growing up in the countryside meant driving was in our blood, and not having been behind the wheel since selling my 320i prior to Hong Kong, I was itching for a spin.

'*No!*'

This wasn't good. No one likes having choice taken away from them.

'Ben, for *fuck's* sake! Let me *drive.*'

'I *can't.*' His lip wobbled.

'Why not?'

'Because Dad made me promise.'

'*What?*'

'You're *not* well, Chris. Honestly, you're *not* well.'

Fucking hell! A bit of a drug problem abroad and my family had to make *such* a big deal out of it. Why couldn't they let me be? As my dad used to say when I'd been subjected to my mother and stepfather's emotional fuckery, there was *nothing* wrong with me.

Benny dropped me at the cottage and returned to the carpet shop. The sun was out, so I sat on the neatly mown grass in the back garden, legs dangling in the leat. Due to blockages upstream, the aqueduct's now-moss-mottled granite slabs no longer channelled fast-flowing water but six inches of slow-moving sludge, a combination of dirt and oil from the nearby shopping precinct.

Dad, bless his rubber wellies, was one of the few villagers who appreciated this unique part of history running through the parish. By way of pressure washer and shovel, he'd be out there twice a year waging war on the muck to reveal the impressive stonework beneath. He was onto a losing battle, though, as none of the other leat owners gave a damn.

Relaxing in the sun isn't possible when you're buzzing on crystal meth and feeling fidgety as hell, so I decided to help my old dad out, although I'd be giving the sludge a miss as it was as solid as a sub-Saharan pancake. Instead, I turned my attention to his vegetable patch. Unlike the nearby aerodrome, which remained undiscovered by the Luftwaffe throughout the war, his cabbages, runner beans and broccoli were taking a good many hits – from the local birdlife.

It simply wasn't cricket, so I put a plan into action and began rummaging through the house and shed. I selected a two-foot length of copper pipe, a wooden coat hanger, two plastic cups, a length of string, six empty milk bottles, a roll of gaffer tape and some nuts – as in the nut-and-bolt variety. Then in the spirit of Barnes-Wallace – or was it Wallace and Gromit? – I set about thwarting the avian invasion.

I shoved the copper pipe into the ground next to a pecked-to-pieces patch of Brussels sprouts. After this, I straightened the coat hanger's hook and, using steel washers as bearings, inserted it into the exposed end of the pipe to create a spinning arrangement – a bit like a miniature two-dimensional version of a rotary washing line. I taped the two plastic cups, facing in opposite directions, to the shoulders of the hanger and waited for the breeze.

It worked. The second the wind picked up, the revolving wooden arms revolved like ... *revolving* wooden arms!

Phase one sorted, I moved swiftly to phase two – if three hours of sleep-deprived confusion counts as swiftly. I filled the milk bottles to varying depths with water and placed them in the path of the spinning arms. Then I strung the nuts from the arms and waited once more.

It was a tense moment. I'd either enter the annals of engineering history, perhaps giving a Reith Lecture on innovation, or be left sitting in a vegetable patch like a nob.

I felt a breeze ...

The rotors came alive ...

I heard the sweet tinkling of music, scaring off *every* feathered invader ... for *four* inches around. *Result!*

My old man wasn't so pleased. Upon his return from the carpet shop, he looked at my contraption and shook his head. He obviously didn't appreciate the complexity of such an undertaking when deprived of a week's sleep by crystal meth.

I first tried the drug in Hong Kong while working in a rather strange traditionally run trading company called Gung Wan Hong. In my tinsel-titled role of international sales manager, I was supposed to be selling computer components to international buyers, but due to the market's fickle nature, I didn't shift so much as a mouse pad during my seven-month charade. So when a colleague, Neil Diamond, offered me a smoke of ice in the gents one afternoon, I thought, *Why not?*

The resultant feeling, utter euphoria combined with immense energy, was like nothing I'd ever experienced. Not having had the most stable of upbringings, I felt normal for the first time in my life, the person nature intended me to be. With my underlying trauma at ease, I was able to relax and enjoy drawing and writing, subjects I'd failed miserably at in school.

Only, fly too high for long and you risk crashing down to Earth – as Icarus found out to his cost. By the time the 14K employed me as a doorman, everything had turned to custard. Too tired and hallucinating, I couldn't have tied my shoelaces let alone kept my life on track.

As such, *almost* managing to protect my father's runner beans should have made him happy. Instead, he muttered something about going up the pub, so I packed his tools away and went in the cottage.

While I'd been away, Dad and Ellen had put some watercolours up in the front room. In one of them, the artist had limned the granite-block wheelhouse of an abandoned tin mine on Dartmoor. A chill come over me ... *menacing eyes ... triads ... evil cult ... communication ...*

The wheelhouse had several glassless windows, which appeared as eerie black voids. These portals exuded the exact dull menace I'd seen in the eyes of cult members and triads, as if under the influence of some kind of satanic mind control.

... your parents ... know all about it ...

Once again, the realisation dawned my parents knew all about the global cult.

... the villagers too ...

Christ, this was all so confusing.

The sound of my stepmother entering the room interrupted my muse. 'Ellen, where did this picture come from?'

'Oh, that? I bought it for your dad. You know how he loves local history.'

'Right ...'

My stepmother was doing her best to deal with the situation, if not for me then for her husband. We sat down at the kitchen table. A quiche warmed in the oven, spits came from the chunky home-cut chips in the deep-fat fryer and an inviting salad bowl sat on the side. For ten minutes, I poured my heart out to Ellen about the confusion I felt. She listened and didn't judge, her body language radiating empathy. Then as the garden gate clicked shut, signalling my old man's return, Ellen shook herself and went back to preparing our meal.

While Dad kept an eye on the chips, I picked up the guitar I'd bought in Hong Kong. Bar strumming three chords, I couldn't play the damn thing, but now seemed a good time to learn. I began tuning the strings, plucking and tightening each one to bring the sound into line. Finally, the instrument produced something resembling a harmony only the top E was a fraction out, so I tweaked it a little more ...

Crack!

The guitar's neck had snapped, its strings splaying like boiled spaghetti.

Looking up from the deep-fat fryer, 'It's too highly strung,' said Dad.

... he's having a go at you ...

I felt certain my father was having a dig at me, insinuating I'd overreacted about this whole Hong Kong business. This was exactly the sort of snide doublespeak the cult employed. As Ellen handed me a plate of food, rather than say anything I hopped up onto the chest freezer and retreated into a private world of hurt. What my old man said next, though, I couldn't let ride.

He began recounting an incident everyone in the pub had been talking about. It involved the Madsons, a feral local family known for their scant regard of the law and those who enforce it. 'So Levi got banned for drink driving recently,' Dad continued, 'and last night he was walking to the boozer with Clint, Delane and Shaw.'

I pictured the four of eight siblings, who were of Romany blood and unlikely to appear on *Mastermind.*

'And the copper that arrested him pulled alongside them in his car,' said Dad.

I started to feel queasy ...

'He said, *"Ha!* You'd better get used to walking everywhere from now on, Levi."'

My heart pounded. I sensed where this was going ...

'The boys were having none of it.' Dad's face darkened. 'They dragged the cop from his car, locked him in the boot, then drove up to Dartmoor and tortured him.'

Adrenaline flooded my body.

The room span.

I could *taste* the police officer's terror, *a resurgence of my own!*

Didn't my dad know the triads set me up for a mock execution in Club Nemo? That I'd experienced the unimaginable fear of knowing you're about to die? Did he think this was *funny* or had the cult put him up to it?

'Poor bloke was terrified,' Dad went on. 'Thought they were going to kill –'

'Noooooo!' I thrust my meal away from me.

My dad and stepmother froze, eyes locked in utter shock, the plate, food and cutlery raining down on their previously spotless Axminster.

'Edward, he's going to kill us!' Ellen screamed, pouncing on the phone.

As she dialled 999 with shaking fingers, my old man dived across the room and threw me to the ground.

Huh?

What the *fuck* was he playing at? I wasn't going to hurt anyone. I simply couldn't understand why my father told that story in front of me. Was he purposely being cruel to provoke a reaction?

'Fucking get *off* me!' I pushed him aside and ran into the garden, standing at the corner of the cottage trembling with confusion. *What was going on?*

In what seemed seconds, wailing sirens filled the country lane and two police cars, lights ablaze, skidded to a halt outside the house. It could well have been a scene from a Hollywood thriller, *The Boy who Ran into the Garden.* In a blur of black, white and blue, three coppers wearing stab vests lurched from the vehicles. Wielding truncheons, they burst through the five-bar gate, crossing the gravel in lightning speed to pin me against the cottage's whitewashed wall.

If they were fast, my kid brother was faster. Having arrived at the cottage to drop the shop keys off, he took three animated steps across the driveway and leapt between us, sending one of the coppers reeling into the leat. Fuming, Ben pushed a second officer in the chest, and as the guy took a step backwards their colleague decided to do likewise.

'There's *nothing* wrong with my brother!' Ben's eyes burned as he put his arm around me.

'It's okay, mate,' said the sergeant. 'We just got a call from a woman who sounded hysterical. She said drugs were involved.'

'*Hah!*' Looking down at my feet, I shook my head. 'My stepmother doesn't know what a drug looks like.'

The sergeant calmed everyone down and went inside to talk to my parents. The officer Benny floored clambered out of the leat. 'Don't hit me again!' He grinned, holding his hands out in a pacifying gesture. 'Can you tell us what's going on?'

I explained how things had gone pear-shaped in Hong Kong, adding I'd not long left the marines. A lot of police officers have served in the military, or wished they had, and so this namedrop always earned you a bit of respect.

'Listen, Chris,' said the copper. 'There's no point locking you in a cell. My sister had a drug problem, so I know it's an illness not a choice. People think calling the police will solve everything, but the station's not the place for people who are unwell.'

He fished in his wallet and handed me a business card for an addiction treatment centre in the nearby town of Tavistock. 'Look, these people helped my sister,' he said. 'Give them a call.'

'Thank you,' I replied, humbled by their handling of the situation.

The sergeant reappeared. 'Look after yourself, Chris. And be thankful you've got a brother like that.'

I was.

The cops had been kind to me, but I wouldn't be going to any treatment centre. There was nothing wrong with me – nothing I couldn't sort out myself. Besides, I only had a small amount of ice left and when it was gone, it was gone. Life would return to Little England normality and I'd start looking for a job – although I couldn't see two O Levels and three GCSEs landing me a dream career.

That night, I got some long-overdue sleep. Upon waking, I snorted the last of the illicit crystals through a rolled-up piece of a paper. I didn't have a banknote – or any notes in the bank. In fact, I owed them £8,000. When I went down to the kitchen, 'Chris, how about popping up to the doctors?' asked Dad, handing me a cup of tea.

'The *doctors?*'

I didn't have a GP, as the military had always taken care of my medical needs, but why did I need to see one anyway? Dad seemed keen on the idea, though, and so to keep him happy I agreed to sign on at the local surgery.

The practice sat adjacent the village shops, shaded by towering fir trees and ringed by a wall of natural slate. My stepmother walked me there, which was generous of her considering she obviously thought I was a psychopath. It felt strangely comforting to have a maternal figure looking out for my welfare.

After speaking to the receptionist, Ellen left me sitting on a leather sofa in the spacious waiting room, my vital organs protected in the event of a bomb blast by the mass of *Ideal Home* magazines stacked on the surgery's coffee table. Scanning around, I wondered what ailed my fellow waitees – a ruddy-faced woman who had obviously been at the gin, and a farmer-type, likely haemorrhoids, erectile dysfunction or anger issues.

A grey-haired horn-rimmed quack appeared wearing regulation corduroys, a hunting jacket and sensible shoes – which was reassuring in case we had to shoot an elk. 'Mister Thrall, this way.'

I read the plaque on his consulting room door and held my palm out. 'Doctor Middleton, how do you do?'

'Oh ... yes-yes.' With a look of surprise, the GP reciprocated. Perhaps he didn't know the pox-ridden peasantry had hands. 'Sit down, please,' he said. 'I spoke to your father and he tells me you got involved in drugs in Hong Kong.'

'Crystal meth.'

'Ah ... right.' The doctor glanced at the serious-looking tome on the desk. He'd obviously done some homework. 'So are you being followed?'

'*Followed?*'

'Yes, do you think people are following you?'

'Well, they did in Hong Kong, if that's what you mean?'

'Can you explain?'

'I worked for the triads. They followed me on a number of occasions.'

'And do you think they're following you here?'

My mind flicked to envisage the large number of Chinese restaurants in nearby Plymouth. I'd read that the 14K, a global crime syndicate with over half a million foot soldiers, extorted money from these establishments and used them to import drugs. I'd upset a good many triads in Hong Kong, and so, 'I suppose it's possible,' I told the doc.

'You are aware you will have suffered irreparable brain damage from using this drug?'

Hmmh ... possible but hardly fucking likely.

In Hong Kong, I'd met managers, lawyers, fashion photographers, to name but a few professionals, who smoked way more meth than I ever did. A gram used to last me a week, but some cats would *inject* this amount twice daily. I reckon Dr Middleton was putting across the worst-case scenario – as no doubt I *was* Helmstone's worst-case scenario, the designer-drug scene not having taken off in the village. I think Panadol topped the charts here ... closely followed by the gin.

Sinbad

'Doctor Sinjin-Jones,' the South West of England's eminent psychiatrist announced at the door of Brook Cottage.

'Edward Thrall,' my dad replied – his turn to remind the medical community we shook hands in this great country.

'Oh!' Sinjin-Jones struggled with his clipboard and pilot's case – the latter a necessary accoutrement for landing a Volvo.

It was clear to see Dr Sing-Sing or Gin Sling, or whatever this clown's name was, went to the Dr Middleton School of Fashion – functional garb ticking all the boxes for banging out Prozac to disenfranchised housewives *or* popping pheasants from the sky with a twelve bore. With his case full of *How to Fix Fucking Druggies* journals, he entered the cottage with two female colleagues. Sister Sandra Yelm was the manager of Plymouth's mental health unit, and Natasha a psychology student on placement.

As we settled in the front room, *This is all quite pleasant,* I thought, but surely these funny-farmers had cuckoo's nests to visit.

'So, Christopher,' Dr Shindig began, shielding his torso with the clipboard. 'Are you hearing voices?'

'Yes!' I beamed.

He and Sandra shuffled forward in their seats, truth dawning they had a genuine mental on their hands.

'And?' the aging psychiatrist pressed.

'I can hear your voice, Doctor Sin Bin – *errh,* Sinjin.'

'No, Chris, the doctor means can you hear *other* voices?' Sandra frowned.

'*Yours,* you mean?'

As the doctor and nurse made eye contact, Natasha tried not to smile.

'Let's put it another way,' said Sinbad. 'Do you hear voices coming from the television?'

'Yes, Doc.'

Frantic scribbling ensued.

Dr Bin Bag peered over the top of his shield. 'And what kind of voices?'

'Oh, you know, actors ... newsreaders,' I told him truthfully.

'But Doctor Middleton tells me you think you're being followed by the Hong Kong triads?'

Yes, and he also wears tweed.

'No, I told the doctor I *worked* for the Hong Kong triads and had a few issues with them.'

'Right ... right.'

And so the meeting continued.

When the professionals left, my old man was surprisingly chipper. He explained Dr Middleton had told him to consider admitting me to a psychiatric ward – but obviously today's assessment had shown this wasn't necessary. Like Sid James in *Carry On Chlorpromazine,* Dad kept double-nudging my elbow and winking. 'Well, that Natasha didn't half fancy you!' he'd chuckle.

As for Dr Singalong-Jones, he fancied I attend a mental health clinic in Plymouth for further consultation.

'Dad, watch this!'

We'd parked outside the NHS head-fixing shed in the city, but before going inside, I wanted to show my pops a trick Yuri the Bolshoi ballerina had taught me in Wan Chai. Dropping down into the splits, I placed my hands flat on the ground and slowly pushed up into a perfect handstand. Then I walked my upside-down self out of the car park and up to the building's entrance, before flipping back onto my feet.

Dad frowned.

After summarising Dr Ginseng's findings, one of his fellow mind mechanics sent us to the in-house pharmacy and we came away with a carrier bag full of antipsychotic medicine. Back at Brook Cottage, I shoved it all in the bin.

Everything was becoming too much and now that the ice had run out I felt tired, sketchy and full of dread. It was always like this coming off the drug. Having not eaten or slept for a week, while expending enough energy to complete a double Ironman, you crash for thirty-six hours and upon waking have to deal with reality while ravenously hungry, chronically depressed and physically exhausted.

I went to my room, lay on the bed and stared up at the Artex. I'd resigned from a secure job in the Royal Marines to run a failing business. Sarah had left me in Hong Kong to pursue a career with British Airways – not that I blamed her. I'd lost a string of jobs, a load of money and my treasured Rolex. I'd been traumatised, humiliated, set up to be executed ... *and* developed a drug problem. Now my family were giving me a hard time, demanding I change who I was to conform to their blinkered protocol.

Fuck ...

Was I a bad person? The whole world seemed to think so. Perhaps this shouldn't come as a surprise. I'd done some stupid, *selfish* things over the years, getting on the wrong side of the law and narrowly avoiding prison. Was this karma? Shit, I *must* be a bad person.

Dad put his head around the door. 'Phone for you.'

I went downstairs and picked up the receiver.

'Hello, old boy. I gather you had a bit of a rough time over there.'

It was Uncle James, my godfather, a thoroughly good guy and a top bod in the Financial Services Authority, based on the prestigious Canary Warf in London's Docklands. He sounded genuinely concerned, but I couldn't help wondering if the evil cult had their hooks into him. Maybe they'd told James I deserved everything I got because I'd robbed things in the past and wronged innocent people.

'James ... am I a *bad* person?' I tendered.

'*No ...!*' he answered without hesitation. 'You're a *good* person, Chris.'

This was reassuring as, despite the confusion, I trusted my uncle.

'Listen, I'm driving down in the morning to see you,' he continued.

'Oh ... thanks.'

Uncle James was an important figure in the City, an extremely busy man, so I appreciated his gesture even more. As I hung the phone up, the front gate clicked shut. I looked out of the kitchen window to see my mother – my real mother – crossing the drive. So caught up in the events in Hong Kong, I hadn't spoken to her for months, bar a brief phone chat the day I got back.

During that call, I'd attempted to obtain some insight into our complicated and untalked-about family history. I hadn't been seeking to lay blame on anyone, only to gain an appreciation of the historical factors, the intergenerational family dynamics so to speak, that might explain why my parents behaved the way they did, *at* times, over the years. In London parlance, it was a plea to 'throw me a *fackin* bone!' I deserved at least *one* nugget, something to help me make sense of the situation – my mental *and* physical state testified to that. Mum had become angry, though, and slammed the phone down.

After a hug, we sat at the kitchen table. She projected a calmness and had an understanding look in her eye. Dad must have said to prepare for the worst, but the situation didn't appear to faze her.

'Mum, am I a *bad* person?'

I felt sure I must be, that my turbulent upbringing and resultant rebellious streak destined me to be that way. I'd upset people as I careened through life experimenting with the good, the bad and the ugly in the hope of finding some answers. Perhaps this was payback.

'Actually, Chris, I've always loved you very much. You were such a special child.' She slid an envelope across the table.

I opened it to find a card with a mountain scene painted in pastel colours on the front and a poem inside.

There may be days when you get up in the morning and things aren't the way you hoped they would be. That's when you have to tell yourself that things will get better.

There are times when people disappoint you and let you down, but those are the times when you must remind yourself to trust your own judgements and opinions, to keep your life focused on believing in yourself and all that you are capable of.

There will be challenges to face and changes to make in your life, and it is up to you to accept them. Constantly keep yourself headed in the right direction for you.

It may not be easy at times, but in those times of struggle you will find a stronger sense of who you are, and you will also see yourself developing into the person you have always wanted to be.

Life is a journey through time, filled with many choices. Each of us will experience life in our own special way.

So when the days come that are filled with frustration and unexpected responsibilities, remember to believe in yourself and all you want your life to be, because the challenges and changes will only help you to find the dreams that are meant to come true for you.

Deanna Beisser

Mum had written, 'Dear Chris. Do hope you are beginning to find the answers to all your questions. We all love you very much.'

The next day was the first in six months I willingly went without ice. I wouldn't be climbing any walls, robbing post offices or shivering in cold turkey. Crystal meth is mentally but not physically addictive and so I only had sheer apathy and exhaustion to deal with. I slept for forty-eight hours and woke up feeling not too bad – perhaps because of my safe environment and the fresh opportunity in England.

That evening, I sat down with Dad, Ellen and Uncle James to eat a delicious chilli my stepmother had cooked. It was kind of James to travel down here, a step into the unknown when you consider none of my elders had ever seen an illegal drug let alone taken one. He even asked me what 'they' looked like.

I attempted to clarify why I had to return to Hong Kong, but couldn't put the experience of living there into words. Only a fellow expat would understand what I was trying to say. My family seized upon this discordance as proof I should stay in the UK.

'But *why* do you want to go back there?' asked a frustrated James, who'd visited the colony on business. 'Hong Kong's a city full of greed and narcissism, where the majority of ventures *fail!*'

He was right on both counts, but Hong Kong was my home. How could I explain the 24/7 buzz, the ancient and exotic culture, the amazing food, the fascinating language, the tight-knit community of expats and a nightclub district that stayed open all night pandering to your every sense and playing host to your inner-most needs?

But then how could I explain living in a dive, losing my mind, going on a ridiculous yomp carrying a boogie box and buying that bloody guitar thinking it would give me all the answers?

Bang on cue those pesky tears returned, *'Uh-huht-huht-huh ...'* chin dropping to my chest as I shrugged the weight of a confused world up and down. I couldn't account for what happened in Hong Kong or how I ended up in this unbecoming state.

And this crying business was beyond me too. I never cried, *never.* It was a sign of weakness only babies and people who felt sorry for themselves indulged in. To paraphrase Mum's card, life ain't always fair and you'd better get on and deal with it. But for some reason, everything I said and did conspired against me, along with the people on the way, and tears were my only release from the unrelenting rejection and pain.

While I spurted liquid hurt into the garlic bread, Uncle James gripped my forearm. 'It's alright, Chris. It's alright.'

Poor bloke, in at the deep end he'd handled this like a trouper.

Only, it wasn't alright. It couldn't be further from it.

After a few days, with the dregs of meth purged from my bloodstream, the old Chris had returned, bar four stone in lost weight, near-bankruptcy and an invisible void in my heart. I say 'invisible' because in the warm rays of British summertime my newfound sobriety papered over a crevasse deeper than the Grand Canyon, my aspirations of returning to Hong Kong now as distant as a cup of Jasmine tea.

Similarly, my mind disengaged from worldwide conspiracies, global puppet shows, vegetable growing guides and conversations with burger van owners. As the drugs left my system, so did the mismatched thoughts, evaporating like breath off a pane of glass, leaving only a barely perceptible trace they'd ever existed.

It felt okay-*ish* to be in the calm after the storm, only the lapping waves of indifference were in danger of pushing the good ship *Thrall* into the doldrums. Rather than reject my dad's advice to take it easy, I actually embraced it. I had to, because as the meth disappeared so did the urgency of finding a job. I wouldn't know where to start.

'Chris, Joe's on the phone!' Dad shouted up the stairs.

'Joe?'

'Says he's an old friend of yours.'

'Okay, I got it.'

I took the call in my parents' bedroom. 'Hello, it's Chris.'

'Ehh,' the caller began, in a Liverpudlian accent, 'I'm phoning from Sheridan's debt-collection agency about the eight thousand pounds you owe Barclays Bank. We don't wanna take yooz to court and get yooz a criminal record, Mister Thrall. So if we can agree to a repayment plan, like?'

Hmmh ...?

Having survived being shot at, bombed and mortared by the IRA, a mass crush in Hong Kong in which forty people died, mugging by Turkish *and* Thai gangsters, rolling three cars off the road and the wrath of the Hong Kong triads, I now had 'Joe' threatening me. What did Sheridan's dick-employment agency care about the upset my family was going through? And when did it become a crime to owe money? I bet no one at Barclays Bank PLC, pre-tax profit £3.4 billion, was losing sleep over it.

'Joe …'

'Ehh, yeah?'

'Go fuck yourself.'

Ellen worked three afternoons a week as a typist in a law firm. She discussed my predicament with one of the solicitors. He kindly contacted Dr Middleton, who wrote a letter stating I was suffering from severe psychiatric illness and the prognosis for recovery was poor. The solicitor forwarded this information to Barclays and I never heard from 'Joe' again.

That evening, I walked up to the Moorland Heights with Dad and Ben. The Heights was one of those character-lacking 'There's a better pub up the road' joints that, as such, was constantly changing hands. It was always the same, though. A new owner would arrive determined to make a go of things. They'd invest their life savings, £250, into revamping the place, which usually entailed moving the pool table three feet to the left or right and swapping salad for peas, or vice versa, in the scampi in a basket. The budget never quite leant itself to replacing the thirty-year-old Wilton carpet, its threadbare Paisley-pattern weave appearing strimmed not vacuumed, or fixing the pipes in the gents, the floor of which you waded across to reach a urinal, a manoeuvre best undertaken roped in pairs.

As I stood in the pub saying 'Cheers!' to my dad and bro, for the first time in a year raising a good old British pint glass as opposed to one of Hong Kong's 330ml bottles, I felt relaxed but not exactly at home. More like on old ground.

Dad's accountant, Richard, entered the lounge and true to his generous form got a round in. Richard loved listening to my military and travel anecdotes. *'Strewth!'* he would say – and a few more strewths came out as we discussed Hong Kong.

'You really ought to write a book, Chris,' he said, sliding a

Scotch along the bar to my dad.

Richard would say this every time we enjoyed a pint together. I always laughed and shrugged it off as flattery. Living an adventurous life was something I'd always done. To me it was normal and I couldn't imagine people wanting to read about it. 'I'll put writing a book on my bucket list.' I grinned.

Dad nudged me. 'You don't half look better now that crystal meth nonsense is behind you.'

'*Hah!* What crystal meth?' I shrugged, as it was no big deal.

'Well, just take it easy. It's good to have you back.'

My old fella meant well, but he didn't understand. I didn't *want* to be back. One year in Hong Kong was worth ten in boring rip-off soap-opera Britain. I'd been on the rollercoaster ride of a lifetime with the craziest scoundrels you could ever hope to meet. Telling me to take it easy was akin to saying to a shipwrecked sailor, 'Hey, you're on a desert island, so you might as well get some rays!'

The first crack showed within a week as I watched a TV program about the upcoming Hong Kong handover. Next summer, Britain's ninety-nine-year lease on the colony ended and the Chinese would take back control of the enigmatic enclave. Despite a fifty-year buffer period known as the Anglo-Sino Joint Declaration, Hong Kongers were justifiably nervous about the future. But there was also an element of excitement, with the biggest parties ever organised in the Fragrant Harbour set to commemorate this unique occasion.

When the time came for Prince Charles and Governor Chris Patten to shake hands with the incoming Communists before boarding the Royal Yacht *Britannia* and sailing into the sunset, eighty tons of fireworks would set the night sky ablaze over Victoria Harbour. Everyone had bagged a spot to witness the spectacular, in favourite bars, restaurants and clubs, some throwing champagne parties on the waterfront or sailing out onto the rippling black South China Sea in traditional junks.

... And where would I be?

As iconic scenes of Hong Kong flashed upon the screen, locals and expats spouting anticipation at the camera, tears rolled down my face. It was *my* Hong Kong, my *beautiful* Hong Kong, and I should be there sharing the experience with my friends. Sitting unemployed on your parents' couch while watching daytime TV is demoralising enough. This unexpected reminder of everything I'd lost was an additional kick in the teeth.

My dad came over from the carpet shop to pick up his lunch. 'You okay?'

I just pointed at the program and sobbed.

Dad put his hand on my shoulder. 'You're not happy, old boy, are you?'

All I could do was nod at the TV.

'But *why* do you want to go back there?' he asked, shaking his head.

How could I explain the adrenaline rush of simply being in Hong Kong, let alone immersing yourself in a culture you love? My father could never understand how it felt to be a *gweilo* who spoke the language, one of the few westerners who worked for the Hong Kong triads. Everything about living in such a remarkable place, including my wonderful Chinese friendships, was eye opening and unforgettable.

I'd love to have talked with Dad about my reasons for returning to Asia – only I couldn't. When it came to meaningful dialogue, my parents avoided it like anthrax. It's just the way it was.

The Miracle of Metherton

Benny lived with a friend in Metherton in Cornwall, a one-cockerel hamlet not far from the engineering shop where he worked as a welder. I still had no idea what that driving ban nonsense had been about, but Dad had no problem with me borrowing the van to go over there.

Metherton sat in the Tamar Valley, ten miles upstream of Plymouth and about forty minutes' drive from Helmstone. As opposed to taking the Torpoint Ferry, the long way around, I drove inland, passing the ancient stannary town of Tavistock, the birthplace of Sir Francis Drake, and crossing the Tamar into Cornwall via the village of Gunnislake's five-hundred-year-old granite bridge. Cruising through the enchanting pine forest bristling along the slow-flowing river's steep upper banks, I was in a much better mood than the previous day. Hong Kong might well be approaching a historic handover, but I was stuck in England and had to make the best of it.

Although not as outgoing as me, my brother got on well with everyone. We had a close relationship, a bond strengthened by the tough times we'd endured as kids. He'd been exceptionally proud of my military accomplishments, but this Hong Kong business appeared to have rocked him. I guess he was coming to terms with the fact his big brother was only human.

Ben looked after Oscar, my pet scorpion, whom I'd inherited from an American-born Royal Marine when he returned stateside. Oscar was good value, particularly at after-parties when I'd pick him up by the tail and freak out my guests. When I left for Hong Kong, my bro offered to take care of him.

Upon reaching Metherton, I located Ben's house, a former tin miners cottage with whitewashed walls and an undulating slate roof that had seen flatter days. I crossed the patchy grass in the front yard and knocked on the cottage's solid wooden door.

The chap who answered grinned. 'Hello, mate. I'm Raynes. You must be Ben's brother.'

Raynes shook my hand, but as I stepped inside a shiver came over me. The cottage's thick stone walls acted like a fridge, resulting in a distinct drop in temperature, another reminder I was no longer in the tropics.

'Ben, Chris's here!' Raynes shouted up through the ceiling's cracked plaster.

Unusually, my brother didn't come bounding down the narrow wooden staircase to greet me, so Raynes ushered us through to the cottage's cramped front room, where we sat on a blim-burned flowery sofa in front of a much-welcomed log fire. 'I'm a landscape gardener,' he said, rolling a joint. 'Self-employed.'

I immediately felt envious. Raynes was obviously one of these disciplined types, grafting outside in all manner of weather to build a solid future for himself. Although I'd demonstrated similar qualities to earn my green beret, I felt a million miles away from that mindset now.

'I quite often need labourers,' Raynes continued. 'I can give you a shout next time, if you like.'

'Sure,' I replied, grateful for the offer.

Footsteps creaked on the staircase. Benny entered the room, but rather than give his big brother a hug, he collapsed in a chair. 'I *don't* believe it,' he groaned, fingertips pressed against his temples.

'What's up, mate?' I asked.

'I *don't* believe it.' He shook his head, a hair's breadth from bursting into tears.

Raynes and I glanced at each other.

'It's *Oscar.*' Ben slammed his fists into his thighs.

'Go on,' I urged.

'He's ... *dead!*'

Well, this was a spinner. I'd come over to say hi to Benny not goodbye to my beloved scorpion. 'Beloved' is a slight exaggeration, though, as it's hard to form a connection with a cold-blooded poisoner who lives under a rock. Ben brought Oscar's lifeless body downstairs and placed him on the mantelpiece. Then he began muttering if-onlys followed by a tearful eulogy.

Oscar had been a strange fish – for a scorpion. He'd lived in a gravel-strewn vivarium, with a rock and a piece of driftwood providing token environment and a milk bottle lid to hold his water. It was weird, though, for when the Giant Desert Scorpion hadn't been hiding under his rock, claws ajar, waiting to ambush his weekly meal of locust, he'd spent a good part of the day *crouching* in his water bowl. Considering the little fella was supposed to be a sand dweller, evolved for arid conditions, something hadn't seemed right.

Raynes and I did our best to console Ben, volunteering to dig a grave in the garden and inviting him to say a few words in the critter's honour. Spying Raynes' barbeque, 'Perhaps we should give him a Viking send off?' I suggested.

Raynes laughed and fetched a spade from the shed. 'Where shall I dig the hole?'

'There.' I pointed to the centre of the lawn, figuring Oscar deserved pride of place.

'How big shall I dig it?'

'About ... *that* big.' I indicated with my thumb and forefinger the approximate length of a Giant Desert Scorpion.

'Fuck off!' Raynes chuckled. 'I mean, do you think Ben wants to bury him in a box or something?'

'Why don't you dig a shoebox-size hole just to be on the safe side?'

'Good idea.' Raynes went to plant the spade in the turf.

'*Wait!*'

'What?'

'Do you need a hand?'

'Nob!'

With the hole dug, Raynes and I stood side by side on the lawn, like a pair of gravediggers showing their respect for the funeral party, only my brother still hadn't appeared with the deceased.

Seconds later, Benny burst out of the front door, eyes as wide as

Clyde's. *'You won't believe it!'* he screamed. *'It's the Miracle of Metherton!'*

Raynes and I glanced at one another.

'Oscar's *alive!'*

Sure enough, my brother was right, but as he ran around the house waxing evangelical, I think I was able to explain the second coming.

Two of the lads I'd served with on HMS *Invincible,* Stretch and Scooter, had bought a pair of rattlesnakes while ashore in the USA. Tragically, the diamondbacks died on the passage back to Britain, so the boys threw them into the North Atlantic. Later that evening, one of the other marines happened to be reading the owners guide supplied by the pet shop. 'Fellas,' he piped up. 'What's the temperature in the ship – in Fahrenheit, I mean?'

'Bout ... fifteen degrees C, so around fifty-five,' Stretch replied.

'Fuck ... It says here rattlesnakes *hibernate* below sixty!'

Armed with this information, Ben took Oscar to a reptile shop in town. The proprietor concurred, saying Oscar had not only gone into temporary hibernation but he wasn't a Giant Desert Scorpion – he was a *tropical* Emperor Scorpion. Jungle dwellers such as these needed a humid environment, not the bone-dry one Oscar had been forced to endure for *five* years. No wonder the poor chap spent most of the day in his water bowl!

Rather than return to Helmstone, I detoured to Plymouth to see an old mate, Morris, whom I'd met in the Warehouse nightclub. A brain injury as a baby had left Morris with damaged hearing, impaired speech and disobedient legs, but this never affected his sense of humour. Back in the day, when the lights came on in the club at the end of night, Morris would lend me his wheelchair and I'd burn around the dance floor pulling wheelies. One time, a girl chased after me, screaming, 'Give it *back* to him, you *twat!'* which we always found hilarious.

Morris was a technical boffin, smart-as when it came to computer engineering and programming. I appreciated how he explained complex PC stuff to me in easily understood terms. I pulled up outside his bungalow and knocked on the door.

'I thought you were in Hong Kong?' he rasped and grinned.

'I was, mate, but I'm here now. So you gonna roll a joint or what?'

He let out a child-like giggle and reversed his chair back along the hall.

Another bonus of being buddies with Morris was he always had a generous chunk of hash. While he skinned up, I made the coffees, and as we slipped seamlessly into conversation it was good to be in uncomplicated company. You knew where you were with Morris.

Just Once

Staring out of the kitchen window, I watched the morning sun breathing life into the lawn ... as it slipped out of me. What was I going to do? What job could I get? Where did my future lie?

I didn't have the answers to these questions, but I did have an old stereo in the loft that might fetch a tenner second-hand, enough to score some base amphetamine. Obviously, I wouldn't go full on down the drugs route again – that would be a bit stupid – but a ten-pound deal would pick me right up and put some poke in my spokes.

As its street name suggests, 'base', aka methamphetamine, is the raw form of speed that's purified into crystal form in places like Asia, the USA and Australia to create 'ice', hence 'crystal meth'. Base doesn't produce the intense, pure and long-lasting high that ice does, but it's the strongest amphetamine the UK has to offer and comes a close but shabby second.

Only the once, I rationalised, *to get me in the mood for some positive action.*

I picked up the phone and called the carpet shop. 'Dad, can I borrow the van?'

'Sure, Chris.'

I walked across the moorland to the business park and told my father I was visiting a friend and might be back late. 'Take it easy,' he replied, handing me the van keys. Back home, I picked up the stereo and headed for Wilkes, a second-hand shop in Plymouth. With a tenner in my wallet, I drove to Simon's, hoping he'd be home with goods to offer.

The door flew open. *'Chrissy!'* Simon beamed, throwing his huge arms around me. 'I thought you were in Hong Kong!'

'It went wrong, mate.'

'Come in.' He flicked his Samsonesque locks aside and thrust a spliff at me.

Simon had made an effort in his new flat, creating a bohemian environment with scatter cushions and psychedelic Goa-style backdrops. A Gibson Les Paul rested against the wall.

'Can you play it?' I eyed the guitar with envy, dying to show off my vast repertoire of A-C-and-D-chorded songs.

'Nah.'

I told Simon about my adventure in the Orient, not going into too much detail but enough to vent some pent-up trauma with a friend who would listen, someone far detached from my strange experience over there.

Sitting on the rug, wearing a pair of board shorts exposing calves larger than Goliath's big brother, Simon let out a plume of yellowy brown smoke. 'That's some shit, Chrissy,' he said, without a trace of scepticism.

This was one reason I loved Simon. He never doubted me.

I picked a Chinese puzzle off his mantelpiece, one of those wire-framed thingamajigs with a seemingly impossible-to-remove loop of string. I contemplated this conundrum for three or four seconds and had the string off in six moves.

Simon chuckled. 'That fucking thing's sat there for *seven* years and no one's ever managed to solve it. You do it in *thirty* seconds!'

Simon often said things like this. Sharing a spliff with him, the sun shining through his patio doors to the sound of uplifting house music, I felt the most relaxed I had in months.

'Erm ...' Scrunching his cheeks, Simon reached under a pile of CDs and pulled out an extra-large scorebag containing an ounce of beige powder. 'Been doing a *bit* of base myself.'

'How much is a bit?'

'Three or four grams a day.'

'*Whoa ...!*'

I couldn't believe Simon managed to keep it together with such a large habit. Three grams of base would get me high for a week. I guess he'd built up a tolerance.

'So can I get a bit, then?' I asked.

'Are you sure?'

'Yeah.'

'How much?' Simon went into dealer mode.

'Tenner's worth.'

My mate tore a small square from a page of Mixmag and fetched a miniature set of brass scales and weights. Then he tapped a gram of powder onto the paper, making a play of selecting me a match-head-sized chunk of 'allegedly' pure base yet to disintegrate in what was probably a sea of glucose. Of course, it was all an act. Scales or no scales, Simon could do this with his eyes closed.

I wrapped a quarter of the gram in a Rizla paper and washed it down with a Coke my host had grabbed from the fridge. With my system free of speed, the base hit the spot, enough to see me reminiscing with Simon about our mad shenanigans over the years, such as the time we'd shackled ourselves together with police handcuffs only to find out he'd lost the key.

'So how did you get back?' From a small red-and-silver fleury patterned cardboard holder, Simon pulled a foot length of Rips cigarette paper, a dedicated stoner's product that always reminded me of the cheap shiny bog roll you used to get in public toilets.

'I was screwed, mate. Skint, homeless, sacked from loads of jobs – even sold my Rolex. Dad asked me to come home and offered to pay for the flight.'

'Good fucking move.'

'Yeah ...' I began to chuckle.

'Go on.' Simon grinned, sprinkling a generous amount of Moroccan flat press onto the bed of tobacco he'd spread evenly along the paper.

'I was bit worse for wear turning up at the airport. Like an idiot, I got there at five pm, when my flight was due to depart. I hadn't even considered the three hours checking-in time.'

'*No!*'

'Luckily the flight was still on the ground. The girl at the Virgin desk called up an immigration official, who grabbed my bags and ran me past all the X-ray machines and into an office to stamp my passport.'

'Shit!' Simon began rolling his foot-long doob, using a split-cane place mat like a Rastafarian sushi chef.

'Yeah, then he asks if I'm carrying anything I shouldn't be.'

'Were you?'

'Erm ...' I frowned.

'Right.'

'When I finally got on the plane, the stewardesses had to shove my gear in the crew locker, because I never had time to check it in. So I sat down – *mega* self-conscious because it felt like it was *me* delaying the flight – and when they began serving drinks, the stewardess asks the guy behind, "Sir, would you like a refreshment?" And he says, "Yeah, a bloody Mary," and then looking right at me, "And can I have *ice* in that?"'

'Ha-hah!'

'I know, that was probably paranoia, but there was *definitely* some weird shit going on over there with the expats and the triads. But the funny thing was, when the stewardess bent down to serve the people across the aisle from me, I'm not kidding, she stuck her bum *right* in my face!'

'Hah!'

'I was so off my head, I thought it was all part of the service, like *"This* is how Branson grabbed such a big piece of the pie!"'

'Ah, ha-hah!'

Simon got up from the rug and threw his arms around my shoulders, making me feel secure for the first time in months. Then I watched him lick the gummed lip of the enormous cigarette paper protruding from the pleat of bamboo mat. He cut the resultant twelve-inch bad boy into three equal lengths, roaching each with rolled-up pinch of card torn from a half-empty Marlboro packet.

As evening drew in, a car pulled up. Simon stopped midsentence and jumped up to investigate.

'What is it –?'

He tore out of the room, returning seconds later. 'Here!' He handed me a meat cleaver and pulled a twelve-inch Bowie knife from its sturdy leather sheath.

'Mate?'

'*Fucking* Scousers!'

Growing up on Britain's roughest sink estates, Toxteth, Huyton, Bootle, the Liverpudlian gangsters migrating south in droves were notoriously sociopathic. They manipulated vulnerable Janners into warehousing and dealing drugs for them and woe betide anyone getting in their way. Their modus operandi involved getting a local girl pregnant, thus rendering the courts powerless to issue an antisocial behaviour order banishing them from the area. Retribution for debts and other perceived crimes against them came by way of gang rape and torture, some of the thugs carrying vials of hydrochloric acid to intimidate their victims.

I wasn't afraid to fight – although I should have been as I was pretty crap at it – but begrudged doing so over fucking drugs.

Simon stood at the window, making a wait-for-it signal with his hand. Glancing at the butcher's knife, I knew I'd only use it if my life was in danger, but should the door come smashing in, would I have time to think? After a few seconds, my mate's sigh of relief broke the tense atmosphere. 'Okay, it's Nige.'

Without further elucidation, Simon opened the door to a chap dressed in smart designer casuals. He spoke in a cockney accent and clutched a small leather holdall, like the ones the triads in Club Nemo carried. After cursory introductions, Simon handed Nige a wad of notes, which he stuffed into the holdall and disappeared.

'So where's the gear?' I cocked an eyebrow.

'It's coming,' Simon replied confidently. 'The goods should never be in the same place as the cash.'

This figured. It obviously gave the police less evidence with which to press charges.

Five minutes later, another car stopped outside. Simon walked up the garden path to greet the driver and came back with a small plastic dustbin. He drew the curtains and peeled off the lid. 'Have a look.'

Twenty nine-ounce blocks of Moroccan hashish, 'nine-bars',

packed the bin, each moulded with a star symbol. I gave Simon a contemplative nod but worried he was in over his head. From what I'd witnessed, drug dealers always ended up in prison or dead.

'Here.' He grinned and handed me one. 'Whatever you can bite off, you can keep.'

Greed kicked in and I clamped down on the bar with my front teeth, only managing to leave two slight indents because the hash was as hard as ebony.

Simon chuckled.

Morning came and Simon threw open the curtains. As sunlight flooded through his patio doors, he slid a Doobie Brothers CD into the hi-fi, selected 'Long Train Running' and cranked up the volume. We had a one-legged no-armed dance off – which we both lost *or* won *or* drew, depending upon your perspective – and Simon asked if I could drop him at a girlfriend's.

'Sure. You can drive.' I tossed him the keys.

Simon hadn't passed his test, but he was always banging on about how good a driver he was, so I thought he'd appreciate a lesson. What happened next made me question my offer.

He slammed my dad's poor van into gear, stomped his size-twelve boot down on the accelerator and released the clutch as if stepping on a landmine. We lurched forward and began careening down the street in a manner that could only mean he was trying to kill us – *after* taking out everyone in Plymouth. It was the reality version of *Grand Theft Auto,* an edit that would never made it past the censors, fellow road users veering onto the pavement and pedestrians diving over hedges.

'Look at *this* idiot!' Simon hollered, honking at an oncoming van. 'You're on the *wrong* side of the road, mate!'

'No, dude, we're on the wrong side.' I reached over and eased the steering wheel to the left.

Fortunately, the bus in front stopped, blocking the road. Unfortunately, Simon drove through the bus stop, scattering the passengers like extras in a Mad Max film.

'Erh ... Simon, can you slow down a bit?' I wondered how to

explain to my old man he had a pensioner stuck in his grill.

'*Don't* worry!' Freddy Kruger grinned. 'I know how to drive.'

I can see that …

It was no good. Despite my continued protestations, Simon hurtled through the city like a homecoming chimp. It was a relief to arrive at our destination.

At Brook Cottage, things weren't exactly relaxed, either. My stepmother continued to make it clear she resented me being there, which put pressure on my dad. I told them not to worry, because I'd soon return to Hong Kong.

'Why the *hell* would you go back there?' Dad slammed his hands down on the washing-up bowl.

There was no point trying to explain, so I packed my bergen and walked out. I called Elsie from the village phone box and hitchhiked to her flat. Following the rapid-fire clack of a doorbell muffled with a folded takeaway menu, her silhouette appeared in the small pane and the latch clicked open.

'Hello, lovey!' She grinned.

We had a hug – only Elsie suddenly pulled away. 'Did *you* shove that cloth through my letterbox?' Her face had darkened.

'Oh … I'm so sorry, Elsie.' I felt fucking stupid. 'I haven't been very well. I was trying to give you a sign I needed help.'

Elsie's eyes instantly switched to project empathy, easing my embarrassment as we went inside. We sat chatting on her black leather sofa, four-year-old Massey playing with toys on the floor. 'I've got a job in an old people's home,' she said. 'Been doing a bit of speed to keep me awake on nights.'

I didn't say anything, but the amphetamine certainly explained Elsie's twitchiness. She called my dad to say I was okay, which was kind of her.

While Elsie slept after her shift, Massey and I went walkabout. It was a gorgeous summer day in Plymouth, trees in full bloom, sprucing up a backdrop of tired townhouses and ugly post-war-reconstruction concrete. Shorts and miniskirts had replaced jeans and tracksuit bottoms, shoes and trainers swapped for flip-flops and sandals. Locals went about their business, smiling and with a spring in their step, looking forward to weekend drinks on the seafront, barbecues in back gardens and picnics at the beach.

'Massey, wannabe a Viking?' I pulled my monastery-plundering face.

'Yeah!' he replied, delight glinting in his tiny brown eyes, and so we snapped broadswords from a tree and began marauding down the street chopping monks in half.

In reality, we were heading for Simon's. I'd withdrawn a tenner from an old Halifax account that still had a few quid in it. I wasn't desperate for amphetamine, but life was boring and getting high seemed a good idea. *Only a ten-quid wrap,* I rationalised. *Something to add an edge to the day.*

Elsie went to work, leaving me to entertain Massey for the evening. 'Who's the *best* guy in the whole wide world?' I joked.

'Me!' He grinned.

'And who's the *other* best guy?' I winked.

'You!'

We giggled at our silly role-play for the umpteenth time that day and chorused, 'High-*five!*'

After Massey went to bed, I tidied the flat as a thank you to Elsie, but in the morning she wasn't happy.

'Chris, I don't like this stuff about being the best guy in the world.'

'Oh ...' This surprised me – it was only a silly game. We'd also played at being the stupidest shark, the funniest frog and the tickliest tiger.

'Elsie, I'm sorry.' I felt foolish and hurt.

'Chris, I'm gonna have to ask you to leave. I can't be dealing with this at the moment.'

'Okay,' I replied ... for the fifth time in as many months.

Chunks

As I packed my bergen in the hallway, Elsie poked her head around the door. 'Your dad's on the phone.'

I picked up the receiver, knowing my old man would be feeling as bad as I did about our falling out. 'Chris, I spoke with the letting agent,' he said, his tone intentionally neutral.

'Uh-huh.'

'I explained the situation and the guy renting your place has agreed to move into another of their properties.'

'Oh, right.'

'He's leaving this morning, so how about I pick you up and drop you around there?'

'Okay, thanks, Dad. I'm sorry about –'

'Ye-ye-yeah.' He met me halfway.

I said goodbye to Elsie and hefted my khaki house out to the pavement. At the risk of seeming ungrateful, I wasn't looking forward to moving back in. It made the prospect of returning to Hong Kong anytime soon seem increasingly unlikely.

Dad pulled up and after subdued hellos we drove to Carroll Road. I entered the two-bedroom new-build to find everything as I'd left it, the only exception being the tenant had taken down the poster of me and Eric Jansen on stage at London's Alexandra Palace. Eric was the world-famous personal-development guru whose 'Break Through the Barriers Inside' seminar I'd attended as part of my military resettlement package. It was a memorable event, with Eric teaching us to walk on hot coals to bolster our goal-getting skills.

Now, however, as I cast an eye over the magnolia walls, deep-pile cream carpet and minimalist furnishing, my previous passion for life seemed so far removed. Perhaps Eric's techniques were slow burners.

Dad entered the front room, interrupting my morosity. He

dumped a large bag of food on the floor and promptly burst into tears. Before I could speak, he'd run back to the van, muttering, 'I'm glad you're home, son.'

I understood why he was upset, but I was far from glad. I lived in Hong Kong, and I didn't want to be here.

There was a knock at the door. Assuming it was a cold caller, I decided not to answer, but the possibility of some mild excitement saw me change my mind. It was Derek, my neighbour opposite, a good bloke and a builder by trade.

'How was Hong Kong?'

'Long story, Del, but not brilliant.'

'Sorry to hear that. Do you need a set of wheels?'

'Wheels?'

'Yeah, come.' He winked.

Del led me across the road to his garage and hoisted the up-and-over door. *'This* little beauty.'

I *couldn't* believe my luck! Derek's Mazda RX7 sat there gleaming, *sparkling,* in as immaculate a condition as the last time I saw it. I guess he must have upgraded to the latest model and be in the process of moving this one on.

'Del, I-I-I *don't* know what to –'

'Save it, mate.' He grinned and ducked behind the mint-condition sports car, reappearing a second later with a dusty purple bicycle. 'Here.' He thrust it at me.

'Oh ...'

It wasn't even a good bike – it had a fucking bell.

Derek explained it was an impulse purchase at the local supermarket. 'Fitness bug not for you, then?' I smiled.

'Never actually ridden it.' He blushed. 'But it's yours if you want.'

I appreciated the gesture. Carroll Road was four miles from nowhere in every direction and only lunatics walk that kind of distance.

'What you doing tonight?' Derek propped the bike on its

sensible stand.

I considered the non-existent agenda in my non-happening life. 'Not a lot.'

'Fancy a pint on the Barbican?' He referred to Plymouth's historic harbour. 'Taxi's booked for seven.'

Come evening, I'd spruced myself up as best I could. With all my money going on meth these past months, I only had one set of casuals, namely a black gilet, T-shirt, grey jeans and Caterpillar boots, plus a black low-profile baseball cap from the junk room in Wan Chai. I hopped in the cab feeling a touch self-conscious, the Barbican representing the upmarket side of a night out in Plymouth.

'Where's Cara?' I wondered why Derek's stunning girlfriend wasn't with us.

'Gone, mate.' He half-grinned and shrugged. 'We got the seven-year itch and called it a day.'

'*Really?*' I envied Del's coolness. He was always self-assured and optimistic.

'Cara always fancied you, to be honest.' He chuckled. 'She loved the way you always take time for the kids around here, fixing their bikes and stuff.'

'Oh ...' I'd never have thought mending punctures and playing keepy-uppy placed me in Derek's tall, dark and handsome league.

The taxi driver pulled up next to one of the hefty iron cleats studding the Barbican's block-granite basin. We ambled along cobbled streets flanked by tall Tudor buildings, their ground floors now souvenir shops, pubs, tearooms and restaurants, and past pleasure craft and trawlers nudging against pontoons in the quay. I pulled open the door to a popular bar, the Maritime, and we stepped into a pack of drinkers enjoying the start of the weekend.

Derek bought round after round of lager, and I spent a token tenner as a gesture of gratitude. Pretty soon I was as drunk as the time I'd visited the Kangaroo Pub with the Filipinas a year ago, yet watching the revellers all doled-up and shouting above the Spice

Girls' 'Wannabe', I felt alienated. They had money in their pockets and jobs to go to on Monday. What did I have?

In an effort to perk myself up, I took a tour of the bar, but lurching around seeing double, I knew there was no chance of bumping my wretched self into Miss Right. When I rejoined Derek, he was chatting to a bubbly blonde-haired girl in a black dress. 'Chris, this is Josie,' he yelled. 'We've just met.'

Derek and Josie were obviously enjoying each other's company, raising my fed-up factor another notch, so I said goodbye and staggered outside. Del came running after me and tucked a fiver in my hand. 'Get a cab, Chris.' He patted me on the shoulder.

I awoke on the sofa at midday feeling rough. I yawned, stretched and opened the blinds to see a police car outside Derek's place. Figuring a garden shed had been broken into and the old bill were investigating the *Mystery of the Missing Flymo,* I went into the kitchen to make a cup of tea.

As the kettle boiled, there was a knock at the door. Del looked unusually flustered. 'Police have been round, mate. Have you seen the news?'

'No, what happened?'

'That girl we were talking to in the Maritime, *Josie?*'

'The blonde one, before I left?'

'She's been murdered.'

'Fuck ...' I invited him in.

'I hope you don't mind, but I gave the police your name. They'd like to speak to you.'

'Yeah, of course.' I began rolling a cigarette.

Apparently, CCTV captured Josie leaving a club on Union Street around 2am and a dog walker found the poor girl's battered body in the park this morning.

I didn't mind Derek giving the cops my name, but it wouldn't be the first time they'd interviewed me for something this serious. During my time on HMS *Invincible,* a crewmember crept into the chief medical officer's cabin and smashed her over the head with a ballpein hammer. Fortunately, the woman lived, and after interviewing the ship's company the Special Investigation Branch narrowed it down to a jealous stoker.

A year later, someone murdered a woman *with* a hammer on a housing estate near mine. Because her husband had served on HMS *Invincible,* the police computer cross-referenced the murder weapon, the ship and my neighbourhood and came up with me as a suspect. In my interview, the detectives attempted the good-cop/bad-cop routine, but *fairly* certain I wasn't a serial killer, I told them to stop trying to intimidate me and provided an alibi. However, when the coppers showed me a photofit the resemblance was uncanny and I could see why they thought I was their man. After last night's tragic event, I bet the police *and* their dodgy computer thought they had struck gold.

Halfway through the week the law still hadn't been around. Hopefully, this meant they'd arrested the fucking scumbag. I slumped on my two-seater sofa bed as it slid sideways into a meaningless abyss. Miserable didn't come near to summing up the sheer apathy, unhappiness and rejection I felt. I couldn't eat and hadn't bothered to unpack. Everything was *shit.* Absolutely *shit.* The only thing capable of lifting this crushing mood was a trip to Simon's flat.

I entered his front garden to find a scene bordering on anarchy. The giant stalks of grass lay slain like warriors on the battlefield. Someone – certainly not Lord Lazybones – had let rip with the eye of a tiger, the blade of a Samurai and the resolve of a worldclass goal-scoring legend underated in his time ... Tommy Tynan, for example.

I found my pot-peddling pal in the front room chatting to the human combine harvester – a rotund chap wearing bright yellow dungarees, Liverpool FC sweatbands and a 'Choose Life' T-shirt. He carried off a Panama hat, gold hoop earrings and purple grass-stained wellies better than anyone I'd ever met.

'Chrissy!' Simon shoved a fat joint into my fingers. 'This is

Chunks.'

I turned to acknowledge the bohemian Wurzel, who wouldn't look amiss selling weed to the cast of *Rainbow*. But before I could shake his hand, 'The *Chunkster!*' he blurted.

'Chunkenstein!' Simon batted a return.

'Chunkfest!'

'Señor Chunkenheimer!'

'Chunky Chunkleton!'

'The Chunkmeister!'

'The Chunkmeister General!'

'Sir Chunkety Chungleton!'

'His Royal Chunkness!'

So it went on, the two of them amusing themselves in what must have been a well-worn script.

Chunks turned to me, waggling his hands like Al Jolson. 'Chrissy, or should it be Kristoff?'

'Kristofferson?' Simon suggested.

'Kris Kristofferson the Third!'

'Kristobell!'

'Kristolo Kristenhammar!'

'The Kristenmeister!'

'Kristen Crusolo!'

As Simon guffawed once more, the Chunkmeister General shook an apologetic head and introduced himself as Paul, a former soldier originally from Dorset. 'Me and Siborg go way back,' he stated proudly. 'I *de-triffided* Centre Court this afternoon with my petrol strimmer.'

'De-triffidified?' Simon proffered.

'Triff-lesstified.'

'Triff-ridded.'

... and off they went again, leaving me wishing I had the tongue-talent to join in.

Chunks' outgoing demeanour was typical of ex-forces. He made a refreshing change from Simon's usual parade of sketchers and their paranoid 'Who's-he?' routines. He looked late-thirties, although years of partying likely contributed to that. Along with laughter lines, he had a permanent grin and wore limp Ravy Davy bob hair under his eccentric straw hat.

We sat smoking joints and howling with laughter as El Chunko regaled us with tales of drug-fuelled derring-do and chemically enhanced stupidity. When I shot Simon a 'Got any speed?' look, he shook his head, and so as night drew in I welcomed Chunks' offer of a lift home.

As I shoved my bike into the back of his hideous hand-painted Mattel-pink Volvo, complete with matching fur upholstery and fluffy dice, 'Cuppa at mine?' he suggested.

'Nice one.' I climbed into the giant vagina.

Chunkeroo drove us north of the city to a council estate on the banks of the River Tamar, about a mile from my house. 'Fort Chunkington,' he announced, pulling up outside a solid-looking post-war prefab on a shadowy tree-lined boulevard.

I followed him up the garden path and under a fifteen-foot-high fibreglass owl with a rope swing, slide and a satanic grin. The backdoor opened into a dinette decked out in pine, its booth-style bench and table giving it a yacht cabin feel. 'Cup of cha, Kristoff?' he whispered, pointing through the ceiling to his sleeping family.

'Rude not to,' I told this highly likeable gent.

Chunks shoved a Prodigy CD into an aging ghetto blaster and screwed down the volume. 'Keith's a mate of mine,' he said, flicking a thumb at the absent singer's vocals.

I wasn't familiar with the track, but it sounded like an excited gorilla bashing a cat over the head with a Yamaha keyboard and certainly not the house music I felt passionate about.

Chunks returned with two mugs. 'So shake out the shizzle-banger.' He gave me an expectant nod.

'Sorry?'

'The rum-dinky-doo.'

'Uh ...?'

'The *gear,*' he clarified.

'What gear?'

'The hooty-tooty, the nasal blazer, the *drugs* you bought from Siborg.'

'He didn't have any, mate.' I could have done without the reminder.

'Oh ...' Chunks frowned. 'Best stick with tea then.'

With 'Out of Space's' psychedelic intro tripping in the background, we fell into an easy chat about drugs, travel and outrageous military experiences. When Chunks got up to make another brew, I took a skeg around the room. There were loads of photos of him and a pretty, demure-looking woman with large brown eyes and long dark hair. As the years progressed, a succession of romper-suited rug thugs boosted the numbers in the family portraits, five boys in total, the oldest now approaching his teens.

'My partner, Chelle.' Chunks placed our mugs on the table. 'And that's Leroy, Kodiak, Benz, Hawk and Jack.'

'Jack?' I wondered why the eldest got off so lightly.

'After the bass player in Cream.'

'Oh, right.' I took a sip of tea. 'And these guys?' I pointed to a photo of a younger Chunks sitting outside a pub with four other lads, all sporting the centre-parted bobs favoured by Mancunian bands and Aunt Sally from *Worzel Gummidge.*

'My old crew.' The Chunkster beamed. 'After the army, I went on a mad one, tearing around the Smoke, snorting coke, popping pills, setting up raves and mixing it large with all the top DJs. Should probably have spent more time at home, but Chelle was good with Jack and Hawk, so it worked out okay.'

Chunks fell silent a moment, as if reflecting on past behaviour. It made me realise how fortunate I was to have gone through my recent turmoil with no dependents. After a time, 'Siborg tells me you lived in Honky Konky, Chrissy-boy.'

'Got back recently, mate.'

'So can you speak any of the ol' Japanese?'

That's a different country ...

Chunkfucious began making a comical chopping motion with his hands. 'I'm guessing you're hoo-hoo hi-*yah* hi-*yah-yah* with the ol' taekwondo!' he continued, knocking over his tea.

That's Korea ...

'I bet you woz *hushty-cushty* with the ol' yakuza. I bet they looked at you and thought here's an ex-Royal Machine that's gonna teach us how to *kick* ass!'

That's Japan ...

'It's the triads in Hong Kong, Chunks.' I tweaked his GPS. 'I was a doorman in one of their clubs and it all went a bit –'

'Nuclear antiques!' Chunks grabbed my arm, nodding to the imaginary distance with a glint in his eye.

'Nucl –'

'Think about it, Chrissenhoff! All those submarines knocking about in the dockyard. We buy one from the MOD, dismantle it and *sell* each part as a collector's item.'

Chunks was referring to the outmoded Cold War subs lying alongside in the naval base while their reactors cooled down, which took – *ooh?* – about a *thousand* fucking years!

'We could melt down the hull and make doorknockers!' He gave me a *'This* time next year, Rodney ...' look.

'Chunks, that shit's radioactive.'

'Exactly! How many people can say they've got a radioactive periscope on their mantelpiece?'

'Or a doorknocker that glows,' I cashed in on his genius.

Call me a spoilsport, but along with the threat to national security, I spotted a potential health and safety issue in the Chunkmeister's plan. I didn't say anything, though. He seemed happy, and I certainly was. Cycling home in the early hours, I couldn't wait to see Chunks – aka Captain Chungleton, Chunksthorpe, the Chunkfest, Sir Chunkity-Chinkity-Changlemeister – again.

Pins and Needles

I awoke at midday and mooched about the house, knowing I should unpack my bergen but not having the will for it. Instead, I crashed on the sofa bed, utterly fed up, directionless and deflated. I was about to do something I'd never done before, switching on the delights of daytime television, when the phone rang. '*Chris,* it's *Neil Diamond!*'

Neil was my drug-loving colleague from Gung Wan Hong, the crazy computer trading company. Born in Kenya to British parents, Neil had graduated from university in the UK with a degree in Geography and Soil Science. Only, with his condition of paranoid schizophrenia going undiagnosed for years, Neil had 'accidently' ended up in Strangeways Prison where he 'accidently' incited fellow prisoners to climb onto the roof during the 1990 riot. The last I'd heard, Neil's parents had sent him to rehab in England.

'*Neil!*' I laughed aloud. 'How the *hell –?*'

'I'm living in Barnstaple. I found your dad's number and he said you're back in Plymouth.'

Barnstaple was in North Devon, seventy miles away, and so the following Friday I hitchhiked to Helmstone and borrowed the van.

Driving across the Dartmoor highlands felt amazing. Long golden grass shimmered in the breeze. Skylarks flitted to and from their nests in the vivid purple heather. The rugged little horses grazed along the rolling highway. As House Music's chopping piano chords cranked up my mood, glorious sunshine enhanced the stunning landscape, filling me with energy.

Slowing occasionally for sheep or speeding up to pass other cars, I couldn't wait to see Neil. He'd lived in Hong Kong a number of years but wasn't involved in this Foreign Triad business, which meant I could be straight with him and maybe get some answers.

Of course, there was another reason I looked forward to

meeting Neil. Since smoking meth together in Gung Wan Hong's toilet cubicle, we'd bashed the drugs at every opportunity. His parents may have sent him to rehab but, like me, there was no way he was ready to knock his substance use on the head.

I followed the south bank of the Taw towards Barnstaple, a former river port and Britain's oldest borough. An enormous stone bridge dating back to medieval times carried me into the quaint market town – quaint in the eighteen hundreds, that is. Now a mismatch of contemporary frontages diluted the original redbrick architecture's Dickensian ambience. Steering with my knee, I double-checked Neil's directions before pulling up outside a turn-of-the-century townhouse.

Neil appeared at the front door, his nicotine-stained fingers evidencing the poor chap's loneliness. *Hiiiii,* Chris!' he extended his usual exaggerated welcome, grinning so hard his ears met for coffee.

'Mate, *this* is alright.' I nodded at his place.

'This is *alright!'*

When Neil was excited, he repeated what you said.

'How are you, mate?' I asked.

'Yeeaah, how *am* I, mate?'

'No, really, how *are* you?'

'I'm, well ... *ha-ha!'* He threw his arms around me. 'I grew a marijuana plant, you know.'

'Wow!'

'Wanna see it?'

'Why not.'

'Oh ...' He stared at the ground. 'My support worker made me throw it away. It was pretty big, though. I grew it from a seed.'

Support worker? This was a surprise. Neil never had one in Hong Kong, perhaps because he'd lived with his parents.

He showed me around the three-story property and introduced me to his fellow tenant, a chap with learning disability. Apparently, the support worker popped in twice a week to check on them.

'Shall we walk around and smoke?' Neil asked.

'Walk where?'

'Along the roads?' He shrugged.

'Let's do it.' I smiled.

Heading up the street, rolling a cigarette, I was keen to get Neil's take on the Foreign Triad. 'Do you know anything about them, mate? They hung around Club Nemo running errands for the 14K.'

'No ...' He took a drag on his roll-up. 'But it sounds a bit pathetic. You don't need to be in a gang to feel good about yourself.'

Spot on!

Beneath Neil's childlike exterior lay pearls of unadulterated wisdom, precisely what I needed to hear.

'And what about their hand signs, code words and coughs?' I pictured the surreptitious exchanges I'd witnessed while working as a doorman.

'Sounds like Iggy Piggy.'

'Go on.'

'Pig Latin. Boys at my boarding school used it to keep secrets from the masters. You swap your letters around and add "ay" to them. So "stick" becomes "ickstay".'

'Right ...' I nodded, mind in overdrive.

Rather than putting the Foreign Triad to bed, Neil's insight fuelled my curiosity. Getting to the bottom of the expat clique was a definite on my bucket list – in between the London Marathon and naked fly-fishing.

A packed school bus pulled up alongside the kerb. Neil grinned and began mimicking a thumping dance track, *'Boom*-bah, *boom*-bah, *boom*-bah ...!' Pumping his fists in the air while stepping from side to side, he looked like a troglodyte performing a tribal ritual.

The kids went into uproar, piling over each other to reach the window, shrieks of laughter penetrating the glass.

I laughed. Neil could be pretty random.

We continued through town. 'How did you end up in Barnstaple, Neil?'

'Oh, my parents got sick of the drugs and sent me to a farm

here.'

'A *farm?*'

'Yeah, with a rehab.'

This was a new one. I'd heard farmers were turning to various enterprises to remain solvent – B&Bs, petting zoos, working holidays – but *rehab?* Talk about jumping on the charity bandwagon!

'It was dead strict, like a convent,' Neil continued, 'and everyone had to work.'

'What did you do?'

'Fed the chickens.'

'Hah!'

'But we'd collect the eggs then sneak into town and sell them to a butcher to get money for cigarettes.'

'Did you do any drugs?'

'Nah, not there.'

Neil looked down for a moment and then his eyes lit up. 'But I've been getting speed off a guy at my NA meeting.'

'What we waiting for, then?'

Neil called his friend in Narcotics Anonymous and got the number for his dealer, a lad called Jamie. 'Come on over,' said Jamie.

Pooling our enormous reserves, we came up with a tenner, not enough for the drug deal of the century but if Jamie's gear was as good as he'd made out it should get us high for some time. I didn't spare a thought for any previous resolutions or my family's feelings. In the same way people drive above the speed limit, eat junk food and pollute the environment, my primate mind ignored the consequences and focused on the short-term gain. I was miserable in Plymouth, alienated from society and desperately missing Hong Kong. Here was a chance to escape those feelings and experience sheer bliss with an old friend, someone who understood and accepted me.

Besides, the *moment* I contemplated getting high there was never any going back. Like a wolf in captivity spotting its cage door ajar, my mind was already running with the pack.

After crossing the old town, passing Victorian buildings and swans paddling in the river, we entered a modern council estate. Neil rang the bottom bell on a smart block of flats, the door opening a few inches to reveal a skinny pale-faced youth in baggy jeans and a tracksuit top.

He eyed us warily.

'Jamie?'

After a nervous nod, he invited us in. We stepped into the living area and sat on a red polyester sofa bed, the kind of flimsy Argos affair a teenager might have in their bedroom. Jamie took the floor and began flicking through a music magazine on the coffee table, revealing wraps of speed secreted in its folds. He passed one to me. 'You gonna pin it?'

I looked to my mate, knowing 'pin' meant 'inject', something I'd done once, with David Niven (not *the* David Niven) in my dilapidated shack in Mong Kok, but Neil never. The way Jamie assumed we'd bang the drug into our arms added a degree of normality to a practice most people found abhorrent. 'Yeah,' we replied in unison, no way our addicted mindsets would pass on the chance to maximise our precious investment.

'But I'm first on the needle, Neil.' I said, recalling the sinister-looking iceberg in the scaremongering eighties AIDS-awareness campaign.

'Don't worry.' Jamie smiled, sliding a Tupperware box and yellow sharps bin out from under the coffee table. 'No one shares works anymore.' He opened the box and ripped two hermetically wrapped 1ml syringes from a strip of ten.

'Where do you get this stuff?' I asked.

'The drug service.' He shrugged, handing me a small packet containing a 'Sterets' alcohol wipe. 'I'm a heroin addict. This shit's free.'

'You don't do speed, then?' I found it strange someone would choose opiates over amphetamine.

'Nah.' Jamie frowned, emptying our gear into the bowl of a

shiny tablespoon. 'Used to do loads, but I 'ad psychosis. I *ain't* going there again.'

Psychosis ... I'd not heard this term before. It sounded like some kind of speed-induced mind warp, one of those weird schizoid conditions that, fortunately, never affected strong characters like me.

Jamie had two syringes ready to go in seconds. 'Do you need a tourniquet?' he asked – as if we were accomplished pinner-uppers who should know such things.

The thought of wrapping a belt around my arm conjured up images from *Trainspotting,* so to avoid feeling a complete deviant I flexed my bicep and a fat blue lifeline answered the call. Our host pricked the spot and slid the hypodermic's contents into my bloodstream. Then I sat back on the couch, a Sterets clamped over the resultant red trickle, expecting a tsunami-like rush to sweep me to victory ... but I felt *nothing.*

Neil was next in the not-even-luke-warm seat. As Jamie pressed the plunger home, I watched for the expected euphoria ... which didn't materialise. This couldn't be *base* amphetamine. It wasn't even as strong as the glucose-laden chaff sold by gurning chavs in dance clubs. I should have called Jamie out for passing off crap deals to fund his heroin habit, only you don't burn your bridges with the dealer because rubbish gear is better than nothing and you never know when you'll be desperate – or stupid – enough to buy some more.

We got chatting and Jamie told us about his life, a revelation that didn't exactly fit with society's image of heroin users as dysfunctional layabouts. 'I get up at eight-thirty,' he said, 'to go shoplifting in town.'

'Every day?' I asked.

'Yeah, 'cept Sundays. Used to be less, but nicking's got a lot 'arder since they started using StoreNet.'

'What is it?' said Neil.

'A shared radio frequency. Barnstaple's got a huge smack problem, so shoplifting's rife. All the shops 'ave walkie-talkies and when they spot a smackhead they track 'em around town.'

'What do you do with the stuff?' asked Neil.

'Sell it in the pub and score three bags of heroin. I bang two of 'em up and gouge out on the sofa for the rest of the day. The other bag's for the morning, when I do it all again.'

Not much of a life ... I thought.

As if on cue, the door opened and two lads in trackies and baseball caps entered the flat. 'Gonna leave some stuff here, Jaimo,' said one of them, unzipping a large sports holdall. Out came six cut-crystal glasses, two leather jackets, a Nintendo games console, thirty packs of Gillette razor blades *and* a Swartz pepper mill.

'Big market for them?' I smiled, nodding at the condiment grinder.

'Nah.' The chap shook his head. 'That's for me.'

Neil and I spent the afternoon at Barnstaple's modest beach, making sculptures out of pebbles, driftwood and seaweed. Bizarrely, the buzz from the speed slowly increased, until it became surprisingly pleasant. Upon our arrival back at Neil's, I asked for the phone book.

'Sure.' He went to fetch it.

Before Sarah left Hong Kong for the air-hostess interview, she'd mentioned her parents had relocated to Barnstaple. I thumbed through the directory and found their address. Sarah's mum, Jenny, answered the door. *'Hello,* Chris!' she said, mouth agape but face alight.

Jenny was a wonderful individual, her kind eyes always smiling behind large clear-framed glasses. Put simply, she loved me because Sarah did. Her husband, Martin, a retired Wing Commander, worked for the Ministry of Defence at Barnstaple's RAF Chivenor. We got on extremely well, partly due to the respect fellow services hold for the Royal Marines. Sarah had two adorable sisters, both of whom had left home. I think the family had quietly assumed Sarah and I would tie the knot and pump out some sprogs.

'So you're back from Hong Kong,' Jenny said softly, appearing interested yet concerned.

'Yeah ...' I shrugged, not knowing where to begin.

'Sarah said you weren't in a good place over there?' Jenny tilted her head.

Figuring honesty the best policy, 'I got addicted to drugs,' I replied – noting the colour drain from her husband's face.

> *He's not smiling,*
> *He's not smiling,*
> *He's not smiling anymorrrrre ...*
>
> Barnstaple's Male Voice Choir:
Anymorrrrre ...
>
> *He's not smiling anymore!*

Martin began rocking back and forward like a reluctant skydiver. 'B-b-but *drugs* are *illegal!'* he blurted, attempting to turn his back on me – tricky when you're sitting opposite someone.

'Oh, *sweetheart ...* 'Jenny patted my knee.

'Yeah, it was fun at first, but before I knew it –'

'But *drugs* are *illegal!'* Martin boomed – at the cheese plant.

Not for the first time, I missed the obvious clues indicating a person felt out of their comfort zone. Desperate to be understood, I regurgitated events, oblivious as to how bizarre my rapid-fire recollection must have sounded – to anyone, let alone two innocents who'd only ever known a polite and humorous commando, good with children and animals.

'But *drugs* are *illegal!'*

In Martin's attempt to turn his back on the conversation, he'd come unscrewed at the hips and now his top half span around spouting the illegality of drugs like a demented Dalek. It was time I left.

Come morning, Neil and I felt the effects of no sleep and crap speed. There was only one thing for it – to buy some more – but our problem was cash. I knew there was a small amount in the

Halifax account, only I didn't have my bankcard, so we decided to try and withdraw twenty quid over the counter.

Heading into Barnstaple's town centre in the bright light of normality, I felt sketchy, scruffy and a total druggy. Neil chewed gum with his mouth open and wore iridescent eighties-style Top Shop trousers tucked into his shin-high Timberlands, a look that screamed playground shooter and cranked my angst.

The Halifax sat in a pedestrianised street packed with meandering tourists and mission-focused pensioners hauling wheeled shopping baskets. To avoid death by tartan trailer, we crossed the busy thoroughfare like *Frogger* to get to the building society. 'We need the customer service counter,' I told Neil.

'Yeah, we need the customer service counter,' he chewed, sounding like the sidekick in a stoner movie.

'Failing that, go in there wearing your Rambo boots and shout, "No heroes, no alarms and no one'll get hurt!"'

'... and no one'll get hurt.'

I approached a young woman wearing a Halifax-blue cravat and a welcoming smile. 'Do you sell lamps for lampshades?' I asked.

'I'm sorry?' Her eyes flicked to Neil and then to a non-existent colleague, seeking a cue to laugh.

I could tell something was wrong.

Realising she had a Grade A mental on her hands, the woman attempted to reply, only embarrassed and confused I grabbed my mate and dragged him outside.

'*Neil!*' I gripped his arm and stared straight ahead. '*What* did I say in there?'

'You asked if they sold lamps for lampshades,' he replied matter-of-factly.

'And did they?'

'No, they're a building society.'

The Perfect Storm

By the time I got back to Carroll Road, thoughts of building societies, lampshades and former potential father-in-laws were far from my mind, replaced by apathy, fatigue and guilt post-speed binge – if you can call half a gram of glucose a 'binge'. As I fumbled with the key, my next-door neighbour, Jane, arrived home with her daughter, Kayleigh.

'Hiya, Jane.' I forced a smile, wishing we'd caught up earlier when I wasn't feeling so perpendicular to the population.

'Hey, Chris!' The attractive blonde beamed.

Obliged to go over and chat, I mumbled something about Hong Kong not going so well, while neglecting to point out I was a drug-munching business failure with no soft-lighting appliances in the bank. I was acutely aware that before moving to Asia, when Jane knew me as a confident young marine, I probably came across as a bit 'cool'. Now, though, I felt shy, self-conscious and unable to look this hard-working mum in the eye. So absorbed by my own shattered sense of worth, I didn't even ask how she and Kayleigh were doing. Instead, I seized the first opportunity to slip inside my house.

Despite representing NATO at cleaning, tidying and ironing for seven years, I couldn't bring myself to unpack my Hong Kong baggage. Instead, I unfolded the sofa bed, dragged a duvet down from upstairs and flicked on my fourteen-inch colour TV. A rerun of *Columbo* appeared, one of the earlier episodes, in which Peter Faulk was still shaping his best-known character. In those days, when his signature raincoat remained relatively unblemished, the young lieutenant presented solely as a bumbling buffoon – as opposed to the shrewd, passively aggressive mind-gamer he would become.

Of course, that raincoat was never just a raincoat. That crumpled coverall, with its unsightly rips, blims and stains, represented justice for the people, for everyday folk who don't go around putting rat poison in Ovaltine or cutting the brake hoses on golf carts. That crass coffee-coloured crusader was responsible for bringing down corporate crooks, greedy relatives, vain celebrities and a bunch of other narcissists willing to commit the ultimate sin to secure their wealth and privilege. That raincoat *was* Columbo. It had a profound effect on public perception, affirming humanity's altruistic nature and keeping base desires in check. Through three glorious decades, *Columbo* winning numerous awards and accolades, it's safe to say that crusty cotton cloak was the real star of the show.

Unlike our wonky-eyed sleuth, I never saw the investigation through. I must have drifted off, waking a day later when hunger forced me from slumber. In my snazzy kitchen-diner, I rummaged through the food Dad had kindly bought, finding tea, coffee, sugar, milk, bread, butter, soup, apples, broccoli, sweetcorn, marmalade, tinned tuna, corned beef, pasta shells, tomato-and-basil sauce and sheets of lasagne verde.

There was a decent meal in there, but preparing it required a will to live – plus it's against the law for twenty-six-year-olds to own pasta in sheet form. So taking the easier option, I emptied a tin of mushroom soup into a black-glass bowl and whacked it in the microwave. Four slices of bread went in the toaster and another four rested on top, pre-browning to speed up the process.

I intended to pack away the sofa bed and enjoy a civilised meal in front of the television, after which I would shave, shower, form an animal charity and generally sort my life out. It would have been a wonderful plan ... had it not involved me. Instead, I stood there, elbow on the worktop, unable to resist dipping toast into steaming mushroom heaven and wolfing the lot down. Life doesn't get much more of a shambles than not being able to join yourself for dinner – especially when you both live in the same house. With this in mind, I retired to the sofa bed for another prescription of unadulterated TV-and-duvet escapism.

Here I was, a *grown man,* a *former commando,* an *international businessman,* behaving in a way that felt downright wrong and yet unable to stop. A loss of purpose and direction consumed me. To make matters worse, my closest friends were advancing in their careers and home lives, making sensible forward-thinking decisions and not rash and myopic ones like mine.

How come the Bobsleigh of Life was always cool runnings for *other* people, who got off to a good start, properly equipped with a determined team behind them, making appropriate adjustments to ace a smooth line to thunderous applause? Whereas, I would rock up solo in a bathtub with ice skates taped to the outside, opting for the easiest route and ignoring all the warning signs to shoot backwards out of the emergency exit and halfway across the car park.

My life had always been this way. I couldn't apply myself at school despite having a clever head and creative mind. I would never have served in the Royal Marines if Dan – now a captain – hadn't led the way. I excelled in sales, but you don't need formal qualifications or accredited training to succeed in network marketing, so I had nothing to show for my efforts.

Sitting under the duvet in the front room, scoffing toast and watching mind-numbing TV, I couldn't envisage landing a job stacking shelves let alone kick-starting a highflying venture. I wasn't feeling sorry for myself or burying my head in the sand. Deep inside, something was seriously wrong and I *couldn't* face reality without drugs.

'*Hiiiiii,* Chris!' Neil yelled down the phone. 'I've got my benefit money, so I can come down.'

I'd never been so pleased to hear from someone in my life. I met Neil off the Barnstaple bus when it pulled into Helmstone and we returned to Plymouth in my dad's van. It was a magnificent day in Devon – not that this was of any concern to us. We wanted to get high not top up our tans.

'I've brought my camera equipment,' said Neil. 'Perhaps we can sell it.'

I knew just the man.

An aficionado of the arts – photography, kung fu, drug dealing – Simon wouldn't hesitate to swap Neil's expensive camera for a questionable amount of amphetamine. We left his place with enough speed to keep two gnats off their heads for twenty minutes and headed for the Cornish end of the Tamar Suspension Bridge. Having parked beneath the impressive half-mile span, we clambered into the back of the van and poured the gear onto a map book.

Once again, Simon had been quick to point out the greeny-grey clusters in the mix were pure sulphate – not that us nobheads needed this selling point. We'd willingly have ingested cat litter if it promised to give us a buzz. With R Kelly's 'I Believe I Can Fly' floating from Radio 1, Neil and I racked the base into inch-long lines and snorted a couple each through a banknote. Then we lay down and stared up out of the van's rear window at the enormous bridge.

'Wow, *so* high!' said Neil.

'Yeah, man ...'

'No, the *bridge.*'

'*Oh* ... forty-two metres,' I played tour guide. 'Hence why people jump.'

'People hit the water from *that* height?' Neil sat up, eyes even wider.

'No, people hit the deck from that height.' I nodded to the shoreline. 'Aiming for that concrete there.'

'Oh, that's sad.' Neil was genuinely upset. 'Have you ever thought about committing suicide?'

'Nah, mate. Suicide is the ultimate sign you hate yourself.'

Despite my shitty situation, I didn't hate myself and never would.

By the following evening, we'd polished off the gear, and so before a comedown robbed us of motivation, I suggested a walk to see a friend.

Chunks yanked opened the door. 'Heh-hey, old bean! How's it hanging on the intergalactic ... *hangy* thingamabob?'

'It's hanging alright, mate.' I grinned. 'And don't call me Bob!'

Chunkmeister threw his head back. *'Ah, ha-hah!'*

'This is my mate, Neil, from Hong Kong.'

'Honkers, hey?' Chunks began bobbing up and down and waving his palms as if dodging snowballs. 'Bet you're handy with the old ju-jitsu, Neil.'

That's Japan ...

Neil let out an imbecilic chuckle.

'Always fancied a trip to Taiwan,' Chunks continued as we stepped inside.

Now, I knew *this* was bullshit – out of all the dream destinations, who the fuck prioritises Taiwan?

'Listen, do you guys fancy a pint?' asked our host.

I looked at Neil and we nodded.

'Chelle!' Chunks shouted up the stairs. 'Chrissy's stopped by. You know, the bloke from Honduras.'

'Oh, right,' came a muffled female voice.

'We're going up the pub.'

Chunks pulled a fluorescent-yellow construction worker's jacket from a row of pegs holding enough fabric to keep the whole of Plymouth dry. 'Get a move on and we'll catch the Eighty-Four.'

The bus driver drove us up the hill Neil and I had just walked down and stopped outside the Backward Parrot, a spit-and-lino affair with a reputation for being the roughest pub in Plymouth. We entered the lounge to the sound of the Verve's 'Bitter Sweet Symphony' and the familiar whiff of hashish. I liked the Backward Parrot.

Chunks introduced us to the barman, a thickset blond-haired chap with a welcoming smile. 'Steve, meet my mates, Chris and Neil, from Tokyo.'

'Hong Kong,' blurted Neil, as I shook hands with Steve.

'What can I get you boys?' Steve patted a pump handle.

Picturing the lone fiver in my wallet, 'Two halves of lager and whatever Chunks is having,' I replied.

As Steve pulled our drinks, Chunks whispered in my ear, 'If you ever need sorting out, Steve's your man.'

In the ensuing conversation, Steve made it clear he didn't sell drugs but knew all the punters who did.

'Can you get hold of any base?' I asked.

'A phone call and it's here in five minutes.' He winked.

'Any good?'

'*Strong* as, mate. Had a dab off someone last weekend.' Steve licked his finger. 'Didn't sleep for two days.'

Hmmh ... I looked forward to my next income support payment.

Neil and I left Chunks chatting at the bar and retired to the poolroom. With us being a little worse for wear, it wasn't going to be the best game ever played, but we cracked on nonetheless.

As I lined up on a difficult red, Chunks burst into the room. 'I've *got* it, Christobell!'

'Got what, mate?'

'*Magma* gnomes!'

I was definitely missing something.

'*Think* about it!' He beamed. 'We make a mould of a garden gnome, tap into the side of a volcano and fill it with magma! They'll be *all* the rage! Ching-pow-ping – we'll earn a *fortune!*'

'*Yeah ...!*' Neil grinned, delighted to be in on the ground floor of this lucrative venture.

'Not too many active volcanos in Plymouth, Chunks.' I hated to point out the obvious.

'Oh ...' He stroked his gold hoop earring. 'Where's the nearest one?'

'Probably Central America or failing that Hawaii.'

'Right ... I better sort out some transport.'

'And sensible footwear.' I smiled, looking forward to making my fortune in molten rock.

Full Speed Ahead

*'Well, it's like this, sir. I knew it was you when you told
me you'd driven up to Santa Barbara for tacos the night
Missus Malone died.'*

'I'm listening, Detective Columbo.'

*'Well, I had to ask myself, why the hell would
someone go all that way for tacos – not that tacos ain't
delicious. I mean, me and Missus Columbo, we just love
tac –'*

'Get to the point, Detective.'

*'Oh, yeah, sorry. The point is, sir, you panicked when I
put you on the spot.'*

'I'm afraid I don't understand.'

*'You lived in Santa Barbara for twenty years before
moving to Long Beach. There's a gazillion places to buy
tacos in Long Beach, but you blurted out your old
neighborhood.'*

'You know, Columbo. I think I underestimated you.'

Columbo. *'A Taco too Far'*

Neil went back to Barnstaple in the morning. With the drugs long
gone, it was all I could do to raise my head off the sofa bed and say
goodbye. I spent the next few days practising my new routine of
being thoroughly miserable, only leaving the comforting aura of my
four-channel Sony soulmate to go and spread an ever-decreasing
amount of butter and marmalade on toast. This somewhat extreme
diagnosis of 'psycho pants' meant I didn't have to seek employment
or provide further sick notes. Instead, I received a book containing
six months' worth of tear-out giros, each for the bank-breaking
bonanza of £102.16 cashed fortnightly at the local post office.

The 16p made me laugh, as if the government was attempting

to legitimise this piss-arse allowance by insinuating there was a complex yet equitable algorithm involved in their miserly calculation. I doubted anyone on Income Support gave a damn about 16p. Living on fifty-one quid a week was the ball-buster.

The following Thursday was benefit day. Bar the lasagne verde sheets and a rotting apple, my food cupboards were empty. Rather than cycle to the Co-op, which sat in a retail park behind Carroll Road, I opted for a shortcut the kids took through a patch of woodland. Having hauled myself over the head-high wooden fence bordering our estate, I picked my way through an army of chest-high stingers and, clinging to a trailing tree branch, used sidesteps to negotiate a steep muddy bank. After squeezing around a futile security grill intertwined with brambles, I climbed down a ten-foot-high retaining wall to emerge near the shopping trolleys.

I intended to splash out with this week's £51.08, stocking up on virgin-pressed-daffodil milk, cream of pike soup, a bacon and elderberry cob, Dutch shark pâté, pigmy-whipped veg, pan-fried koala and an onion flapjack. I'd treat my luscious locks to a bamboo-root-with-yew-tree-oil deep-follicle cleanse, followed by a Madagascan-peach destresser, soothing my tired skin with a shelled-almond-husk rejuvenator – because I'm worth it – not forgetting a bottle of Weedol for the lawn.

Pah! Who was I kidding? No amount of pampering could rescue me from this unrelenting torpor and certainly not a tin of pretentious soup. I needed some magical life-giving powder. With a bit of speed, I wouldn't have to waste my precious time on Earth lying on a shitty sofa bed. I'd flutter in the air like Roadrunner – *'Meep-meep!'* – and then tear around cleaning the house like Superman in a pair of Marigolds – *rock n' roll,* baby!

I'd empty the bins and wash the dishes stacked along the sideboard. I'd play house music on full volume and dance around the lounge, throwing in handstands and Michael Jackson spins for good measure. I'd crack a broad grin and say hi to the neighbours I'd so far managed to avoid. I'd whip out my musky Cantonese books and be fluent in the language, likely Mandarin too, by the end of the day. I could visit my family, catch up with old friends and look in the employment section of the *Evening Herald.* The moment amphetamine entered my bloodstream, my love of life would shunt into gear and I'd be *firing* on all four once more!

Unbeknown to me, my 'learned psychological condition' or 'maladapted programming', aka 'addiction', had already begun to 'act out' the process of taking drugs, triggering my brain's primitive reward mechanism and a state of anxious anticipation. Like a starving lion spotting a big fat gazelle, I was powerless to focus on anything else, making a trip to the Backward Parrot inevitable.

I left the post office with my cash but found myself staring at the shopping complex's pharmacy. *Needles!* If I scored some gear, what better way to ramp up the experience than to inject it? This method sent the drug hurtling towards the brain's pleasure receptors, maximising the high and making the gear last longer.

Entering the pharmacy's sterile environment, I felt inferior but dismissed it with an invisible shrug. If the white middleclass staff judged me that was their problem. These folks didn't know my story. They had no idea what I'd been through in my life and why I relied on amphetamine to seize the day. I'd *tried* to go drug-free and ended up no good to anyone. Besides, why wasn't there a law against eating junk food and sugar-laden snacks or drinking a bottle of wine a night, practices that place a huge burden on society and are guaranteed to shorten your life?

I approached the woman at the counter. 'May I have a packet of syringes, please?' I asked politely, as if buying a box of sticking plasters.

'*Syringes!*' she announced, unnecessarily shocked, as they obviously sold the fucking things. 'What size?'

'Erm ...' I didn't have a clue, screwing up my cover story of being diabetic. Recalling my Barnstaple experience, 'the small ones, please,' I continued, 'with the orange caps.'

'You mean *microfines.* We don't have them, but we've got one-mil barrels and separate needles.'

Shit, this was getting technical! I needed a hit not open-heart surgery. 'Yeah, they'll be fine,' I mumbled. 'And do you have any Sterets?'

'Only boxes of five hundred.' She turned to the pharmacist.

His eyes flicked to me and then to save us all the embarrassment, he nodded to his colleague and she dropped a handful of freebies into the plastic bag.

I cycled to the Backward Parrot, hoping Steve was good to his word and I wouldn't end up scoring a bag of salt and vinegar crisps. As I entered the near-empty pub, he looked up from his newspaper and grinned. 'Hi Chris, you after a bit of fast?'

'Yes, mate, please.'

'How much?'

With a hundred pounds in my wallet – not exactly Scarface – I knew a gram of base cost around twenty quid but had no idea about larger amounts. Steve explained a quarter of an ounce, approximately seven grams, cost a ton. 'It's *strong* old stuff,' he added.

'I'll go for four grams, then.' I figured this would last a fortnight, leaving me enough cash for a butter dish I'd had my eye on in the charity shop, plus a set of antimacassars and one of those ceramic chicken jobs you put eggs in.

'Right-o.' Steve reached for the phone. 'I'll call Damo.'

To be polite, I ordered a half of lager – not that Steve cared whether I'd come into the pub to buy beer or blood diamonds – and stood at the bar tapping my feet to 'Wonderwall' by Oasis. Hong Kong nightclubs catered to a wide-ranging clientele and therefore played mostly trashy dance and pop, so I'd missed the recent explosion of Northern druggy bands. I was aware of the Stone Roses, the Verve and the Happy Mondays, and that they all wore bobbed hair, Mod clothes and hated Robbie Williams, but it was Oasis that struck a chord with me. Here was a band loved for their abstract yet meaningful tunes, *true* rockers who didn't give a shit and snorted cocaine for breakfast.

Oasis's meteoric rise to fame was a distinct reminder I was an insignificant nobody. I wanted to be famous and recognised by adoring fans. I wanted to drink beer and get off my head while doing something I was good at. I wanted to *be* somebody.

A white BMW pulled up outside and an unassuming chap stepped out and made his way into the bar. He nodded at Steve, who reached for a Stella glass, and then turned to me. 'Four grams, yeah?' A bag of white powder appeared. 'Has to be twenty a piece. It's top gear.'

The usual sketchy protocol around buying drugs in public was noticeably absent from this exchange – I guess my friendship with Steve vouched for me. I had no doubt it was top gear too, as Damo didn't look the type to mess around cutting his product with shitty glucose. More likely, he shifted larger quantities at a price reflecting its quality.

'Ta.' I handed over the cash.

A thrill came over me as I imagined boiling the gear in a spoon and releasing Utopia into my arm with a syringe. Excitement wanted me to bug out of the pub immediately, but I stayed to finish my drink. Damo picked a blue-Perspex bong off the bar, filled its bowl with hash and took a good long pull.

This place was *brilliant!*

Back at Carroll Road, it was like stepping through a magic portal into a different dimension. How could it be possible to go from Grade-A pissed off to insanely happy simply by slipping a packet of powder into your pocket? Soon that naughty needle would lift my life above worry and strife, filling the *real* me with energy and passion, like Noel and Liam playing to an adulatory crowd.

I had intended to take my time preparing the syringe, revelling in the moment and getting everything just right, but it was never gonna happen. Instead, I rushed into the kitchen, grabbed a dessert spoon from the drawer and shoved a pint glass under the cold tap. After laying everything out on the living room floor – syringes, needles, alcohol swabs, spoon, scissors, water, cigarette filters and lighter – I retrieved the scorebag from my boot and tapped enough speed into the spoon to get sufficiently high without overdosing.

I clipped a needle onto a syringe barrel, sucked water from the glass and squirted it over the amphetamine. The powder dissolved immediately, but I heated the mix with the lighter nonetheless until it bubbled like a witch's cauldron. I snipped a four-millimetre slice from the end of a Swan cigarette filter and dropped it into the spoon, just as David Niven had done in my rat-infested pad that time. With the needle resting on this improvised strainer, I sucked up the liquid, thus preventing any migraine-inducing particles from entering into the equation.

After wiping the crook of my arm with an alcohol swab, I picked up the syringe, only its contents were too hot, so I waved it in the air like Sooty's wayward cousin. When the liquid had cooled, I pointed the needle skyward and flicked the syringe's barrel with a fingernail to release the tiny bubbles trapped in the syrupy elixir. Three or four of them shot upwards to join the air pocket in the top of the syringe.

I gently squeezed the plunger, purging an air bubble the size of a pea, enough to cause a lethal embolism. Good to go, I clenched my fist a couple of times to get my bulging vein up even more.

Stop!

What the *hell* was I thinking? I needed to make the most of the moment by playing some uplifting house music. I should light a cigarette too and take long slow drags to add to the euphoria. I no longer had the luxury of knocked-off Marlboro from the triads and so as Jon Da Silva's remix of 'I Will Survive' soared from my Sony stack system's speakers, I rested a roll-up in the ashtray. *Now* I was good to go.

The situation felt surreal, conducting a thrilling yet potentially life-ending act on my own for the first time. Sitting on the floor, leaning against the sofa, I slid the syringe at a forty-five-degree angle into my arm. I felt its razor-sharp tip pierce my vein's rubbery architecture, conscious to stop there and not to accidently shove it through the other side. I pulled the plunger back a fraction and a blob of dark red blood blossomed in the barrel, confirming I was 'in'.

I pressed the plunger with my forefinger, not rushing for fear of going over. Before the little black rubber piston had reached the barrel's halfway mark, I felt an insane rush, a million angels coursing through my blood to enrapture my soul with their loving caress. Wanting more of this intense high, I pushed the plunger home, knowing Death rode a pale horse and it was galloping towards me.

Strewth ...

Words fall short, like trying to recreate the Iguassu Falls using Lego bricks. It was as if my body's decaying molecules instantly connected with the universe, reabsorbing its energy, leaving me full-on-and-mental, the person I was born to be.

Holding my arm aloft to lower the blood pressure around the wound, I slid the needle out and – on the clumsy side of swift and needing three hands – pressed a Sterets against it. Then I lay back, soaking in the experience of being reborn, completely alive and feeling brighter than a bright afternoon on a bright day in Brightsville. I felt awesome, so *fucking* awesome, as if the world was an oyster and me the pearl.

The high plateaued, morphing into boundless energy and a newfound positivity towards my post-Hong Kong existence. It was time to get my life back on track. I sprang into action, sliding the orange cap onto the syringe, licking the amphetamine residue from the spoon and cleaning the soot off it with the blood-specked Sterets. With a clinical, or a 'military', focus on neatness, I stowed the works in a Pyrex oven dish and slipped it under the sofa. Attention to the smallest detail had suddenly become ever so important as I went about my long-overdue chores at lightning speed.

I flitted around the kitchen like Hummingbird Man, whacking the mixer spout over the sink with a deft slap and flicking on the hot tap, simultaneously opening the cupboard below with an upturned toe. I grabbed a bottle of Fairy Liquid my lodger had left behind and spun it in the air, cocktail-waiter-style, squirting green gunk into the washing-up water like a shot of crème de menthe.

Three minutes later, I'd blitzed a week's worth of dishes.

I hefted my trusty orange beast of a hoover around the house, tidying bits and bobs as I went. Although high as a kite, I couldn't resist the exciting acting-out ritual and so fetched my works and a fresh glass of water for another supersonic hit.

Neither of my lodgers had bothered to mow the strip of grass out front or the lawn to the rear, both now waist-high with stalks and weeds. Out of sight behind a redbrick wall, the back garden could wait, but if I were to keep up with the Joneses the front patch definitely needed a trim. Soon I was mowing away as if property prices in this popular cul-de-sac depended on it, stopping every so often to lift the machine and plonk it down on the more obstinate clumps. Having finished my half of the lawn, I started on Jane's adjoining jungle –

'*Ere!* Why you cutting '*er* grass?'

I looked up to find a little girl giving me a puzzled stare. I smiled and nodded at Jane's door. 'Well, *that* woman in *there* is a *wicked* witch from the *West,* and if I don't cut '*er* grass, she will turn me into an '*andsome* frog.'

The tot's eyes widened and a neighbour watering her flowerbed looked over and chuckled.

'What's your name called?' I asked the half-pint.

'My name's called Jolene,' she replied in her 'Proper Janner' accent. 'Can I cut the grass?'

It was a bit of a stupid request, as I wouldn't wish this godless forest on my worst enemy, let alone an innocent midget. Spotting a dad-looking figure grinning at us from two doors away, 'O-*kay* ... ' I sighed. 'But do you know the first rule of cutting grass?'

'Ut-uh.'

'You must *never* go near the lawnmower's blades.'

'I won't.' Jolene gave a determined shake of the head and reached up to grab the handlebars. I showed her how to squeeze the ON-OFF lever and helped shunt the feeble machine into the remaining thatch.

As we charged a patch of dandelions for a third time, the dad approached. 'Not bothering you, mate, is she?'

'Hah, no bud.' I shook his hand. 'She could never do that. I'm Chris.'

'Nice one, Chris. I'm Paul.' He turned to his daughter. 'Five more minutes, Joley, okay? Mum's got tea on the go.'

After Jolene left, I pulled up a few rogue weeds and re-varnished the sun-bleached lounge windowsill, all at lightning speed while higher than life. The front of the house looked great again, but there was one more task ...

Until now, I'd buried my Hong Kong experience in my subconscious, as not being in a position to return to Asia had been too painful to bear. However, in this euphoric state, I felt an overwhelming urge to commemorate my time over there, to revel in the nostalgic recall of a magical land steeped in an honourable culture, one forever spiking the blood pumping through my aching heart.

Somewhere in the back garden's sprawling green clutch was a piece of slate the shape of a large chocolate bar. I shoved it under the kitchen tap and used my washing-up brush to scrub off the mud. Rather than waste time letting the stone dry naturally, I held it under the fan heater on my kitchen wall. Then I fetched my Cantonese dictionary, along with some paint, varnish and brushes from the hallway cupboard.

After flicking through the pictograms in the lexicon, together with their respective translations, I settled on 'Happy Valley', *Pa Ma Dei* in Cantonese. Happy Valley was the home of Hong Kong's spectacular floodlit racecourse, not only a great name for my house but a welcoming one that brought back treasured memories. I painted the Chinese characters onto the slate using red paint with a black border, adding the English translation below in case my postman's Cantonese wasn't up to scratch. After protecting the plaque with a coat of varnish, I drilled two holes and screwed it to the wall by the front door.

The next task was to spruce myself up. In the Royal Marines, we showered every day without question – unless in the field, in which case a splash in a river would suffice. We'd take another upright bath after physical training and one more in the evening before going into town for drink-fuelled hijinks. I shaved each morning too. Since arriving back from Hong Kong, I'd relaxed this routine, lacking the will to live let alone fuck about with soap. Besides, what was the point in cleansing my body only to crawl under a manky duvet to watch reruns of *Columbo?*

Now, what with this mad burst of energy, personal hygiene suddenly became the number one priority on my turbo-charged agenda. I shaved using my last Gillette Mach 1 blade and trimmed my hair with a pair of scissors, making a mental note to buy a set of clippers at the first opportunity as there was no point spending my precious benefit money on something I could do myself. After this, I showered in the functional manner taught to commando recruits, hand-squeegeeing the excess water from my skin to avoid drenching the bathmat.

On a Hi-Fi Cabinet and a Prayer

Every so often, in a soft supportive whisper, the cherub on my left shoulder suggested making inroads into the future – perhaps visiting the Job Centre, writing a CV or brushing down a suit. However, the fallen angel on the right would tell me I was having too much fun and could do all that shit later.

As such, I spent Thursday and Friday tinkering around the house, cleaning at random, unpacking my Hong Kong luggage and fetching possessions, such as CDs, from the attic. I unpacked my books and placed them in order of size on the black-ash bookcase in the lounge. Fiction went on the second shelf down and non-fiction below that, keeping the top and bottom shelves free for ornaments – but no more than four or five as I didn't want my place looking like the Old Curiosity Shop.

This should all have taken no more than two hours, only I kept stopping for ever-more-generous hits of speed, sometimes two at a time because I was hooked on the whole injecting business. On each occasion, I stowed the Ziploc bag of white powder alongside my works in the Pyrex dish, depositing the used syringes and bloody Sterets in the bag from the pharmacy.

My place was only four years old and still had that new feel and fresh plaster smell to it. Tiled in champagne, the bathroom had an immaculate lilac suite and extra-thick Victorian-chequered linoleum, the offcut from my L-shaped kitchen-diner. The hall, stairs, lounge and landing enjoyed luxurious deep-pile cream carpet Dad had sold me at cost, with smart anthracite-black cord in the bedrooms. The lounge looked impressive too, with the silver-flecked-black-velour sofa bed, a large black floor cushion and black furnishings and electrical items. My kitchen's white ceramic hob, charcoal-grey units and Swedish-made table and chairs made it feel especially state-of-the-art.

I would have given anything to be back in my tiny top-floor

hovel in Wan Chai, but spirits high and mind occupied, I was only able to focus on the now.

On Saturday, I picked up the phone to see if Simon was home.

'*Chrissy!*'

'Mate, I was gonna pop over?'

'Yeah – you driving?'

That wasn't an inquiry into my welfare. Simon was fishing for a lift to pick up drugs.

'Nah, I'm running,' I replied, the bike having a puncture.

'*Running?*' Simon chuckled.

It was five miles to Simon's from mine. I set off at a gentle pace, which quickened after a mile when I flicked my roll-up aside. Most athletes would eat or drink something prior to exercise, but with the amphetamine initiating my body's fight-or-flight mechanism, suppressing appetite and thirst, I'd done neither in forty-eight hours. Reaching the halfway point, I realised nicotine probably wasn't a performance-enhancing drug. In fact, the soreness in my lungs and near-death in my head told me it was pretty rubbish.

Simon shoved his head around the door. 'Mate, I'm under *attack!*'

'Who by?'

'*You!*' He thrust a Beretta 9mm at me.

I stared at the pistol.

Simon pulled out another and shot me in the head.

Fucker!

I charged after him, pulling the trigger as fast as I could, smiling to see tiny yellow balls littering his place.

By the time I'd crossed the lounge, Simon had vanished. The bedroom door was wide open, so he must be in the bathroom. I pulled the pin on an imaginary grenade and lobbed it around the door. '*Fire in the hole!*' Following an almighty great non-explosion, I went in blatting plastic death.

Nothing…

This was weird.

As I stood on the landing wondering how Simon had achieved such a feat, two BB pellets slammed into my face.

'You *fucking* loser!' I cursed, spotting nobhead emerge from under his duvet like a shit version of Rambo.

'Game over.'

'Yes, mate,' I agreed – and shot him in the nuts three times.

'So what's with the guns?' I asked, as we sat rolling a spliff.

'Protection,' Simon replied.

'Protection?'

'I'm a drug dealer, Chris.'

'Really? I thought you were a brain surgeon.'

He held the BB gun up. 'The Scousers will think twice when they see *this.'*

'What, in case they've forgotten their eye protection?' I tried not to laugh.

'It looks like the real thing – at least until I can get a proper one.' Simon shrugged with self-assured naiveté of someone unfamiliar with firearms, death and imprisonment.

'Mate, we live in Plymouth *not* South Central LA!' I shook my head. 'Do you wanna get arrested?'

'Ah ...' Simon took a drag of the spliff.

'Go on.'

'I have been.'

'What?'

'While you were away ... I got busted. Twelve coppers smashed the door down.'

'And?'

'A couple of nine bars – luckily I'd harvested the plants by then.'

'You grew weed?'

'Check these out.' He rifled through a drawer and handed me a photo of veritable triffids taking over the bath.

'They didn't find any Class As, then?'

'Nah.'

Simon stood up, grabbed his keys and disappeared, returning

two minutes later out of breath. 'Check this out.' He tossed a can of WD40 at me.

Turning the can in my hand, I guessed it was some kind of receptacle.

'Twist the end.'

Unscrewing the base revealed scorebags packed with pills. While I'd been in Hong Kong, Simon's party lifestyle appeared to have spiralled out of control.

'You're not worried about getting caught?'

'*Nah.* That thing sits in the shed out back. *Nothing* to do with me.'

I wasn't convinced.

Time for a confession of my own. 'Simon, I've been injecting base.'

'Good, innit?' He winked, passed the spliff and retrieved a daypack from behind the couch.

'You've been doing it too?'

'Yep.' He emptied the bag onto the coffee table.

Whoa ...! There was a pharmacy's worth of 1ml syringes and alcohol swabs, as well as packets of Swan cigarette filters and disposable cooking-up spoons.

'Look under the couch.' He nodded, his face deadpan.

'Mate ...!' There must have been two thousand syringes there, all with telltale red pucks in them.

'Been bang at it for months.' Simon flashed me a swollen red lump on his forearm. 'See that? *All* those hits went in there.'

'What!' Even with my limited knowledge of injecting, I knew you were supposed to rotate sites, thus lessening the risk of infection and blood clots.

'Because when all this is over,' he continued, 'I want a little scar on my arm not a body covered in the fucking things.'

I understood his point, but the 'when all this is over' seemed wishful thinking. I couldn't imagine a life without speed and, having witnessed the amount of syringes beneath Simon's sofa, I couldn't see how he ever could, either.

I left Simon's at eight in the morning, still buzzing off the previous afternoon's hits. Feeling fidgety, I decided to visit a car boot sale at Stonehouse Creek on the edge of town.

After a brisk ten-minute walk, I inserted myself into the throng of bargain-hunting early birds meandering around a maze of bric-a-brac-laden tables. A few mavericks had set up camp on the fringes, showcasing their free-market fare on carpets unfurled on the ground. Here bikes, skis, golf clubs and rollerblades competed with jaded outdoor furniture, garden ornaments and overly ambitious exercise equipment likely bought in January. Clothes rails bent under the weight of burgundy jumbo cords, green-and-mauve shell suits and polyester knitwear from leading fashion houses such as Burton, Giavanno Mancelli and C&A.

Amateur sellers sat in the boots of Ford Sierra estates, drinking coffee from thermos flasks while chatting to enlisted help and passively willing you to buy an item of crap – a snowglobe from Majorca, a 997-piece jigsaw puzzle, unwanted Christmas aftershave. Caught up in the thrill of private enterprise, these trestle-table tycoons were simply content to turn enough trash into cash to cover the ten quid admission price.

The professional sellers were a breed apart. You couldn't intimidate them with a 'Fifty p for this, mate?' Unhindered by morals and unaffected by gravity, they zipped up and down tables overflowing with bulk-bought stock like astronauts on the International Space Station. If you're ever in need of five sizes of paintbrush from China or batteries that last 'longer and longer' – only *not* as long as decent ones – or an ex-rental-shop video tape of any film you wouldn't want to watch twice, hit up a car boot professional. Should you require a B-lister adhesive or a complete CD collection of one-hit wonders, or perhaps you simply fancy seeing eleven Jason Donavan albums side by side, pay a visit to a car boot professional. You will not be disappointed.

Cruising the open-air flea market, off my tits but not *too* self-conscious at this early stage in the binge, I attempted to adhere to the Boot's unwritten protocol, the most important rule being to keep your hands firmly in your pockets and stay at least three inches from the table. This prevents the seller – likely a Satanist – from launching into a sales pitch that will draw you in quicker than the tractor beam on the Death Star: 'Good little batteries those DuraZells, sir. Company's breaking in at the top end of the market.'

It's important to understand the Boot is not about selling the Rocky saga on VHS or banging out hammer drills with missing chuck keys. The boot seller, aka 'Lucifer', only cares about driving away from the crime scene with an empty car and a full wallet, knowing he's mindfucked total strangers into buying absolute toss. If you don't believe me, try going back next week and asking for a refund. You'll *never* get one. That's the car boot equivalent of trying to check in five minutes late for a Ryanair flight.

The Boot is about *power.* It's a *power* game – *hence the importance of stating your offer and walking the fuck away!* By doing so, you gain the respect of the seller and they'll soon call you back with a counter-haggle. Keep walking and you'll get a 'Quid-fifty's the lowest I can go, guv', cutting to the chase and saving you both a world of pain.

In this hyperactive state, I must have lowered my guard, because I left Stonehouse Creek hefting a black bin bag containing a CD player and amplifier, a stack of *Boxing's Greatest Legends* videos and a spinning world globe. The seller had assured me the globe was an original seventies illuminating one, a highly sought-after collector's item worth four hundred pounds – and that I could have it for twelve. I haggled, offering a fiver and bagging it for seven. I was now the proud owner of an original seventies illuminating world globe I neither needed nor could afford. It was cool, though, and I looked forward to lighting it up in my front room and reminiscing over all the places I'd visited, such as Paris, New York and Torpoint.

The problem I faced was getting all this junk the five miles home, a glass-fronted hi-fi cabinet I'd stupidly bought only making my dilemma worse. I didn't know the bus routes and would have begrudged forking out my dwindling cash if I did. Besides, we're not talking Hong Kong, where buses pass you by as if they're coming off the production line. This was Devon, *on* a Sunday, where buses arrive so infrequently their tax discs expire on route.

I hoiked the bin bag over my shoulder and began trudging up the road, pushing the hi-fi cabinet in front of me. I looked like a homeless person who'd had their stereo nicked. It was no good, though, for every time I crossed a crack in the pavement the castors threatened to rip out of the cabinet's crappy chipboard.

A change of tactics, I opened the door and hung the case on my spare shoulder, managing three hundred yards before I had to stop for a rest. Perhaps I should lighten the load by shedding a few boxing legends, but *nah!* Having bought all this stuff, I'd get it home somehow. Speed has that effect on you.

After half a mile, I passed the College of Further Education, a sour reminder of the many avenues I'd explored in an attempt to rectify my messed-up education. In this huffing, puffing and sweat-drenched state, I couldn't recall what I'd studied there. Was it the O Levels required to join the Royal Air Force or something to do with my electrician's apprenticeship? Regardless, it reinforced the feeling almost everything I'd done in my life was hotchpotch, off my own back, outside the norm and destined to fail.

Drawing upon a commando's resolve, I hefted my bounty all the way to Crownhill – the 'hill' part a clue as to the incline I'd climbed. Now a mere half-mile descent stood between me and my estate – and *boy* did gravity shine! Plymouth's fine city councillors, whose passion for potholes is rivalled only by their counterparts in Phnom Penn, had gone mental, splurging the budget and *re*tarmacking the road, a game-changer for a former marine with physics on his side.

I placed the hi-fi cabinet on the pristine liquorice-black surface and crammed it full of videos to lighten the bin bag. Then, clutching the bag between my teeth, I climbed astride my trusty chipboard charger. After glancing over my shoulder, I began to roll in the direction of home.

The cabinet's tiny castors worked to my advantage at first, keeping the speed down. I tried to recall the theme tune for *Easy Rider*, but never having seen the film, I settled for *The Dukes of Hazzard* instead. 'Just two good 'ol boys ...' I hollered, as other road users passed me on their way back from church.

As I picked up speed, a Peugeot 305 pulled alongside, its passenger frantically pointing in the direction I'd come. I flashed a look over my shoulder, expecting to see a police car, only the carriageway was empty. Turning back around, I experienced immobilising *panic* upon realising my body was travelling faster than my legs could stop. I had no choice but to ride this baby out.

Throwing caution to the wind, I thrust my arms to the sides, hoping this human crucifix would act as an airbrake. With my long stubble and overdue haircut, I must have looked like Jesus when he rode into town on a hi-fi cabinet. I attempted to steer with brazened leans, ignoring wild gesticulations from the occupants of cars flying by, knowing the luck that got me out of Hong Kong was about to run out.

I passed a red-and-white roadwork sign advising 'RAMP' –

The General Lee flew over the three-inch drop, its castors promptly giving way, the chipboard digging into the rough scraped surface to create a pole-vaulting effect launching me into the air.

Luckily the original seventies illuminating world globe saved the day, buckling beneath my weight and preventing me from smashing my face in. I picked myself out of the gutter, amazed to see the hi-fi unit relatively intact, bar four missing castors, and its glass in one piece. In a state of shock, I overlooked the rip in my jeans, a gashed knee and grazed palms.

What did register was the trail of Mike Tyson videos spread at ten-metre intervals along the road, the urgent pointing of my fellow travellers suddenly making sense. By the time I'd picked all the films up, I was back at the top of the hill. So much for the military maxim of improvise, adapt and overcome.

Why Does Bird Suddenly Appear?

I entered 46 Carroll Road physically drained but still raging on amphetamine. With a sigh of relief, I dumped the boot sale gear in the front room. I was severely dehydrated, my cheeks sunken and my pee dark orange. I should have necked a pint of water, but sticking a needle in my arm was far more important, so I filled a glass for a hit. Once I felt that euphoric rush, manhandling twenty kilos for five miles on no sleep would become a fading memory and I'd be ready to do it all again – not that I needed another original seventies illuminating world globe.

Careful not to spill the water, I walked back across the kitchen's immaculate marble-effect linoleum and – *'Ooph!'* – put my foot right through it. My lodgers must have ignored the aging sealant around the sink and a year's worth of splashes had dripped down the back of the unit and rotted a fair-sized section of the chipboard flooring.

Had I still been an enthusiastic young homeowner with money in the bank, I would have shot up to B&Q and bought the necessary materials to replace it. As it was, I took another hit of the potent potion and pondered how to rectify the situation with an excess of energy yet a deficit of cash.

There was a sheet of chipboard in the loft. Without further ado, I ripped up the lino and, in between gags, dumped the foul-smelling pieces in the back garden. After levering up the rotten wood with a claw hammer, I sawed a new piece to size, nailed it down and smeared Polyfilla into the gaps. To save money, I stained the entire floor using leftover fence protector, intending to score lines in the 'African Cherry' finish when dry to create a parquet flooring effect.

I'd been careful to paint my way backwards out of the room to avoid stepping in the wet woodstain, but greedy for another hit and needing the pint glass to cook up in the comfort of the lounge, I ignored common sense and tiptoed to the draining board.

Idiot! Tackiness underfoot told me the stain had stuck to the soles of my boots. I'd have to touch in the imperfections later and clean my Caterpillars using turpentine.

'*Shit!*' Further disaster as I crossed back over the floor. The bloody nails weren't long enough to secure the chipboard to the joists. Just like in a *Laurel and Hardy* skit, the patch had flipped up, ejecting the filler and splattering my jeans with woodstain. I filled the pint glass, stamped the repair down and strode out of the room, ignoring the imaginary stepping-stones of a moment ago.

In the sanctuary of the living room, having left African Cherry bootprints on the previously spotless cream carpet, I pulled the Pyrex dish out from under the sofa. With my mood still ultra-positive and energy abound, I didn't need another hit, but like an aunt who can't leave the Quality Street alone at Christmas, I couldn't resist.

I'd almost finished attending to the puncture on my bike when the doorbell rang. Through the swirled-glass pane, I could see a small person, Jolene, the girl who'd helped cut the grass. An idea formed, so I rushed upstairs ...

My tenant had left an Emu behind in the airing cupboard. It was identical to Rod Hull's feathered fiend only smaller. I had no idea why my lodger owned a glove puppet – unless, of course, he *was* Rod Hull – but that didn't matter. What did was shoving my hand up through Emu's neck, opening the front door a few inches and poking his head out. 'Harro, mayte!' I did my best Australian bird impression, which came out as a cross between a Chinese laundryman and Spit the Dog.

'Is the man in there?' Jolene remained unfazed.

'Wrich wrun?' Emu curled his beak.

'The man who cuts the grass.'

'Erh ... there's been a lirrel pwoblem.'

'Why?'

'He's gone to the moon.'

'Why?'

'To get some green cheese.'

'Why?'

'His fridge was empty.'

'Why?'

'Because it had nothing in it.'

Jolene peeked around the door. 'It's *you!*' Her face lit up.

'No, I just came to see who Emu was talking to.'

'Why've you got blood on you?' She eyed the rip in my jeans.

'Oh ... I fell off my hi-fi cabinet.'

'What's a high-fly cablinet?'

'It's like a rubbish skateboard.'

'Joooo-lieeee ...!' a woman hollered from a few doors down. *'Teeea tiiiime!'*

'I gotta go!'

'See you layer, arigator,' said Emu.

'Larigator!' Jolene grinned and skipped off.

I put on a pair of shorts and used a clump of wet toilet paper to wipe the dirt and congealed blood from my palms. The gash in my knee needed proper medical attention, but there was no way I would interrupt a speed binge to visit A&E, so a Sterets had to do. The alcohol stung like hell and made the blood flow once more.

There was a packet of washing powder under the sink, so I bounded downstairs to fetch it. Then, using a nailbrush, I attempted to scrub the blood from my grey jeans. It was a token job, leaving a crimson stain in the cotton, a sign I was suffering sleep deprivation. I chucked the jeans over the back of a chair and turned my attention to the hi-fi cabinet.

I'd bought my Sony sound system, TV and video on interest-free credit at seventeen. Almost ten years later, they still functioned okay, but the TV had a green tinge and the video jammed every so often. The stereo stack sat directly on the floor, its two speakers at opposite sides of the room. After disconnecting the cables, I placed the stack in the hi-fi cabinet ... and the whole thing looked ridiculous – like your parents' Dolby dinosaur that blasted out the Carpenters in the seventies.

Another random item my lodger left behind was a pastel paint set. Feeling creative, I began thumbing through a *Watchtower* magazine the Jehovah's Witnesses had shoved through the letterbox. Despite failing art at school and being long overdue some sleep, I knew intuitively I could come up with something rewarding while on speed. And what better canvas than my living room wall?

The artwork in the *Watchtower* was exceptional. I hoped to capture its vivid colour and wonderful detail. The first picture I attempted was a South Pacific Island girl, her back to the artist, kneeling on the beach in gently lapping waves while staring out over the sea to a fiery sunset. Topless and wearing a garland of yellow flowers in her long dark hair, she gave the impression of waiting for her man to return from a vast and tempestuous ocean.

I guess deep down I chose this painting because it represented my future soulmate, that special person longing for me to step out of *her* dreams too. I wasn't desperate for female companionship, but that didn't mean I wouldn't like to find someone to share this uncertain existence with, a girl who accepted me unconditionally and understood my life choices.

I sketched the seascape in pencil on the wall, making sure to get the proportions right. Anyone who's watched *Crawshaw's Watercolours* knows the knack is in mixing and applying the paint, but you don't have to be Rembrandt to copy someone else's art. You simply isolate each brushstroke and replicate them accordingly. In what seemed no time, I'd reproduced the image on a larger scale and was extremely pleased with the result.

However, upon checking my G-Shock I realised it had taken several hours to complete, as it was now five in the morning. I'd still not eaten anything or drunk more than a few glasses of water in four days. I had just chain-smoked roll-ups. Conscious of drawing attention to my non-existent sleeping pattern, I made sure the blinds in the living room were drawn and the curtains pulled over them. I didn't want a neighbour spotting my light on all night and thinking I had a drug problem.

After a slug of water from the tap, I began painting another picture from the *Watchtower,* two beautiful Macaws perching on a jungle tree branch. This time I used a different technique, first drawing a ten-by-ten-centimetre grid on the original artwork and then one scaled up by a factor of five on my wall. From there it was a simple matter of transposing the detail in the smaller squares to the larger ones. The result was beyond spectacular, the birds looking surreal in their feathered splendour and jungle backdrop. I glanced at the Casio. Eleven hours had passed.

Rummaging through the Pyrex dish, I realised I'd used all ten syringes. Although the pharmacy was still open, I couldn't face the stigma around asking for needles, not in this sketchy state. Simon got an endless supply from a drugs charity in the city centre, but even cycling flat out I'd never make it in time. Besides, I didn't want any so-called 'professionals' interfering in my life.

Adopting an alternative arrangement, I sucked water into one of the used syringes. Sealed from the outside air, the millimetre or two of blood in the barrel had yet to congeal and turned the water pale pink. So as not to contaminate the fresh water in the glass, I squirted this in a wide arc over the carpet. I simply lacked the will to fetch a separate container or walk over to the nearest plant pot.

This time, I felt a distinct tearing sensation as the blunt needle ripped through my skin to puncture the vein. I wasn't overly concerned about the internal damage, only that this second-hand usage would likely bruise my arms, showing the world I was a 'junkie' – to use society's hate-laden terminology. So I could tell which syringes had been used twice, I snipped a sliver of plastic off the thumb press using the scissors.

Back up to warp speed, I turned my attention to the CD player and amplifier from the boot sale, smiling as I recalled my short-lived experience as a DJ in China. By leveraging upon my *extensive* knowledge of next-generation consumer-electronic design, while implementing a non-sequential-thought matrix and a mission-focused top-down bottom-up approach, I intended to quasi-synchronise the player's dynamic binary output with my hi-fi's intelligent plug-and-play interface and reconfigure the amp's internal architecture to create a hyper-blasé DJing platform … with my O Level in Control Tech.

But for some reason, such endeavours always seem easier in theory when you're on speed than they pan out in reality. I had a soldering iron but couldn't figure out a circuit that would allow me to cue in a track through my headphones and then crossfade between discs. I removed the balance and volume controls from the amp and placed them in a virtual circuit diagram along with the two CD players. Then I sat there pondering a way forward. Twelve hours later, I still sat there pondering a way forward.

In the end, I plugged the auxiliary CD player into the line-in jack on the hi-fi and used the input selector knob to flick between a Ministry of Sound compilation and a Brandon Block and Alex P album. It was like mixing for five-year-olds, but it brought back the incredible sensation of DJing to hundreds of people in a Chinese nightclub.

It was now 4pm on Tuesday. I had been on the go for five days without food and sleep. Since the boot sale, I hadn't spoken to another of the planet's six billion inhabitants, either in person or by phone. I didn't feel lonely or dejected, as amphetamine was my best friend and our relationship solid. Speed made me feel the person I wanted to be, my true self as nature intended. It got results, and if people would only stop judging my choices, life would be a lot easier.

Life would get even better if I could finish my projects. I'd have a tidy house, a mural to rival the Sistine Chapel and a set of DJ decks to blast out classic tunage and impress the ears of all around.

… Yet the mural wasn't finished and the mixing-deck project hadn't even got off the ground. My once-perfect house now had no lino in the kitchen, a big hole in the floor and woodstain, pastel paint and electronic components trashing the expensive carpet. To make matters worse, the fat bag of speed I bought had but a few crumbs left in it, the hits reduced to token gestures that no longer kept me at my peak.

Tiredness took hold and in my increasing confusion I tinkered around the front room, making grand plans for my debut onto the world stage ... until life became one big unproductive blur. Too screwed up, I shouldn't have been in charge of a sandwich let alone a complicated electronics project. I stared at the near-empty scorebag, knowing this last shot of energy *had* to count. If I failed to achieve something, my justification of 'getting stuff done' while on speed would prove imbecilic. With this in mind, I embarked on my next project – to take down the stairs.

Who needs stairs anyway? I rationalised. *Surely, it's far better to have a rope.*

I mean, while living in harmony with the natural world our cave-dwelling ancestors never bothered with such sugarcoated indulgences. 'Erh sorry, Stig, I can't hunt stegosauruses today because I've got to go upstairs.'

So it was sorted. I would replace the stairs with a rope, the urban equivalent of the vines my childhood hero, Tarzan, used to swing on. I didn't own a rope, but no great plan should mire in the detail. I'd have the only house in Devon – and possibly most of Cornwall – with a rope instead of a staircase. How *cool!*

First, I needed the final bit of speed to keep me going a while longer. By now, I'd used each syringe at least three times and had snipped their thumb presses accordingly. Desperate to stay high, rather than suck water into the syringe and spray the crimson contents over the floor, I emptied it into my mouth to avoid wasting the precious amphetamine contained in the bloody dregs. *No different to licking a cut finger,* my addiction rationalised.

This time, I squirted water directly into the scorebag, sealed its ziploc and massaged the plastic to wash off the sticky speed residue. Then I poured the milky liquid into the spoon.

As speed leaves the body, your blood pressure drops, so my usually bulging vein proved almost impossible to locate, particularly with a ridiculously blunt needle. I pushed the point in again and again, probing at different angles, hoping to achieve the satisfying sensation of penetrating the rubbery hose and seeing a reassuring red rose in the syringe's barrel. However, every time I thought I was in, I pressed the plunger and experienced an awful stinging pain. I think I even pushed the needle right through the vein a couple of times by mistake.

Finally, I slid the scarlet gore into my arm and hoped for the best. A gobstopper-sized swelling developed immediately, but as I returned to the rope ladder project my sole annoyance was that the speed hadn't gone directly into the bloodstream, thus ruining the hit.

The stairway itself formed a sloping alcove, to add space to the living room. I removed the decorative beading from the pine carriage panel and began levering off the plasterboard with a chisel ...

This is Planet Earth

'Hello and welcome to Ready Steady Cook!' says host Fern Britton, looking a deal more scrumptious than the gigantic polystyrene tomato hanging above her head. 'It's the show where two competitors attempt to create Michelin-star dishes on a not-so starry budget with the help of our celebrity chefs.'

'Whoop-whoop!' Clap-clap-clap-clap …!

'It's time to meet our contestants!' Fern forces a smile, knowing a pair of kitchen biffs are about to knock up tripe you wouldn't feed a compost heap. 'Let's welcome Barry and Sandra!'

'Whoop-whoop!' Clap-clap-clap-clap …!

'So, Barry.' Fern flutters her delicious eyelashes. 'What did you spend your five pounds on?'

Geordie joker Barry opens his Kwik Save carrier bag and dumps six cooking apples and a bottle of vodka onto the counter.

Fern mock-frowns into Camera 2.

'Ha-ha-ha-ha!' The audience go wild. Pure comedy gold, they absolutely love it!

Sandra removes quinoa, broccoli shoots, a freshly caught salmon and quails eggs from her basket and gives Fern a guilt-free smile.

'And you bought all that for under a fiver?' asks our incredulous host, knowing full well Sandra is a devious lying witch.

Ready Steady Cook. *Series 4, episode 142*

I awoke on the sofa. My Chinese-style table lamp, a moving-in gift from my great aunt, Kay, was still switched on, as was the dimmed main light. I heard the tape player clunk as a Graeme Park Hacienda mix repeated for the umpteenth time. I couldn't find my watch and had no idea if it was night or day. I must have sat down for a moment and crashed and burned.

Besides a raging thirst and the initial pangs of hunger, I didn't feel too bad, still slightly high. This was depressing in itself for as I started moving about the amphetamine in my system would peter into insignificance, initiating a massive comedown. I peeked through the curtains to find it dark outside. *What day is it?* I wondered, turning to survey the utter carnage.

Electrical components, tools and painting apparatus littered the floor, along with screws, wire and broken plastic. There were tinges of colour all over the lush cream carpet, a result of my half-arsed efforts to clean up splashes of paint. The mural itself was stunning, but its Hawaiian angel and parrots seemed distinctly out of place in a relatively new house on a fairly upmarket estate. A sense of unease came over me. What if neighbours caught a glimpse of my antics and mistook me for a weirdo, particularly as the unfinished pencil sketches looked as nutty as a squirrel's shopping list?

Then I spotted the plasterboard levered away from the stairs. *What the fuck was I thinking?* I cringed. *What a fucking cock-dick!* Not only was it ludicrous to expect guests to climb a rope every time they needed the bathroom, but how was Morris supposed to get up there in his wheelchair – fucking *fly?*

I vowed to put the staircase back together after a cup of tea and a smoke and went to put the kettle on, further dismayed to discover the woodstain footprints in the hallway. The badly patched hole in the middle of the kitchen's now-bare floor only compounded matters.

In an attempt to boost the vestiges of speed in my system, I chucked four teabags in a pint glass and added boiling water, milk and ten sugars. Such was my thirst and calorific need, I glugged it down and added a burned mouth to my growing collection of wounds. It's impossible to do justice to that sugary sweet caffeine quench using words. It was simply the most satisfying drink to ever pass my lips and I immediately made another.

I smoked a fat roll-up, but it was no good. Incessant yawns rose from the depths to rock my exhausted self at ever-decreasing intervals. The slight high I'd experienced upon waking had got off the train, leaving ravenousness behind in the seat pocket.

In Hong Kong, I'd wolf down raisin bread and condensed milk, but pasta shells and lasagne verde slices were the only items in my food cupboard. Opting for the pasta, I filled a pint glass and boiled it in the microwave. Then I replaced the water with full-fat milk, margarine and a heap of sugar and heated the lot back up.

It was a lack of choice to beat all others. *Starving,* I wished my mouth was bigger so I could shovel the pasta shells in quicker. I could taste the durum wheat like never before, sensing each and every molecule satiating my animal desire. My body shuddered in ecstasy, its billions of cells screaming as they absorbed the glucose and fat from the sweet oily fix.

I was about to make a beeline for the sofa bed when an empty Sterets packet on the floor caught my eye. *Fucking hell, Chris, sort it out!* I imagined the shame I would feel if a visitor saw this telltale foil envelope and the hurt it would cause my family.

The packet reminded me I hadn't checked the state of my injection sites. The fresh needle jabs had left almost imperceptible red specks on my skin, whereas the blunter pins had made marks the size of beestings. An ugly yellow bruise had developed where I'd missed the vein and pumped blood and drugs into the tissue of my arm.

I didn't want to think about any of this or that I'd spent eighty quid on gear and not achieved a damn thing – the beginnings of a questionable mural excepted. I wanted to climb under the duvet on the sofa bed and blot out a miserable life without amphetamine. I'd be in a far worse place physically and mentally when I awoke, yet another reason to crash out and not think about it.

Come Monday afternoon, I'd slept for three days, only rising from the sofa bed to boil more pasta. Sitting back under the duvet, I drank the last of the milk in a criminally strong and sweet pint of tea. I felt tired and hungry, but fortunately base was nowhere near as potent as crystal meth, which would have left me exhausted and unable to function for a week. Yet, despite the easier comedown, I experienced something I never had in Asia. I was unhappy ... *extremely* unhappy.

As Lou Reed's ode to drug addiction, 'Perfect Day', played on the radio, I had never felt so numb. I'd had some bad – others would say traumatic – experiences in my life, but I'd always shrugged them off and never felt miserable. I'd learned from a young age life ain't fair, and this philosophy had kept me grounded. But it wasn't working now. I couldn't function without drugs. I lacked the will to do anything.

Letters sat on the doormat for days. I couldn't face opening them for fear of a demand on my damaged finances and broken self. As for getting a job, *hah!* I had nothing to offer an employer – unless they needed an Emu impersonator or their house trashed. I hated living in Prison England and couldn't see a way out.

Luckily two things cocooned me from the harshness of my circumstances and made this sad existence bearable – rolling tobacco and television. If I couldn't afford to inject amphetamine, I'd inhale nicotine and carbon monoxide instead. Smoking provided a reassuring crutch, little highs to raise my mood and allow an element of control over a small part of this life.

Where TV was concerned, I'd always preferred reruns of seventies crime series, vintage films and documentaries. But now I found myself sitting through utter rubbish, like *Jerry Springer, Judge Judy, Supermarket Sweep* and *Neighbours*. I wasn't sure what was worse, watching programs intended to anaesthetise the minds of skiving students, bored housewives and the long-term unemployed or the realisation I was in one of these groups myself.

The pasta shells ran out, forcing me from my comfort zone to go and buy food. A rummage in my wallet turned up £1.87. I negotiated the estate fence and clawed through the undergrowth to reach the Co-op. Walking into the busy supermarket and seeing so many 'normal' citizens going about their business overwhelmed me. It was tempting to feel second best, but I immediately shook it off, *Hah!* People could think what they liked. They didn't know me. I would live my own life and not conform to their social constructs. And if I needed speed to function and achieve my goals, then so be it, end of story.

A shopping basket is pretty much redundant when you've only got £1.87 in your wallet, but I picked one up nonetheless. This way I hoped to look less like a shoplifter, what with my scabby knees and ripped jeans. I wandered the aisles, calculating prices in my head like a contestant on *Supermarket Sweep* – the X-rated version, where contestants have to do a weekly shop on a mega comedown with what little money they have left after buying super-strong drugs and shit from a car-boot sale.

After cruising up and down, peering into the other shoppers' delicacy-packed trolleys, I settled on a white sliced loaf, a tub of margarine, an extra-large bag of porridge oats, pasta shells, teabags and four pints of full-fat milk, all from the No Frills range. With the few remaining pence, I bought a small chocolate bar.

When I crossed back over the estate, Jolene was playing in the front garden while her mum sat on the front step enjoying the sun. 'There's the *man!*' the little girl shrieked.

Despite feeling far from sociable, I went over and introduced myself. 'Hello, Mum. I'm Chris.'

'I'm Maggie, Chris, and thanks for letting Madam here cut the grass.'

'Hah, my pleasure.'

'Can we cut the grass again?' Jolene asked.

'Don't you bother Chris!' said Maggie.

'She could never bother me.' I smiled. 'But the grass is too short today. Want some chocolate instead?'

'Yeeeee!' She clenched her tiny teeth.

'Listen, you must never accept stuff from people without asking your mum first, okay?'

'O-*kay.*' Jolene threw her arms around Maggie's knees and made pleading eyes. *'Mum?'*

Back home, I'd just settled under the duvet with a plate of toast when the roamer-phone rang. I saw Dad's number on the display but felt too out of sorts to speak to him. Nor could I listen to the message he left in case it required something of me. I'd have to call back when I had some speed and could function properly.

In the days that followed, I slept a lot and scoffed tea and toast while exploiting *all* four TV channels. When the bread ran out, I invented the Devon Doldrums, a subtle blend of exotic shell-shaped pasta and lovingly machine-rolled oats, skilfully microwaved in a tall – *pint* – glass along with white cow-flavoured milk, a scoop of *marge de la tub* and a liberal sprinkling of genuine West Indian sugar granules – processed on the Stover Trading Estate just outside Bristol. Yet, despite these fancy calorie-rich cocktails, I continued to lose weight and was now nine stone.

Thursday finally arrived and I couldn't wait to cash my giro to score speed. Like a life raft to a drowning sailor, the drug represented salvation. I could finish my mural and DJ decks, fix the stairs and kitchen floor, tidy the house, learn more Cantonese and write that CV. Once again, the sun shone into my wretched cave, replacing the gloom with an aura of infinite possibility.

I threw off the duvet, hurried into the hall and rummaged through my mock-antique writing desk to find the telephone directory. I'd bought the sturdy little word horse at auction when I first moved in. Although shabby, its timber construction and classic orange-leather worktop exuded a literary richness that appealed to the writer inside me – quite deep inside, as the writer hadn't actually written anything.

I rang the Backward Parrot, heart thumping and fingers tightly crossed, oblivious to the fact my previously outgoing team-player persona only interacted in one-on-one drug-seeking relationships these days, my global interactions shrivelled to the sphere of this call. To my relief, Steve answered. 'I'll buzz Damo,' he said. 'Pop down in half an hour.'

I fixed a smoke but passed on food and drink, figuring I'd sort that later. I still felt rough, but the thought of injecting gear and getting my life on track was more than enough motivation to cycle to the post office and on to the pub. I arrived out of breath, having overtaken all the traffic in my path and stealth-crashing three red lights.

I hopped the bike up the pub's three steep concrete steps and chucked it to one side, entering the lounge to the sound of the Verve's 'Lucky Man' on the jukebox. I'd seen Richard Ashcroft on TV recently, clearly spandangled on the red carpet at some award ceremony. Listening to his genius blaring through the bar was a touch disheartening, yet another reminder I'd missed the boat to Bad Boy City. I wanted my fifteen minutes of fame, the respect of fans and the best drugs available.

Steve grinned and immediately made me feel welcome. A hardworking and devoted family man, he looked out of place behind the bar of the Backward Parrot, considering the scallywags who frequented the dive. He didn't profit from the drug deals and was only helping me out because I was a mate of Chunks'.

'Damo's on his way, Chris,' said Steve. 'Have you met Donnie?'

I turned to acknowledge the chap at the bar. Twice my age, he wore a donkey jacket, work-blackened jeans and steel-toe-capped boots. With his Romany complexion, he looked like Ian McShane from the TV series *Lovejoy,* only he'd obviously had a much harder paper round.

'Alright, Donnie?' I smiled.

'Alright, Chris?' His eyes flitted about me. 'You wanna pint?'

'Oh, thank you.' I shook his hand.

It was kind of Donnie to buy me a beer, but I think it was only because he felt awkward. Plymouthians tend to have a mistrust of strangers, which is not surprising when you take into account the number of invasions the city has been subjected to over the years. The French, the Bretons, the Cavaliers, the Spaniards, the Vikings, the Germans, the Torpointers, every Tom, Dick and 'Harald' has had a pop at this place, leaving a healthy dose of xenophobia in their wake.

Unfortunately, this sketchiness peaked in scenarios involving drugs, like this one now. The patrons of the Backward Parrot were by no means the Cali Cartel, but a significant amount of the Liverpudlian gangs' product passed through the pub, as did gold, silver, jewellery, counterfeit banknotes and dirty cash. A lot of the punters had spent time in prison for drugs or violence, most remaining ambivalent to the possibility of serving more.

'What do you do with your days, Don?' I asked tactfully.

'Council worker,' he gruffed. 'You?'

'I've just come back from Hong Kong.'

'Hong Kong?' Donnie pulled back in a polite gesture of surprise.

'Yeah, I moved over there to run a business after leaving the marines.'

My insecurity was obviously namedropping. I just didn't want people thinking my sole achievements in life consisted of ripped jeans, gaunt cheeks and an amphetamine habit. However, in the Backward Parrot, I don't think anyone gave a toss – so long as you weren't old bill.

Damo entered the lounge, 'Gents,' and headed for the communal bong. He took an enormous draw, the super-hot hash smoke raking the filthy water into frantic bubbles, before passing it to Donnie.

'You might need to fill that up.' Donnie coughed, handing me the peace pipe.

'No, it's fine.' I sucked on the remaining mix and blew out a yellowy-brown plume. Truth be told, I wanted a stimulant not a suppressant, so I glugged my beer, scored another eighty quid bag from the dealer and left.

The Girls from Brazil

By the time I hopped on the bike, the killer exhaustion had vanished, my mind gripped by the thrill of acting out. I should have gone to the pharmacy for fresh needles and Sterets, but the allure of the hit was way beyond my authority. Cycling home, I pictured the wonderful things this big bag of amphetamine would help me accomplish, promising myself I would go at my tasks flat out and focused and not waste time over-thinking or getting sidetracked.

I'd long since run out of Sterets, despite cutting them in two and crimping one piece back in the packet. So with a roll-up at hand and music on the stereo, I wiped the crook of my arm with toilet paper soaked in Christian Dior Fahrenheit. I cooked up a generous sprinkling of gear and shoved an ultra-blunt needle into my black-and-blue wing, the syringe's thumb press clip-marked so many times only the shaft remained.

The resulting high was far from supersonic, likely due to my underlying exhaustion and increased tolerance. Disappointed, I tapped five times as much speed into the spoon, intending to drop the dosage for subsequent hits. If I didn't, I'd be through the four grams in no time.

Later that day, the doorbell rang. Jolene stood on the step with two mini-henchmen, a boy and a girl. '*Where's* Bird?' she cut to the chase.

'Bird's in the airing cupboard.'

'*What's* 'e doing in there?' She fixed an accusatory eye on me.

'Having a sleep.' I mimicked a yawn.

Jolene peered past me. 'Why you painting on the wall?'

'It's better than painting on the floor.' I shrugged. 'Is that your football?'

'Yeah.' Jolene held it out.

'Fancy taking penalties?'

'Uh-huh!' There were smiles all round.

At the back of the house was a large square of tarmac bordered by parking bays and our estate's tall wooden fencing. So long as we didn't boot the ball at the cars *too* hard, it was a safe place for a kick around.

'What's your name called?' I asked the droopy-eyed boy.

'Arfur.'

'And what's this one called?' I pointed to the slightly older girl.

'Amber,' she replied, confident beyond her years.

'Okay, let me get this right. *You're* Barfer, *you're* Bamber and *you're* Joley the Goalie who eats roly-polies?'

'*Noooooooo!*' they screamed.

'That's *Arthur*, that's *Amber*, and I'm *Jolene*,' said Joley.

'*That's* what I said!' I shook my head at the sky. '*Arfur* McBarfer, *Amber* Hamburger and *Jolene* Tambourine who *bounces* on a *trampoline!*'

'*Noooooooo!*'

I stood corrected ... *four* more times.

'So you guys can play football?' I continued.

'*Uh-huh!*' they replied in unison.

'Okay, penalties from the spot.' I marked it with a pebble and designated a fence panel for our goal. 'Right, if you go any closer than this little stone then your head is probably gonna fall off.'

'Our *head* will fall off?' Jolene face screwed up.

'Yep, if you do any cheating.'

'Can our head fall off?' Arthur asked softly, staring up at me in earnest.

'He's *joking*,' said Amber.

'*No* I'm not! The other day my head fell off in the supermarket.'

'How did you get home if you didn't even have a head?' Jolene scrunched her eyebrows, skewering me with a beady.

'*I-I-I*... put it under my arm and it gave me directions.'

The kids giggled and the shootout got under way – only there was a problem. I simply *couldn't* save a penalty. Even shots travelling in the wrong direction somehow deflected off my clumsy self and went in the goal. This team rivalled Pele's Brazil.

'Joooo-lieeee ...!' came a familiar call and the future of English football went home for tea.

With my mood back on track, I listened to Dad's telephone message. He was inviting me to the cottage for Sunday lunch. I'd still be fidgety and unable to eat anything then, though. Besides, speed was better company than a stepmother who hated me. I called the shop number and excused myself. My old man was fine about it, but as I went to say goodbye, '... And is everything alright?' he asked.

'Fine, Dad.' I knew what was coming next.

'You haven't ...?'

'Taken drugs?'

I'd always been honest with my father. Surely, he understood I needed speed to function. I mean, what parent wouldn't want their kid to be happy?

'Yeah, I've been doing a few, Dad. I –'

'Oh ...! Oh –'

The line went dead.

For fuck's sake! I slammed the roamer phone back on its base. *Why can't people leave me alone!*

What *harm* was I doing? *Who* was I hurting? I'd tried living without drugs and it didn't *bloody* work! Now that I'd found my magic potion, everyone – particularly those who had never touched a substance in their life – wanted me to give it up! For crying out loud, *everyone* did this shit! Noel and Liam sniffed for England. Members of the royal family shoved it up their snoots. Children's TV presenters snorted like horses. Why the *fuck* couldn't I?

I wouldn't let my old man's negativity get to me. I'd found the secret to happiness and if it meant dying a bit younger at least my time on Earth would be spent productively. I put the phone call out of my mind and began sewing up my jeans, capitalising on the concentration speed induced to create ridiculously neat stiches. I clipped my original seventies illuminating world globe back together and replaced the burnt-out bulb with the one from my microwave.

Now the fun *really* began! I wheeled my bike into the front room, intending to turn it from a naff, sensible affair into something nifty. I considered protecting the carpet with an old sheet, but caught in the moment, I opened my large plastic toolbox instead. Out came a size ten spanner and off came the bike's play-it-safe mudguards ... bell ... dynamo ... lights ... milometer ... chain guard ... go-slower decals ... and front brakes, leaving me with what the Yanks call a JEEP – Just Enough Essential Parts.

I raised the seat an inch and set the handlebars at the sort of rakish angle that makes other road users jealous. Then I bolted brackets above the stairs and hung the bike upside down on them. I felt like the guy in the Gillette advert, the one who lives in a cool loft conversion and spends his days drinking diet coffee, doing topless pull-ups and scraping off his face fuzz while standing under a shower to rival the Niagara Falls.

... But Gillette Guy probably didn't have oil, grease, nuts, bolts, bike parts, brick dust and plaster all over his floor, as well as bits of sticky-backed foil that when pieced together spelt 'Raleigh Shopper'.

I can tidy all that up later, I figured, *after I've worked on my CV and got fluent in Cantonese.*

I fixed up a hit with an ever-blunter needle and turned my attention to the mural project. The chattering parrots and lovesick Hawaiian were really rather good, but the wall needed something to represent my affinity with Hong Kong.

Shoved down the end of the sofa was a paper file containing the poems and pictures I'd composed over there, as well as a selection of Chinese comic books from the mysterious junk room. In Hong Kong, reading comics is predominantly an adult pastime. You'd see commuters on the MTR engrossed in their often dark, dry and erotic storylines. With my understanding of Cantonese writing not *quite* up to scratch – at least not for a couple more hours – I couldn't read the captions and speech bubbles, but the illustrations gave you a good enough idea of the narrative.

It was the illustrations that I appreciated most of all, particularly Hong Kong's triad outlaws, depicted as tattoo-covered muscle bosuns sporting slick Elvis quiffs. I loved the artwork's sheer simplicity – deft strokes of crisp black ink, the odd flick here and there, touched in with no more than three or four colours. So simple that embarking on a picture of a fearsome-looking triad boss, shirtless, muscles rippling, wearing purple pantaloons and shin-high slip-on boots, I didn't bother with grid squares, instead sketching the dude's outline *near-life-sized* using freehand.

My efforts ground to a halt as there was not enough paint in the watercolour set to cover the vast areas of wall space. Not wishing to splash my nonexistent cash on art equipment, I scouted the house and attic and returned with a five-litre tub of magnolia, a pack of felt-tip pens, some blue-ink cartridges, a sachet of decaf coffee and a bottle of red food colouring. I daubed magnolia onto a black-glass dinner plate and mixed a blob of ink from a colouring pen cartridge into it. The result was a gorgeous turquoise. I discovered that differing combinations of the assembled ingredients fulfilled all of my colour palette needs.

In the comic book, the triad leader looked the business. He sat in a throne-like chair surrounded by foot soldiers, his huge legs planted firmly on the ground as if to say, *'Cross* me if you *dare!'* For the chunky outlines, I applied black radiator enamel using a small decorators' brush trimmed to an italic point with a Stanley knife. The lines alone looked awesome, but the cartoon came to stunning life with colour.

The result was unbelievable. It felt as if I'd gone from never having painted a picture in my life to becoming an accomplished urban artist overnight. Using my imagination, I painted a sprawling dragon tattoo across the triad's torso, rewarded from this life until eternity by my nascent creative talent.

Fuck the education system and *fuck* my six schools.

The Kids are Alright

On Saturday morning, the street sounded like a school playground. The door knocked and I peered through the textured glass to see my three soccer stars had multiplied into ten – so *technically* I was the captain of an England team. I had an idea ...

In the back garden, I fashioned a bunch of weeds into a large nest and bound it with string. I shoved a washing-up glove inside Emu's neck and taped its opening to my hoover's long chrome pipe. The machine itself was the canister type, an industrial version of 'Henry', AWOL from a military camp thanks to a mate of mine. You had the option of screwing the flexi-hose onto the air outlet – for blowing dust and cobwebs away – so I did this.

When the kids moved off, I placed the nest on top of my six-foot-high garden wall and thrust Emu's body up through it, leaving the hoover pipe hidden from view behind the brickwork. I set the vacuum's wheeled base on the ground and ran the electrical lead inside, plugging it into a socket on the landing.

Peering out of the upstairs window, I smiled. Emu really did look like a bird on the nest, its neck drooped over the side. Then I waited ...

When the kids returned, I ... *hit* the switch!

Emu bolted upright like an angry pterodactyl, the hoover adding a dinosaur-like roar.

The little ones stopped in their tracks, gobsmacked, before shrieking and pointing.

As I chuckled and cut the power, Emu's head flopped back down like a scene from *Jurassic Park*.

'*Bird!*' Jolene screamed.

So I let rip once more.

I took a break from the mural to check out a compact disc from the boot sale. It was a collection of well-known sounds, the sort inserted into radio plays as background noise. Track 7 on the CD's jacket was 'Fire Truck' and *blimey* it was realistic! The louder I cranked the volume, the more the *wah-wah* effect mirrored an actual fire engine. Track 12, 'Bee', left me further amazed.

A set of car speakers I'd bought at the boot sale came with enough cable to run outside the house. I wasn't sure if the speakers would work when connected to my hi-fi, but they did, and the sound quality was phenomenal. Feeling mischievous, I placed one speaker in the back garden and the other behind my dustbin out front. Then I took up the remote control and stood to the side of the lounge window. 'Helicopter' had to be the one. Slowly upping the volume, I swear it sounded exactly like the police chopper that often hovered over the area.

Net curtains began to twitch.

I increased the volume until the house literally pulsed, stopping there for fear of blowing the speakers. Neighbours had come to their doors and were peering at the sky. I toyed with the volume and balance controls, creating the effect of a police bird zooming around the sky looking for dirty rotten criminals.

I assumed I was the only person in on the joke but spotted Derek in his bay window, in hysterics and shaking his head at me. I phased the helicopter out and selected Track 4, 'Machinegun', spraying the street with some of Wan Chai's invisible ammunition. As my neighbours ran for cover, I whacked on the Fugees' 'Ready or Not', hoping they'd see the funny side and not report me to the actual police.

Saturday arrived and Steve had mentioned a fancy dress party at the Backward Parrot. During the day, I worked on the mural, in between digging into my arms with dulled needles. When evening fell, I climbed into the loft and rummaged through a seaman's kitbag containing the fancy-dress gear I'd accumulated in the marines – studded wristbands, leather joy-boy shorts and dresses from charity shops. I chuckled, recalling many a 'silly rig' run-ashore, not to mention the ensuing fistfights.

To keep things simple, I opted for a pink cowboy hat, a chunky faux-gold chain with dollar-sign medallion and an ultra-butch leather jacket I'd bought in Istanbul's Grand Bazaar. T-shirt could go, jeans could stay – at least until the second beer. As 'Dreamer' by Livin' Joy played on a mix tape compiled off the radio, I danced around the front room, feeling full on, funky and raring to rave.

I cycled to the pub in the dark with no lights on my bike, walking into the lounge a little after 10pm to find the place buzzing. All the punters had dressed up and were off their heads, singing and swaying to Boyzone's 'Words'. 'Al*wwwight,* Cow*boyyy?'* slurred a not-so-super hero, slapping me on the back and spilling beer over Princess Leia's grandmother.

'All good, Batman,' I replied, sidestepping a Chicken off its beak on acid.

Unable to spot Steve, I headed for the bar, squeezing between two oompa loompas busy pouring diamorphine into their JD and Cokes. I ordered half a lager from Jimmy Krankie – clearly stoned off his pack-lunch box – and turned drink in hand to purvey the scene. The joint *rocked,* and I was pleased I'd made the effort to come out. It was hard to believe the Backward Parrot was a regular pub, what with every customer drugged up to the eyeballs.

'*You!*'

The bellow came from the far end of the bar. Sensing trouble, the copycat funsters parted as a nurse with padded boobs, red fishnets and five-day stubble made a rubbish beeline towards me. '*You!*' the accusation continued – as if I didn't know this twat wanted my attention.

Now, if there's one place in the world you don't want a wonky transvestite on your case, it's the Backward Parrot. Just last week a pissed-up 'foreigner' (from a mile away in Whitleigh) made a comment the regulars didn't appreciate. They dragged the guy outside, beat him unconscious and went to douse him in petrol – until someone with a degree of fucking sense put a stop to it.

So here I was in danger of being cremated by a hairy nurse, but no one else knew what the problem was – until, that is, Nurse

Ratchet screamed, *'He's a copper!'*

Jimmy Krankie *killed* the music, adding a 'You're *fucking* fucked, mate' edge to the already tense atmosphere. The drugged-up pissed-up contenders all appeared to lean inwards, forming a leering tunnel of hate. A *copper* in the Parrot was unquestionably wrong, my mind flashing back to the murder-mystery night in Club Nemo.

The angel of death made her way over, wig awry, eyeliner and lipstick smudged, bulging black eyes projecting palpable paranoia.

Then I realised – it was *Donnie.*

'He's a *copper!*' the council worker screamed.

Desperate Dan puffed out his chest.

Kermit the Frog shuffled closer.

Shit! I bunched my fists, praying I wouldn't have to punch a Muppet.

'Stop!'

I turned to see a pirate sitting under the jukebox, a huge beard stuck to his face and a French maid clinging to his arm. 'He's with *me!'* the buccaneer boomed.

It was a relief to hear Steve's voice, only Donnie ignored him. Bracing up to me, 'Who the *fuck* are you?' he sneered.

I rested the rim of my pink Stetson against his nurse's cap and whispered in my best Wild West drawl, *'I'm* John Wayne.'

The bar dissolved into laughter, taking on a 'friend of Steve's' vibe. Jimmy Krankie cranked up the volume and 'School's Out for Summer' belted around the bar.

Donnie looked embarrassed and confused. 'Chris, I'm really sorry.' He put his arm around me. 'I got a bit para, you know?'

'It's okay. Did you do a trip?'

'Nah, coke and mushrooms.'

'Got any spare?'

'Follow me.'

The flat upstairs was modest at most and in serious need of redecoration. The floor was bare boards and the main room only had a couch, a crappy table and chairs and a large TV. It was strange to think the city's biggest drug deals took place here.

Two bald-headed bruisers slumped on the couch, enjoying an enormous conical spliff while watching *Match of the Day*. When it came to pleasantries, one of them was obviously telepathic, but the other had to actually nod to say hello. Shouldn't judge, but life's hard enough as it is without having facial tattoos.

My host pulled a bag of shrooms from his pocket. We scoffed a handful each and then he chopped out two fat lines of cocaine on the table. 'Sorry about all that back there,' he said.

Donnie didn't need to apologise again. Besides, the generous offering of chang spoke for him. Jeeze it was strong. I returned to the bar, bouncing off the ceiling, experiencing a nicely mellow buzz as the mushrooms kicked in. To the tune of the Chemical Brothers, I bopped around the lounge, yapping to flimsily suited Marvel characters, Chewbacca, a baggy hotdog and a bloke who didn't even know what he'd come as – nor did anyone else.

A teenage mutant ninja Damo beckoned me over to his table. 'Can you roll a bifta?' he yelled. 'I'll get the drinks in.'

'Cowabunga!'

'What?'

'Never mind.'

Damo reached into his shell and handed me a bag of weed. I rolled five spliffs at lightning speed as the drinkers around me watched in bemusement. Then I formed a slightly tapering three-inch-long tube from the flap of a Rizla packet and rolled a paper around the outside to prevent it unfurling. Holding the five spliffs side by side, I squeezed the roached ends and slid them into my Rizla-packet stem. The result was a five-pronged fan, which I presented to Damo to light. Ten minutes later, I could still see the glowing tips as the pentaspliff passed around the bar.

I cycled away from the Parrot, spannered yet looking forward to getting home for another hit. A petrol station marked the midway point of the journey and as I approached the Esso tiger's predatory eyes stared down at me. The giant poster sat in a display case high up on a pole, right below the current fuel prices. The eye shot alone captured the majestic creature's uncompromising beauty and I knew exactly what I would do with it.

The sole CCTV camera pointed at the fuel pumps, so I dumped my bike on the forecourt, checked the coast was clear and leapt at the pole. It was no good. I reached the poster and started to force off the casing's rubber seal, but the pole's burnished metal was too shiny to cling to with only my legs and I began slipping back down. For the sake of art, I took off my jeans and leather jacket and clad only in boxers, cowboy hat and gold chain was up the pole like a spooked cat. I unclipped my treasure and dropped it to the deck along with the Plexiglas pane.

Congratulating myself, I began to slide back down –

Headlights lit up the scene.

Shit!

My heart thumped. At this time of night, the odds of the lights belonging to a police car were not in my favour. It would mean a night in the cells charged with public indecency and poaching an endangered species – worse if they searched my house and found the speed – and all for a *stupid* poster! Dropping to the ground would only attract attention, so I did what commandos do when caught out by a flare. I froze.

The vehicle slowed.

My bare knees weakened.

It pulled to a stop.

Phew! A Citroën 2CV.

The driver wound down his window. 'Excuse me?' he said, ignoring the fact I was clinging to a pole dressed as the Gay Caballero. 'Do you know where Carnham Caravan Park is?'

No, piss off!

A woman leaned over. 'Apparently, it's near a petrol station, so we thought we might be close.'

'I don't know it. *Sorry!*'

My arms tired, my grip loosened, but sliding back to Earth would only draw attention to the stolen poster – as if being up a pole half-naked wearing a pink cowboy hat wasn't suspicious enough. To my horror, as I willed the holidaymakers to bugger off, a taxi drew alongside them.

'Alright, me 'andsome,' the cabbie greeted the wayward tourist. 'Where are you heading to?'

'Carnham Caravan Park,' the man replied. 'Rented an eight-berth with an electric hook-up.'

'*Carnham* Caravan Park?' the cab driver muttered.

Oh, fuck off, you moron! I slipped a foot down the pole. *You don't know where it is, so just fuck off!*

'There's a *Plym Valley* Caravan Park,' he stabbed in the dark.

Oh, super, like they're really gonna book into the wrong fucking holiday camp!

'... but *that's* permanent residents only.'

Moron, moron, moron! I slid another two feet.

'Near a petrol station,' said the woman.

'*Ahhh ...!* Near a *petrol* station?' he raised the couple's hopes.

'*Yes!*' they chorused, all beams and nods.

'Well, that's *not* near no petrol station,' he dashed those hopes.

The futile exchange continued, until I'd dropped all the way to the tarmac, where I remained motionless, arms wrapped around the pole. Fortunately, the couple realised the taxi driver was either bored or stupid – or both – and assured him they'd be fine. But as the cab drove off, the man in the Citroën looked at me, puzzled. 'Why are you *hugging* that pole?'

'Oh ... *practice.*' I shrugged.

'Practice?'

'Fire practice. I'm joining the fire brigade.'

'But why in the dark?' the women queried.

'I might have to work nights.'

'And why have you taken your clothes off?' she continued.

'So they don't catch fire.'

'Well, we wish you the best of luck,' said the husband. 'The country needs people like you.'

'Thank you,' I replied.

Free Drugs!

'G'day, Lou!' Harold Bishop is in fine spirits – the sort of spirits where you walk straight into your neighbour's house without knocking. 'How ya going?'

'I'm not going flamin good, mate.' Lou Carpenter has been up all night watching elephant porn. He's got a banging Victoria Bitter and painkiller hangover and is one angry bear. 'Some flaming dil's done a floater in me spiggin chlorine!'

'Oh gosh!' Bishop's pudgy face drops. 'You mean, someone's blocked your dunny?'

'No, rack off, you flaming galah!' Lou is not in the mood for Bishop's theatrical crap. He's never forgiven Harold for shacking up with Madge. 'I mean someone's dropped an arse biscuit in me blue lagoon!'

'Blue la ...?'

'Me spiggin swimming pool!'

'Oh ... I see.'

Neighbours. *Episode 3046*

I picked up my sexy cream-plastic roamer phone, flicked it to ON and whipped out the telescopic aerial. The latter measure, although unnecessary, made me feel like a Columbian drug baron. I pictured myself sitting by the pool of a Medellín villa, sipping an umbrella drink, smoking a Cohiba and making tough decisions – flip-flops, espadrilles or blow up the mayor.

'Hi, Chris.' My dad didn't sound *too* upset. 'I spoke with Plymouth Drug Service – nice bloke called Julian.'

'Okay.'

'He said I shouldn't worry. Reckons addiction is a phase many people go through. I told him I keep expecting to get a phone call to say you're dead, but he said it's hard to overdose on amphetamine.'

Thank heavens someone's talking sense! I thought, although I still couldn't envisage a life without speed.

'Listen,' Dad continued. 'He wants you to pop in for a chat. Holland Square, a week on Wednesday at two.'

'Sure.'

I doubted Julian could do anything for me, but appreciated my dad's efforts. It made a refreshing change to see my family acting positively instead of throwing the baby out with the bathwater ... *and* the bath ... *and* the bathroom ... *and* everything in it.

It was Monday lunchtime – for people who ate lunch. I hadn't done so since Thursday or slept a wink, either. In the thirty-six hours since leaving the Backward Parrot, I'd not achieved much else, bar removing the reflectors from my bike's former mudguards and bolting them to the frame. To keep things in order, I shovelled all the nuts, bolts, screws, nails and electrical junk into my military suitcase, leaving the carpet covered in paint and grease and littered with debris.

In between monster yawns and increasingly larger hits, I stuck the Esso tiger's eyes behind the glass in my front door, screwing the screen over the top. I drilled holes through the Perspex *and* the beast's pupils and plugged red bulbs from my Christmas lights into them. I wired the bulbs into the twelve-volt doorbell circuit so that when the bell rang the tiger's eyes lit up.

I could do with some more Perspex to make frames for my paintings. There was a petrol station next to the Co-op in the nearby retail park, so after it shut at 10pm I cycled down there. A waist-high billboard advertised an offer for engine oil, but the screen had cracks in it. With the amphetamine fuelling my curiosity, I cycled to an adjacent superstore, Furniture World, hoping there might be something in their skip worth scavenging. To my delight, it was full of carpet offcuts and broken-up display furniture. I cycled home with two large pieces of upholstery foam, knowing exactly what I'd do with them.

I'd paid sixty quid second-hand for my smart black sofa bed, chuffed it fitted with my bachelor-boy colour scheme. Now, though, I reckoned it needed turning into a sophisticated corner suite. If I sawed the frame in half, repositioned the two halves and made up some centre cushions, I'd have the couch of all couches and likely an influx of marriage proposals from here to Russia – well, probably just Russia.

My problem after six days without sleep was focusing. I went into the kitchen to fill a glass for a hit but found myself staring for an hour at the broken floor. Finally, I tore myself away, promising to re-patch the hole after finishing the corner suite. I fetched my saw from the hallway cupboard and returned to the lounge. Conscious of the neighbours, I double-checked the blinds and was in the process of redrawing the curtains when –

... sshoerighthemanotherestooutatyou ...

I froze.

Phantom neighbours were *talking* about me.

Everything came flooding back – that *whispery* voice from Hong Kong. Not the backstabbing Cantonese taunts in my building in Mong Kok, people criticising Vance and yelling stuff about the *gweilo. They* had been real. I mean the one in my *head* – like someone else's thoughts spoken in *my* inner voice. *Whoa ...!* I must have been ill, as Dr Middleton wrote in his letter.

I put the voice out of my head and sawed through the couch. Splinters and black lint flew everywhere. I placed the two sections in a corner of the room, one facing the window, the other the TV, and plonked myself on a cushion to get a feel for how to proceed. Two hours later, I still slumped there. *What am I doing? Have I really sawn my sofa in half?*

I retrieved my works, knowing there was only enough gear left in the scorebag for two pathetically small hits. Tired, confused and hallucinating, I stared at the blunt pins, knowing I'd used them all at least ten times each. *Can I sharpen them on the record player?* I wondered.

Having set the machine to forty-five revolutions per minute, I laid the needle at an angle on the spinning rubber mat, hoping the burring effect would bring back an edge. Trouble was, I couldn't focus on keeping the syringe at the factory angle and when I stabbed my arm the pain told me the tip was duller than before. I was cold and tired and finding a vein proved impossible. In desperation, I punctured my arm several times, still with no luck. I finally pressed the plunger down with shaking hands and a swelling the size of a sprout developed. *Fuck it!*

So tired yet still too high to sleep, I staggered around the house, pausing for ever-longer reflection, while squinting at my projects. I *had* to achieve something before I crashed, but couldn't decide how to spend my dwindling energy. *Perhaps I should eat. The calorie intake might pick me up.*

It took me *two* hours to prepare a pint of pasta and porridge and a split second to drop it on the kitchen's filthy floor. Loath to let my efforts go to waste, I inspected the smashed glass and conducted an impromptu risk assessment based on stunts I'd seen on *Record Breakers*. I figured if Monsieur Mangetout could eat an aeroplane, I could handle a bit of dirt and glass, so I picked out the obvious shards and spooned the cereal into a bowl.

Lacking the focus required to paint the mural or finalise my designer-furniture range, I turned my waning attention to the kitchen floor. Rather than face the hassle of fetching my drill from the hallway cupboard, I hammered the chipboard mantrap down using four-inch screws. My tub of wood filler had dried to a stale-yellow nugget, so I knocked up some papier-mâché using watered-down PVA glue as a binder and pressed into the gaps.

Sunlight seeping through the venetian blinds told me I'd wasted hours on a simple task that should have taken minutes. Undeterred, I lay propped on an elbow, daubing African Cherry fence paint on the wet papier-mâché, before lurching to the cupboard for a metal carpet strip and a nail. By scribing lines in the woodstain, I created a crude parquet-flooring effect – crude being the operative word. It was completely fucking shit.

I awoke on my completely fucking shit floor in the afternoon, having become quite attached to it. Not in the sense of admiring my duff workmanship *or* developing a fondness for completely fucking shit floors. I mean, after lying with my face in the paint for hours, I'd become stuck and had to wrench myself away. *How many people have managed to glue themselves to a house while taking a nap?* I wondered, knowing the answer was probably 'one'.

Peering in the bathroom mirror, I saw a dark-orange splodge on my forehead. I looked like Mikhail Gorbachev when he auditioned for *Stig of the Dump.*

You probably shouldn't scrub your face with petrol, but to get the stain off my grid, I soaked a flannel regardless. Being in the bathroom reminded me to turn off the hot-water storage tank to save money. My shower and Economy 7 heating ran on mains electric and I could always boil a kettle to wash the dishes. As for washing my hands, cold water would have to do.

A bizarre law applies to Class A drugs. Regardless of how many kilos you *think* you've got before going to sleep, there's never much left when you wake up. I'd planned on a powerful last hit and a productive day working on my projects, but the tiny line of white powder in the bottom of the scorebag put that idea to bed. I felt gutted and wished I had the money to buy more.

Instead, I began a meticulous process of sucking a little water into each syringe to loosen up the amphetamine-laden blood, squirting it into the scorebag to dissolve the drug residue. Ten rinses later and the dessert spoon brimmed with scarlet dregs. I dropped in the slices of speed-saturated cigarette filter and boiled the disgusting concoction with a lighter, pleased to see the blood congealing into a single lump in the bubbles.

Can injecting blood harm you? I wondered, reassured to find the filtering process removed all visible traces. Not daring to waste this last hit, I selected what I thought was the sharpest syringe and made damn sure it was in my vein before bidding bye-bye to Berty. The resultant high certainly wasn't worth the effort, but try telling that to my addicted inner twin.

Before the comedown overpowered me, I incinerated the

syringes in the back garden. Now I wouldn't be tempted to reuse them, nor would I suffer the guilt of having the scaggy things in my home. After some porridge and pasta and a strong cuppa, I wandered around the mess I'd created, intending to piggyback off the remaining buzz to clean everything up. A huge yawn kicked the knobs off that idea, so I crawled under the duvet on the sofa bed and prayed that drifting off wouldn't be torturous.

It was.

The last thing I recall was bleating like a dying lamb as my sleep-deprived mind locked in a dogfight with Baron von Amphetaminehausen.

The doorbell rang.

Assuming it was the kids, I didn't get up but felt awful letting them down. My ability to interact with young people on their level was my proudest achievement, I just couldn't face entertaining right now. Whoever it was pushed the bell again, something the dinky diamonds never did.

'Mister Thrall?' said the anorak with a clipboard.

'Sorry, who are you?'

I don't usually bat questions back at strangers – it makes you sound like a dick – but I wanted to check the guy wasn't a debt collector.

'I'm from the TV licencing company.' He held up identification.

My mind went into overdrive, figuring a way to avoid paying the £115 fee.

'Do you own a television?' he continued.

'There's one in the house,' I replied – as he and I both knew there's one in every fucking house in the country.

He raised his clipboard and slid out the pen of doom.

'*But* I don't live here.'

'Oh ...'

'I'm away travelling – with the circus. It's just that we've had an incident with one of the clowns.'

'Clowns?'

'Yeah, funny fellas, red noses, crap cars.'

'Yes, I know what clowns are.'

'I don't know *how* many times I've told Coco not to stand so close to the lion's cage – not with those *bloody* long shoes on – but you know clowns ...' I shook my head. 'They seem to think life's one big joke.'

The TV man nodded vaguely.

'Well, the shoes on the other foot now – least it would be if Leo hadn't eaten it.'

The poor guy continued to look flustered, staring alternately at the form and me.

'So while the job centre finds us another clown, I thought I'd come back here and do a bit of redecorating – before renting the place out again, I mean.'

'Oh, so this is a *rental* property?'

'Yes, sir,' I replied, knowing it's the tenant who pays for the license.

'That's fine. I'll-I'll-I'll ...' He flapped his clipboard and fled.

Julian was a good bloke. He laughed when I called him 'Doc', a gesture of respect marines extend to anyone in the medical field. With a modest grin, 'I'm a lowly caseworker,' he joked, ushering me to a comfy chair in one of the drug service's counselling rooms. 'Fancy a cuppa?'

Going by previous encounters with professionals, I'd expected someone cold and distant who would try to fob me off with happy pills. But as a substance-misuse specialist, Julian was streetwise, upfront and approachable. His body language alone told me he cared about his client's wellbeing and understood the bigger picture. After listening intently and asking a few gently probing questions, 'You're self-medicating,' he said, 'for clinical depression and PTSD –'

'PTS ...?' I leant towards him.

'Post-traumatic stress disorder – from your time in the military, perhaps.'

I thought back to my unit's hectic tour of duty in Northern Ireland. We'd faced improvised explosive devices, snipers and similar attacks on a daily basis, with one of our brothers shot dead before we'd even found our feet. Soldiers often say *everyone* gets scared in such situations, but I loved active service and honestly never was. Perhaps the events in Hong Kong had affected me – my life *was* in danger over there on more than one occasion. But *PTSD?* I'd stick with the belief there was nothing wrong with me.

'Is there a way to get a prescription of Dexedrine, Doc?' I referred to the pharmaceutical brand of amphetamine.

'There is,' Julian replied, 'but only for people in treatment.'

'Okay, I'll come into treatment.'

I felt as if I'd struck gold. *Free* frickin drugs! I pictured the stability a never-ending supply of dexys would bring to my life. No longer spending every penny on gear and shoving filthy needles in my arm, simply popping a pill in the morning and going about my day like everyone else. *Yes!*

'*Ah…*' Julian shuffled in his chair. 'We have a twelve-month waiting list.'

'You're *joking.*'

'I know. It's bloody ridiculous.'

I shook my head and asked to join the back of the queue. In the meantime, I'd eat toast and watch episodes of *Neighbours.*

Seventy Bastards

And so my perfect life continued, right through the summer, surfing a syringe along the crest of Chaos or sinking on a sawn-in-half sofa bed into the depths of Despair. The highlight of my week alternated between spending eighty pounds on drugs or nineteen pence on a tin of No Frills soup. Coming down off amphetamine, which was most of the time, I had no option but to sleep or watch television. I only washed the dishes when high, the same with showering – unless I had an appointment to attend.

Of course, all this would change in twelve months' time when the drug service put me on a much-needed prescription of Dexedrine, effectively giving me my life back. Each time I handed my income support payment to Damo, I vowed to finish my projects, thus turning my home into a place of wonder for guests ... but with the exception of the kids asking for a game of footy, not a soul knocked on my door.

On one particular comedown, I felt so desperate I phoned an old business colleague. Lionel was a switched-on Black chap from Torpoint, a hard-working family man who'd always held me in high regard. Perhaps the smartly dressed financial advisor would have some words of wisdom to help me sort my life out.

When I answered the door, Lionel's jaw dropped – and not because of the Esso Tiger's illuminating welcome. I wasn't sure what shocked him the most – my appearance or the state of the smart house we'd once held business meetings in. Perched on half a sofa bed, Lionel went through the motions of friendship, but upon hearing about my drug problem, he lurched towards his car, muttering something about keeping in touch.

Where have I heard that before? I thought, feeling foolish to have trusted someone with a cry for help.

The drinkers in the Backward Parrot now considered me a regular because of all the halves of lager they witnessed me drinking – which is slightly ironic as I only bought them as a courtesy while waiting to bug out of the place. And as anyone with a drug problem will tell you, it's the hanging around that's the hardest part, akin to an eternity in Hell digging your eyeballs out with a marrow.

You can be fucked about for any number of reasons, the complexity of which would blow Mr Spock's Vulcan brain. 'It's coming' might mean the gear was on its way down the M5 *or* with one of any number of dealers in the distribution chain, each of whom needed time to divide, bash and bag their investment before selling it on. 'It's coming' might also mean the dealer had no gear on the horizon but was trying to source a supply so they didn't lose your custom.

If you were lucky, 'I'm on my way' meant exactly that, but more often than not the dealer was watching *EastEnders* or being dragged around Morrisons by the long-haired boss and would be with you in a couple of hours. Regardless of this cheating lying bullshit, I hung on these words like an obedient dog waiting for a non-existent walk in an invisible park, as powerless as a supermarket battery on Boxing Day.

Despite travelling halfway around the world on several occasions, the furthest I now ventured was a pharmacy three miles away. I'd attempted to buy syringes there one day and the women serving said they distributed ten-packs of Microfines and swabs free of charge as part of the government's harm-reduction agenda. I still reused the pins until they were as blunt as bananas, though, so desperate to whack the speed in my arm I would put off the trip over there.

Upon receiving my benefit money, I'd cycle ever-faster to the Backward Parrot, taking my works with me. At the back of the pub, a latched wooden gate opened into a high-walled courtyard full of empty beer barrels, drinks crates and large waste bins. After scoring my life-giving powder, I'd sneak in there and cook up a hit, before taking a leisurely ride home cocooned in bliss.

Late one Saturday night, I pelted down the pub on my bike. The usual suspects spread around the bar, all having a good time to the sound of the Fugees' 'Killing Me Softly'. I sought out Damo and following our brief transaction went back out to my walled hideaway to have one for the road.

I laid my works on the lid of a wheelie bin only the spoon sat at an awkward angle, so I bent its handle slightly to level things up and prevent spillage. I tapped a generous amount of powder into the spoon's bowl, making a mental note to hide the scorebag in my boot before leaving the courtyard. I'd stuck to this practice religiously in Hong Kong after a British lad received a twelve-year prison sentence for possession of a single ecstasy pill. Having prepared the syringe with a splash of water from a Jif lemon bottle, I lifted off into the euphoric state I'd been craving for days.

A police siren blipped in the distance. Picturing one of the area's villainous pensioners shoplifting Scotch eggs in the Co-op, I put it out of my mind, stowed the works in my bomber jacket and reached for the latch on the gate –

Vehicles *screeched* to a halt.

Doors *crashed* open.

Boots *thudded* on the tarmac.

Oh shit... I thought, as equipment jangled, rattled and banged.

I hopped onto a beer barrel and peered over the wall to see an ocean of blue flashing lights converged on the Backward Parrot. *The pub was being busted!*

In a panic, I grabbed my bike and contemplated making a break for it, but they obviously had the place surrounded. A quick change of plan, I whipped out the scorebag and chucked it under a beer barrel.

Radios *blared* and orders *barked* as riot-clad officers leapt from their vehicles and charged into the lounge. What should I do? If I attempted to waffle my way out of this, they might search the courtyard and find the gear. Heart pounding, I considered my limited options. So limited, I only had one ...

I climbed into the largest waste bin, its lid swinging shut as I hid under the filthy rubbish bags. Rancid liquid soaked my clothes, the stench of stale beer and fag butts filling my nostrils. I prayed the police would focus their search inside the pub, but as my breathing calmed the thought occurred I might be stuck in here for ages. Police raids don't take five minutes. There'd be evidence to collect, people to arrest, witness statements to record.

Minutes turned into hours as I pickled in alcohol, nicotine and cheese-and-onion, the pub's usually blaring music replaced by the sound of black-jumpsuited agents-of-the-state going about their search. I bet the coppers were *dead* proud of themselves, busting the hard-working class for letting their hair down at the weekend.

What about those *above* the law, though? Members of Britain's parliament off their gimp-masked faces on cocaine in sex dungeons right about now? Celebrities laying on trays of the bloody stuff at their VIP parties? Aristocracy snorting it up their toffee noses on country estates? Why weren't the police going after them? Just like me in the marines, acting on behalf of a capitalist elite, the coppers lacked the life experience to see through the rhetoric and consider all sides of the debate.

Without warning, the gate to the courtyard crashed open, scattering beer barrels like bowling pins. A panting mutt strained at the leash, its handler shouting encouragement in doggy-speak.

My mind went numb, body limp. Life morphed into a kaleidoscope of *terror,* slow-motion screenshots cascading towards an inevitable conclusion.

The bin's lid crashed open, revealing an umbrella of irrelevant stars and Rover's sniffing chops silhouetted in the moonlight.

Anticipating a frantic barking, I felt a sudden, *desperate* need for closure ...

Ruff-ruff-ruff!

'Don't move!' The stunned handler yanks the dog back by its harness. 'Lads, quick, some bloke's hiding in here!'

The coppers haul me out of the skip sans ceremony. Two of them slam me chest-first onto a beer barrel, pinning my arms behind my back.

'Arrrrh!' I overplay the pain, putting up zero resistance in the hope they'll go easy on me.

The handcuffs bite into my wrists.

'Right, mate. You can start by telling us why you were in that bin!'

'I-I-I…'

The lid slammed shut and pitch-blackness reigned once more. Trained not to interact with humans, the faithful canine had done just that.

I sat there in squalor well into the early hours, listening to the intermittent crackle of police radios and vehicle movements. Each time a van departed, I wondered if one of my mates was being carted off to the nick. Every so often, I shifted position to prevent cramp, until the search finally quietened down and I heard the last police car leave.

I clambered out of the skip, soaking wet and covered in filth. My first thought was the drugs. I should really leave them here, but the prospect of arriving home without a hit was more than I could bear, so I retrieved the scorebag and slipped it in my boot. Then, after a quick peek around the gate, I wheeled the bike out and hopped on.

'Oy!'

I turned to see a uniformed copper standing under the pub's swinging sign.

'Over here *now!*'

I was away, pedalling up the road like Lance Armstrong's drugged-up cousin. At the first set of traffic lights, I cut left, bombing downhill for half a mile and ducking into a woodland reserve. Gasping for breath, I ran the bike up a track through the trees, a detour that brought me out by the junction for the Co-op. I could see Carroll Road five hundred metres further up, but with the cop shop less than a mile away any patrol car responding to the officer's sighting would intercept me before I got there. My best option was to cross the junction and enter the estate through the coppice to the rear.

Praying the police helicopter wouldn't appear overhead, I hopped my bicycle off the kerb and onto the barren highway.

Headlights swept around the bend, the reflectors I'd insisted on bolting back onto the bike lighting up like Christmas decorations.

Perhaps they haven't seen me …

A blaze of crystal-blue reflected off walls and hedges as the angry blip of a siren ordered me to stay put.

In a panic worthy of *Tom and Jerry,* I powered over the junction and skidded to a halt in a Kingdom Hall car par. Hefting the bike on my shoulder, I charged up the muddy bank, tearing through weeds and branches, reassured the tarmacked path at the top lead straight to my estate.

The police car screeched to a standstill and out jumped a copper. 'Alright, *stop* there!'

I would love to have rattled off a reply, something deep and profound like, 'Up yours, *spotty* face!' but too terrified, I jumped on my bike and dashed the final thirty metres to my house.

Not wishing to get caught fumbling with the key, I pelted past the front door and shot behind the street's electricity substation. Crammed between the grey-painted aluminium and a neighbour's fence, I had an inch of space on either side of the handlebars but was hidden from the road.

Sure enough, the cop car entered the street and drove right past me. If the officers got out and walked around, they'd have found me in seconds. But after a circuit of the estate, they drove off.

Later in the day, as I stared at a fortnight's worth of dirty dishes, there was a knock on the door. Fearing a visit from the local constabulary, I'd stowed my syringes and scorebag in a Tupperware container and buried it in the back garden. This precaution did nothing to prevent my already racing heart from stepping up a gear, though. I'd taken the Esso Tiger down as the kids kept pressing the doorbell to make his eyes light up, so I could see through the textured glass once more. Two youngsters stood there, which came as a relief.

'Got any jobs?' the fair-haired lad asked.

'We're trying to earn some money for our 'alf term 'oliday,' the redheaded girl explained.

'What are your names?'

'Lee.'

'Claire.'

'Ah, nice one. I'm Chris.'

High-fives and grins broke the ice.

Lee and Claire looked about ten years old and lived on a nearby council estate. 'So how many doors have you knocked on?' I asked.

'All of them,' Lee replied.

'And how many people gave you a job?'

'None of them.' Claire shook her head.

'You any good at washing-up?'

'Uh-huh,' they replied.

'Well, I've got *loads* of it!'

Lee and Claire were cracking kids. They asked if I owned the Fugees debut album. I didn't but had recorded 'Ready or Not' from the radio. We sang along, Lee standing on a chair to reach the sink and Claire drying the dishes.

'What pub do you drink in?' asked Lee.

'I don't really have a local.' I smiled. 'But I go in the Backward Parrot sometimes.'

'Awh, do you know my Uncle Damion?' Lee's face lit up. 'He's *always* stoned and he walks like this ...'

I laughed at Lee's zombie impression, which could only be Damo, but pretended we hadn't met, for obvious reasons.

'His uncle got *arrested* last night!' Claire's eyes widened.

'The Backward Parrot got *busted!*' Lee added.

With events at the pub all too real, I reflected on how socially aware these kids were compared to their cohort in my street. 'Who told you that?' I asked.

'Mum's boyfriend,' said Lee. ''E read it in the 'Erald.'

'Oh.'

I never bought a paper, so it hadn't occurred to me the bust might make the day's edition. 'Can you pop to the shop and get us a copy?' I handed Lee a quid fifty. 'And split the pound between you.'

Not only had it made the paper, but also the front page. 'SEVENTY POLICE IN RAID ON DRUG PUB'. Scanning the article, I expected to learn the boys and girls in blue had seized umpteen kilos of coke, a ton of gold bullion, a stack of blank passports, several AK-47s and a sex slave from Moldovia. Gobsmacked, I read that along with a small bag of marijuana, they'd confiscated three pills and five grams of 'a white powdery substance', while making one arrest.

When my fortnightly speed buy came around, I dragged myself off the sofa bed and cycled to the Parrot. Phil, the landlord, stood behind the bar. Phil was a hard-nut wide boy, the type of guy who ends up owning a rough pub and a big dog. No surprise, he hated the police and probably their parents. 'Damo got nicked, Chrissy.' He scowled. 'Seventy *black* bastards smashed the *fucking* door in!'

By 'black' bastards, Phil *obviously* referred to the cops in their protective kit, a morally appropriate choice of adjective and not in *any* way a racist juxtapose indicative of a parochial worldview and underlying prejudice – the fucking *xenophobe!*

Evidently, the local police chief was under the impression the Backward Parrot crawled with evil drug dealers on a Saturday night, their pockets overflowing with Class A poison. Anticipating a showdown at the Okay Corral, he'd sent seventy officers piling into the pub – only for them to find the place half-empty. And not only that, but it was *10pm* at night and, with the exception of Damo, the few punters present had no substances left on them.

As with Old Man Jakes, Professor Penfold and all the other fright merchants giving it the big one in *Scooby-Doo* over the years, Damo 'would have gotten away with it too' had his attempt to ditch his goody bag not hit the skids when a copper spotted him flicking it under the pool table.

'He'll get a three-stretch,' said the landlord, nodding behind me. I turned to see that on every wall was a handwritten sign with a cannabis leaf drawn on it in green felt-tip pen. 'NO SMOKING WEED ON THE PREMISES OR SEVENTY BLACK BASTARDS WILL SMASH THE FUCKING DOOR DOWN!'

Phil offered to source me some base, saying it wouldn't be anywhere near the quality of Damo's. He said the better dealers had gone to ground, following a recent string of busts. I cycled home fed up and so desperate for a hit I tried to think of people from my past who might know someone who could sell me amphetamine.

The Itches

'*Chris!*' screamed my favourite paranoid schizophrenic.

Ordinarily, I couldn't bring myself to answer the phone on a comedown, but spying a Barnstaple number, I knew it was my drug buddy.

'Hello, mate. What's happening?'

'I've been doing loads of speed,' he replied. 'I've been injecting it.'

Wow ... Neil had hit the pins too.

'Can you get hold of some whizz, Neil?'

'Yeah, I can get hold of some whizz. I've been buying quarters for fifty from a bloke called Mousey.'

What! He'd been getting the same amount I bought from Damo but for thirty pounds less.

'Is it any good, Neil?'

'Yeah, it's good, you know?'

I did know and immediately boarded a double-decker bus for the two-hour journey to Barnstaple.

Neil met me at the station, trousers tucked into his boots. We went to the nearest pub to make a call and begin the waiting game. Out of respect to the landlord, I bought a half of lager, but Neil was happy to sit there practising his chewing.

Mousey turned up half an hour later, which was a good start. Thickset and unassuming, he had a bob haircut and wore a long thin denim jacket like Liam Gallagher. According to Neil, Mousey had a heroin habit but wasn't a rip-off merchant.

'Let's go to my flat,' said Mousey.

Neil and I followed him like obedient puppies.

Jeeee-zuss! I'd never seen such a fucking craphole. Mousey's pad made the Mother Superior's gaff in *Trainspotting* look downright palatial. There were no carpets, furniture or appliances – bar a grotty couch and an aging crate of a TV. Draft racing between the rotten window frames abducted all of the antiquated oil radiator's meagre heat. Mousey had bypassed the flat's coin-operated electricity meter – with a sledgehammer – and substituted sheets of newspaper for toilet paper in the mould-infested bathroom. The only thing of value, a king snake, lay coiled under a lightbulb in a vivarium in the corner. Despite its owner not having to pay for energy, the coldblooded reptile was probably the warmest creature in the room.

'So have you got the gear?' I asked.

'It's coming,' Mousey replied.

It wasn't what we wanted to hear, but Mousey seemed honest enough and Neil had scored speed off him before.

'It's not going to be bashed to fuck is it?' I frowned.

This wasn't a question but an indirect way of telling Mousey not to piss us about. He wasn't doing this out of kindness, only to support a heroin habit, and his cut had to come from somewhere.

'Don't worry.' Mousey scrunched his nose and shook his head. 'I put business this guy's way and he sorts me with a bit of scag.'

I still had my suspicions about Mousey and the miracle deal on offer, especially as at 8pm we were still watching his hand-cranked TV because his mate hadn't turned up. The guy eventually arrived, allaying my fears, for the cling-filmed wrap was a good weight and smelled as strong as the Devil's dandruff. Mousey gave me the number of the pub so I could get hold of him when I needed to score again, which in view of the generous deal on offer would be as soon as my next payment arrived.

Back at Neil's, two days went by in a blur of injecting. Despite each other's presence, we drifted into separate worlds, pursuing individual missions, such as drawing and writing. I came up with the excellent idea of injecting tobacco in the hope it would make our gear last longer. If amphetam*ine,* coca*ine* and caffe*ine* were all stimulants, I reasoned, then surely nicot*ine* must be an upper too. I boiled a pinch of Cutter's Choice in the spoon and banged it into my arm without further thought.

My heart began to thump like a three-legged ferret

breakdancing in a cement mixer. Nausea washed over me, my mouth filling with metallic-tasting drool. As Neil's bedroom span, I became *extremely* cold.

'N–N–N ... *eil* ...' I tried to get his attention but could barely whisper.

Terrified, I wrapped myself in Neil's duvet and prepared to clock out of this merry parade but fell asleep instead. It was a frightening experience, definitely one of my stupidest endeavours. I later learned the nicotine in a single cigarette is enough to kill you if taken in one hit.

In the morning, I felt lucky to be alive, happier still when my buddy returned to Plymouth with me.

'Neil, I'm itching.' I sat on half a sofa bed, scratching my arms.

'Itching?' Neil looked up from preparing a hit.

'Yeah, like I've caught fleas. Do you feel anything?'

'No.' He shrugged.

I felt pinpricks all over my body, as if minute bugs were burying into my skin. My eyes wandered around the room. Perhaps I'd contracted lice from Mousey's place or a skip or the car boot sale. I shuddered, regretting ever hoarding a single piece of junk.

'Neil, I'm not sure what to do.' I inspected my skin. 'I'll need to delouse the whole place.'

My fretting increased. I peered at the sofa bed, trying to see any movement that might indicate an infestation. There was nothing, but that didn't stop my hair from coming alive. *They're burying into my scalp,* I feared. *What if they lay eggs?*

I reached over and grabbed the largest book on the shelf, *Tattoo: The Exotic Art of Skin Decoration,* which I'd bought at a boot sale with my mural in mind.

'What are you doing?' Neil asked.

'I need to see what they are.' I ruffled my hair, attempting to dislodge one of the critters onto my improvised specimen tray. Scanning the light dusting of dandruff, I was unable to spot any livestock and so fetched my Swiss army knife and levered out the magnifying glass. Nothing, only tiny threads of white power, which I guessed was my body ejecting amphetamine.

'Go to the doctor,' said Neil.

'I haven't got one in Plymouth, mate.'

I looked up the number for my nearest medical centre, Parkside Surgery in Whitleigh, relieved when the receptionist offered me an emergency appointment. Whitleigh was half a mile away, so I left Neil at home and cycled over there.

'How can I help, Mister Thrall?' asked a male GP named Adams, who seemed nice enough.

'Doctor, I'm itching all over, like I've picked up lice or something.'

'Do you take drugs?' he replied without hesitation.

'Yes ... amphetamine.'

'Then you're imagining it.'

The doc wasn't being offhand, but I felt powerless to tell him his snap diagnosis was wrong. I had no doubt people visualise all kinds of weird stuff when nutted, only I *wasn't* hallucinating. My body physically *itched* and I still had no idea why.

Usually, taking speed represented my 'up' time, the happy part of my otherwise miserable fortnight, a period when I could at least try and get things done. Now, though, I couldn't relax. If the quack wouldn't help me end this nightmare, I would have to take matters into my own hands.

When Neil left the next morning, I went to the Co-op and bought two cans of flea powder and a large bottle of bleach. My duvet was too big to fit in the washing machine, so I chucked it in the back garden and doused it in petrol from a red-plastic jerry can I used to keep in the car. For good measure, I splashed on some more ... and more ... and a *wee* bit more ...

Whooomph! The fireball engulfed me, singeing my hair and eyebrows. I leapt through the kitchen door in shock and had to plonk myself on one of the black-ash dining chairs to calm down.

After a minute, I put my clothes on a hot wash cycle and

sprinkled my boots with flea powder. Then I filled the bath with cold water, added two cups of bleach and hopped in. It wasn't an ideal scenario, but how else could I annihilate the vicious little squatters making themselves at home in my skin? I made sure to submerge my frazzled mop and splash water around the tiling to catch any fugitives.

Dressed in an old T-shirt, tracky bottoms and Adidas flip-flops, I began to delouse the house, giving the bedrooms a miss as I hardly spent any time in them. I shook flea powder over the carpets, couch and skirting boards, figuring the fumes alone should kill these guests from Hell.

It was then that I noticed the smell ...

A waft at first, impossible to place, it couldn't be the burning duvet because I remembered shutting the back door. I walked around the house, sniffing the air, my nose receiving mixed messages ... *coffee ... bleach ... biscuits ... crumbs in the toaster ... bread ... rubbish in the bin ... black bags under the sink ... amphetamine ...*

So *peculiar,* a whiff morphing from benign one moment to acrid and chemically the next. If I didn't know better, I'd say a poltergeist had taken up residence and the smell was the scheming phantom's malignant breath. I inspected the rooms once more, shoving my nose in drawers, cupboards, bottles, jars and boxes. Every time I congratulated myself on finding its source, the odour transformed into something else. How *weird ...*

Don't waste time on this sideshow.

Something told me to get on with my jobs. The problem was I'd run out of base and the shivering-tired sickness plaguing me in Hong Kong returned with a vengeance. Every so often, a gigantic jolt rocked my torso – *'Uhh!'* – leaving me stunned and confused.

Panic crept in. I knew a crash was inevitable.

Ordinarily, I'd crawl under the duvet and Groundhog Day would commence its predictable scroll. This time it was different. If I didn't get the flea powder hoovered up, how would I know if I'd defeated the bugs? On top of that, I had wet clothes to hang out and needed to find some kind of cover under which to sleep. If I allowed myself to drift off I'd die of hypothermia, leaving behind a pallid pockmarked corpse overrun with lice.

The word 'frightened' came to mind. The part of my life I usually controlled with magic fix-all medication was now off the leash, leaving me with a sense of foreboding. Laurel and Hardy syndrome had kicked in big time, so when I took a step forward a metaphorical plank slammed into my face, sending me reeling backwards. I *had* to get a grip.

I sat on the edge of the sofa bed, cringing at the thought it crawled with mites. *Could the horrible smell be coming from inside me?* I wondered. Perhaps the amphetamine had upset my system's fragile balance and I had developed cancer. My diseased cells would explain why the smell always managed to follow me around.

Still, I'd have to worry about my health later as putting the house back together took priority. That way, when I awoke from a coma I'd only have miserableness to cope with and not a guilt-inducing shambles. Before continuing, I needed a nicotine fix and reached for my pouch of Cutter's Choice.

'Tpuh!' I spat the cigarette smoke out and retched.

Something had contaminated the tobacco, leaving a vile taste in my mouth like Vosene shampoo. I sat there pondering what it could be, when – *fuuff!* – an ash-like particle shot from the roll-up's burning tip. I watched as it arced in the air before floating down to the carpet. *What the ...?*

I took a second drag and sure enough – *fuuff!* – the same thing occurred.

As rank smoke spilled from my lips, I realised what the problem was – *the bugs were in the tobacco!*

I shoved my nose in the plastic pouch and smelt that god-awful odour of earlier. Further sickening, the next time I sucked on the cigarette's cardboard roach a bug shot into my mouth. I could feel the wicked little blighter latching onto my tongue and had to scrape it off with a tooth and spit it out.

I rolled another cigarette, this time using a filter to stop me inhaling the tobaccic trespassers. The smoke still tasted awful and every so often – *fuuff!* – a toasted mite leapt for its life, a sign my pouch was riddled with the bloody things.

A shivering spasm juddered up through my body, followed by a gurnblaster of a yawn. If I didn't score some speed forthwith, I'd crash in the middle of this nightmare. On my last visit to Fort Chunkington, the Colonel had shown me a bottle of yellow medicine prescribed by his GP. I couldn't recall what it was for, Chunkfest having more ailments than a doctor's waiting room, but I did remember him saying it was amphetamine-based *and* that he always had a spare bottle.

I grabbed my keys and crossed the road to a neighbours' house. Steve and Mandy were a pleasant couple and although we were not bosom buddies, I knew them well enough to ask Steve for a lift.

'Sure, mate,' the former squaddie replied, a little surprised.

We jumped into Steve's Astra and I gave him the address. A short way into the journey, 'Is everything alright, Chris?' he asked. 'It's just you've kept to yourself since Honkers.'

'Not really, mate,' my unbridled honesty replied. 'I picked up a drug problem over there.'

'Oh …'

Steve's discomfort told me he'd never done drugs, but at least he didn't piss his pants like Lionel.

When I knocked on the Chunkmeister's door, his wonderful and adoring partner, Chelle, answered. 'Oh hi, Chris. Paul's out at the minute.'

Chelle was calm, non-judgemental, unassuming yet street-smart, the perfect ying to Chunkenheim's madcap but loveable yang. She knew about my substance use, so I cut to the chase, telling her about my battle with the mites and asking for a drop of El Chunko's medicine. 'So I can tidy the house up before crashing,' I added. 'If it doesn't get you in trouble with Paul, that is.'

'I'll worry about him.' Chelle smiled, handing me a full bottle along with a large packet of bootleg Golden Virginia.

Back home, I couldn't wait to drink the amphetamine-laden

prescription, knowing the resulting high would take me *up* and the lice *down*. I rolled a smoke first, though, and placed the fresh packet of tobacco in a Tupperware box dusted with flea powder for additional protection.

The tonic itself tasted like the banana-flavoured syrup mums spoon into sick kids. I took a couple of sips and waited for its speedy effect to take hold. In the meantime, I dragged on my ciggie and watched for scorched bugs pinging into the air. I couldn't see any, but the smoke tasted just as revolting as before. *How the hell did the tobacco get contaminated already?* I cursed.

Whatever evil spirit had descended on my place, it was always one step ahead and just thinking about the plague of mites it had spawned made my skin crawl. I scratched every itch with a fingernail – shoulders, ears, scalp – certain I could feel the pesky invaders like specks of dirt. They were driving me out of my mind, so I did the thing with the tattoo book again, raking my hair and inspecting whatever dropped out.

Wow! In amongst the detritus, I could see tiny dead creatures that looked like aliens. Peering through the magnifying glass on my Swiss army knife, I was shocked to see their heads, bodies and limbs in detail.

I was at a loss what to do. Like in *War of the Worlds,* the Martians were winning. I had no gear left and the yellow banana shit hadn't worked – no surprise there. I gulped the remainder and whacked my Golden Virginia in the microwave for ten seconds to nuke any extraterrestrial insurgents that might have found their way in there. Then I sat on the filthy flea-powdered carpet in the lounge, leaning back against the wall, smoking a roll-up and staring at the ominous state of the room.

It was midwinter, but to save money I'd only switched on one of the property's three Economy-7 storage heaters. Previously, with strong speed rushing the blood around my body, I'd been fine in trackies, flip-flops and a T-shirt, but now as the effect of the drug waned and the radiator gave up the last of its precious heat the sub-temperate air sapped the warmth from my body. My core temperature plummeted and I started shivering uncontrollably, teeth chattering like a wind-up toy. I'd never felt so cold, not even when pinned down by blizzards in the Arctic Circle.

Recognising the onset of hypothermia, I had to act fast but my panic-stricken mind faced an awful dilemma. Bar the toaster, the only source of portable heat in the house was a cheap hairdryer left behind by an ex-girlfriend as she sprinted to freedom. However, it was in the airing cupboard upstairs – where *all* the radiators were off. I was so *bitterly* cold, I couldn't move from the spot for fear the chilly air brushing against my skin would leach another critical degree of core body heat and I'd lapse into unconsciousness.

Die here or die trying…

I bolted upstairs and wrenched the airing cupboard door open, grabbing the hairdryer and a velvet tiger-themed throw I'd bought in Cairo. In my growing confusion, I made sure to clutch both before sidestepping slowly back down the stairs, yowling like a pelted cat.

With the throw wrapped around my shoulders, I crouched by the failing storage heater and shoved the nozzle of the hairdryer down the neck of my T-shirt. The result was *instant* euphoria, the warm air eddying around my skinny frame like a much-missed friend. It was sheer bliss, total relief, a wonderful life … until the hairdryer tripped to prevent me going up in flames.

Then shock took hold, transforming me into a nauseous ghost in a foreign room with a sterile white glow. In a primal effort to soothe my battered psyche and rejected existence, I whimpered like a wounded dog. For the first time since arriving back from Hong Kong, I reflected on my actions, namely the amount of speed I'd consumed and still managed to fuck everything up. I thought about the isolation I felt and how sideways life had become.

In that moment, juvenile self-pity attempted to take advantage of my exhausted mind and I found myself on the verge of being upset.

Hah! I grinned. I'd come through a terrible ordeal, almost freezing myself to a house, but no one ever said life was fair. I was doing my best in the most adverse of circumstances and making sure to remain proud of the person I was. Besides, I had a tin of value-range tomato soup in the kitchen and a jar of Bovril – and *I* think I deserved a treat.

An hour passed before I felt warm enough to venture from the radiator's tepid embrace. I slotted four slices of bread into the toaster and microwaved the soup, making sure to cover the bowl to prevent the miniature aliens wading in for a feed. I didn't put the telly on. I simply sat with my back against the Economy-7 heater, dipping Bovril on toast into tomato delight. In the calm after something of a storm, a sense of contentment washed over me. How could life get any better and why would you want it to?

Busted

Beep-beep
 ♪ *'Let's check out!'* ♪
 'Are you ready to do your supermarket shop?'
 'Yeahhh-whoooo-yeahhh ...!'
 *'Then step inside a rather unique supermarket. There
isn't another on the planet that gives you money!'*
 'Yeahhh-whoooo ...!' Clap-clap-clap ...!
 *'One thousand pounds is sat in our cash register ready
for you to check out!'*
 'Whooooooo ...!' Clap-clap-clap-clap ...!
 ♪ *'Let's check out!'* ♪
 *'It has to be won by one of our lucky contestants, right
here in this store!'*
 'Well, hello! I'm your host, Dale Winton.'

Supermarket Sweep. *Episode 67*

When I awoke the next afternoon, lying by the heater and clad in
the tiger throw, the itches had vanished along with the urgency to
get rid of the bugs. After some strong sweet tea and a ciggie that
strangely tasted normal, I pulled my clothes from the washer and
hung them on the bookshelf to dry. I made a pint of porridge and
pasta, eyeing the blemishes on the oats with lice-induced suspicion,
and ladled on the sugar.

Now that I'd slept and eaten something, the remaining buzz
from Mousey's amphetamine left me feeling surprisingly chipper.
This was one reason not to fester on the sofa bed, forgetting about
life – another being the twenty-quid-plus-change in my wallet. If I
scored one of Simon's deals to see me through, I could then blast up
to Barnstaple on payday and get some more of the good stuff.

After a phone call, I cycled to Goldilocks' place, the crisp

December air keeping my sweat to a trickle. I arrived at his gate and hopped off the bike, but something didn't feel right.

A black van appeared over the brow of a hill and hammered towards me. I turned to my left to see another screeching around a mini-roundabout.

Time froze.

I was about to be *busted!*

There was not a lot I could do. I stood there holding my bike, waiting for the cops to bundle me into the van and read me my rights. I thought about the disgusting syringes they would find in my house and wondered if this was enough evidence to get me jail time.

The police vans skidded to a halt, bonnets either side of me. Doors flew open and black-clad members of the drug squad poured out. *'Stop there, bud!'* shouted the first cop to reach me.

I rested the bike on my hip and held my arms to the sides, *gutted ...*

He pushed past me carrying a battering ram and legged it up the garden path.

'Simon, you're being raided!' the girl next door screamed from her living room window, the scenario suddenly made sense.

My heart went out to my mate, for busting him a second time the cops only had to find a bar of hash and the judge would lock him up for years. I'd *told* Simon his blasé bloody attitude would get him in trouble.

I wheeled my bike to the corner, expecting Simon to appear in handcuffs at any moment. Then I remembered the WD40 can stuffed full of drugs. Hadn't Simon said it sat innocuously in a shed in the rear courtyard? The sniffer dog was bound to find it and a judge would have a hard time believing the contents weren't his.

There were no cops in the service lane – not a priority what with Simon living on the third floor – yet my chest thumped like a bass drum nonetheless. I knew Simon locked the back gate but not the shed – he reckoned a padlock suggested its owner had something to hide – so I hauled myself up the wall and dropped down the other side.

For the love of Horatio, I *couldn't* find the can. It wasn't on the shelf with the MaxiGrow plant nutrients and PH Perfection soil additives – all of which pointed a suspiciously green finger at Farmer Fucking Giles. Nor was it in amongst the weightlifting equipment and let's-punch-each-other kit piled on the floor. Feeling frantic, I figured the drugs must be in the flat and was about to bug out when a five-kilogram bag of mulch beckoned. I opened its loosely twisted neck and in the words of Steve Coogan's latest comedy offering, 'Ah-*hahhhh!*'

As I cycled away from the crime scene, phoney WD40 can shoved in my waistband, I took a last look over my shoulder. A movement on the roof caught my eye – Simon sitting astride its spine, *yapping* on his roamer phone!

I placed the spray can in the gutter and distanced myself from it to watch events unfold.

Ten minutes passed, Simon remaining undetected, and I was about to pedal off when the sound of a blowing exhaust came into earshot and a hand-painted pink Volvo shot into the service lane.

Simon skipped across the rooftop, scrambling down his neighbour's frontage to join Chunks in the car.

While they sped off in the Pink Panther, I retrieved the WD40 can and cycled home to inspect its contents – two grams of base, twenty ecstasy tablets and five blue Valiums.

I called Chunks' number.

His phone rang for ages, and then, 'Hello!'

'Mate, it's Chris.'

'Chinkity-bingle-ping! How's it going, you old flugleheimer?'

'It's going alright. You just drove past me –'

'Flinkity-bisquits! I don't owe you money, do I?'

'No.' I chuckled. 'You don't owe me money.'

'And you don't do drugs – catnip, Weedol, bit of the old sniffity-whiffter?'

'Nah, I don't do drugs.' I smiled.

'Good, then it's about time we fandangoed flantastic into the flinkity-fluglesphere.'

'Yes, mate, we should, but I was ringing to say –'

'*So* if you'll *Chunk*-kindly leave a message, me or the Chellemeister will call you back.'

... Beeeeep.

Twat!

My plan was to bus to Barnstaple when my money arrived the next day and pinch a wee bit of Simon's base in the meantime. I'd explain everything when I managed to get hold of him. With a gentle buzz, I could work on my projects for a couple of hours and then crash out, perking myself up with another smidgen of the greeny-grey powder before my two-hour journey in the morning.

Right, but only a little ...

One of the bargains I'd nabbed at the boot sale, something *no* homeowner should be without, was a large black tarantula with wicked orange stripes – a rubber one, I hasten to add. I thought I could have a laugh with it at some point, perhaps dropping it down from the eaves of my house on a fishing line attached to an electric motor. For today's exercise, though, I started sketching it in pencil on the wall, opting for a scale of 1:10.

An idea formed and I began to draw the creature's right-hand side in bionic form, a combination of titanium struts, hydraulic pistons, hoses and springs, adding four mirror-shiny picks at the ends of its legs. Adopting a palette of Kiwi shoe polish, chrome-effect spray paint and ruddy-orange primer, I came up with my own pretentious colour shades – Doc Martin Dazzle, Exhaust-Pipe Pomp and Rusty Rooster.

Upon inspecting my bio-robotic tarantula, I felt pleased with the result, but on the downside I'd dug into Simon's speed a good few times. When 4pm arrived, I allowed myself a final hit, promising to get some sleep after its effect wore off.

How about crushing a pill into the spoon with the base?

What a fabulous idea, up there with the best of them, but harder to carry out in practice as the binding agent in the Love

Dove insisted on clogging the needle. It took ages to spike my vein and a while again to depress the plunger due to the viscosity of the mix. In fact, the rubber piston was still only halfway down the syringe's barrel when the cocktail began to hit home.

As I hadn't taken a pill for months, my high shot off the scale, achieving a state of ecstasy matching that of the early raves. After sliding the needle out of my arm, it was all I could do to hold myself down and clamp a Sterets in place.

I floated on a Class A cloud, content to lie back and enjoy the ride for a while. Only, I liked to achieve things on drugs – sawing sofa beds in half, pulling staircases down, thwarting alien invasions – and therefore needed adrenaline not dopamine. I knew Simon wouldn't mind if I had another little dibby dabby doo of his speed. *Only a tiny hit. Just to get an edge …*

Come morning, I'd banged up his entire bag of base and necked all the Love Doves. Fortunately, the alien bugs appeared to have gone and, considering I'd taken enough drugs to make a Tyrannosaurus gurn, the mural had come on leaps and bounds. With Simon off on his toes and Damo banged to rights, I had to get to Mousey's place. If not, life would become as much fun as a corpse at a picnic. The only drugs left were Simon's double-strength Valium. I'd only ever taken a tranquilizer once before and it mellowed me right out – so best scoff all five of these things now.

Having swallowed so many downers on top of a rave's worth of uppers, I felt as sideways as a space hopper. I stared at the £100 in my wallet, unable to remember going to the post office. Now I had to get myself to North Devon before the chemicals wore off.

After rolling a ciggie, I set off on the half-mile walk to the bus stop. In my spannered state, I spent a stupid amount of time trying to read the miniature listings on the Enigma-encrypted timetable before asking the good people in the bus shelter for help.

'It just left, mate,' said a middle-aged chap in a Plymouth Argyle beanie. 'Next one's not for a while.'

'*No …!*' I spoke my dismay aloud – as that usually makes a bus come back and get you.

It didn't, so I walked away in the direction of the shops, sensing the speed draining from my body and the Valium coming on top. If I waited for another bus, I risked falling asleep in public and waking up in a police cell. There was only one thing for it – I would have to steal a car.

Actually, it wouldn't be so much *stealing* as *borrowing*, because upon my return from North Devon, I'd leave the vehicle in exactly the same spot I'd found it. Like in films when a frantic protagonist commandeers a hockey mom's station wagon to save the world, it would be a mercy mission and certainly not the self-centred behaviour of a drugged-up idiot.

However, my plan had a slight flaw, as during my chequered youth I'd only learned how to hotwire Fords.

By the time I'd entered the shopping precinct's car park, the allure of Mousey's base had convinced me to bring my deviant knowhow out of retirement. I wasn't ignoring the voice, albeit a feeble one, telling me I was out of control and hurting random strangers. My heavily sedated mind was simply too uninhibited to act upon it.

Spotting a white Ford Escort, I took a glance around and then removed the rubber seal from the driver's-side window. I yanked the door skin outwards to expose the rod to the interior opener, but no matter how hard I pulled the latch wouldn't disengage. Swapping to a Mondeo estate, I got the door open but forcing the steering lock proved impossible. I needed the right tools, namely a socket wrench, sharpened screwdriver and electrical tape – or a scaffolding bar.

A car started up two spaces away, startling me out of my benzoed-up state, so I walked back to the bus stop to reassess the situation.

The sound of distant sirens carried across the dual carriageway from the nearby police station, but floating around the bus shelter I failed to make the connection. Seconds later, an ear-splitting two-tone screech broke out as high-spec diesel engines roared across the flyover overhead. Only then did my chemical bubble burst, speared by the piercing blue light on the patrol cars speeding towards me.

You stupid fucking idiot!

What had I been thinking? *What* was I doing? By stealing innocent bystanders' property, I'd crossed back over a despicable line, a sign my drug use was way out of control. Picturing the shock on those poor car owners' faces ... I felt sickened and ashamed.

When I finally arrived at Mousey's flat, there was no answer. I hung around outside for a while, wondering if he might be in his local. After a second knock, I was about to head to the pub when the door opened.

'Alright, Chris,' said Mousey, surprised but unfazed. 'What you after?'

'Quarter of base, mate.'

'Come in. I'll need seventy.'

It was twenty quid more than he'd charged on the previous occasion, but in ten minutes time I would have the coordinates locked in for a lift-off to Planet Me, so I willingly handed over the cash.

'Make yourself at home,' said Mousey. 'Back in two ticks.'

'No worries,' I replied, relieved the mega-strong gear would soon be in my possession.

I sat on Mousey's dilapidated couch and stared at the sole poster on his wall – Che Guevara. I didn't even switch on the TV, knowing the dealer would be back at any moment.

An hour turned into two, then three and four, until I was desperate for a hit. The horrible convulsions began smashing through me like barrels on Big Wednesday, intense hunger returning with all its mates. *Is there any food in the house?* I wondered.

Mousey's kitchen made the students' in *The Young Ones* look Michelin Star. No appliances, not even a cooker, and all the cupboards empty bar a box of value teabags. Mousey must have sold the kettle, so I had no way of boiling water – not that a cuppa without milk and sugar on a comedown was in any way appealing.

Back on the couch, I looked up at Che Guevara and shook my head. Who the fuck was Mousey trying to kid? I reckon he'd never been out of England, or even *Devon,* in his miserable existence. I bet he didn't even know who the man in the beret was ... not that I really did to be honest, although I'd definitely be visiting Argentina and Cuba at some point to find out.

Perhaps I was being a touch harsh, as after today's events I didn't exactly have the moral high ground. I was angry, though, because it was obvious the cheating bastard wasn't coming back. If he'd taxed the deal by skimming a tenner or keeping a bit of base for himself, I wouldn't have minded, but *lying* to my face?

How could drugs be someone's *entire* existence? Okay, so I took a lot of the bloody things, but not to gouge out on the sofa all day doing the jack shit part of bugger-all. Speed freed my spirit from this confounded mental dungeon and injected pre-Hong Kong passion into my miserable life. It didn't *blot* it out!

I sat on the couch, tired, hungry and sketchy, coming up with plausible yet unlikely explanations for Mousey's prolonged absence. *It's normal to stop for a hit with the dealer,* I told myself. *He's probably having the time of his life and has put me on hold.* I could live with this so long as Mousey returned with my gear at some point, but as 3am rolled into town even my hackedoffness became hacked off.

I prayed to every god and goddess up there – even inventing a few of my own – for some divine intervention, until sunlight shining through holes in the flat's moth-eaten curtains forced me to accept the truth. Mousey had Foxtrot Oscared and spent my money on heroin.

Maybe five more minutes ...

At five past ten the next morning, I heard a key in the lock. 'Alright, Chris?' said Mousey, as if nothing had happened.

'Yeah, good, mate,' I lied, my needy pathetic mind conveniently overlooking the telltale flash of shock in his eyes.

'Gonna be a bit longer, I'm afraid. The first guy took the money 'cause I owed him from before.'

My excitement clattered on the deck. The wanker dealer hadn't reclaimed cash Mousey owed him – he'd simply *stolen* mine.

'But I'm waiting on someone else. Got these to be going on with.' He held out a couple of Es. 'Fancy banging one up?'

'Why not,' I replied, relieved the speed was on its way.

Mousey prepared two syringes, burning Sterets supplied by the drug service to heat the spoon. As he handed one to me, I spotted a bulbous cling-filmed wrap of white powder concealed in his palm. 'What's that?' I nodded.

'Oh, glucose for bashing gear,' he replied with a shrug, before joining me on the couch.

Strange... The wrap appeared to be the same weight as my speed, but I didn't pull him up on it. Instead, I pressed the syringe's plunger home, a feeling of bliss washing away the hideous comedown. 'Thanks, Mousey ...'

No answer.

I turned to my right. 'Mate that's –'

He wasn't on the couch.

Must have popped into the other room ... I got up to look for him.

Mousey had done a runner.

Sneaky little fucker!

He'd even left the front door ajar so I wouldn't hear it click. Everything suddenly made sense. There was never any dealer or outstanding debt – Mousey had simply taken me for the mug I was. No wonder I spotted a look of surprise when he'd waltzed in expecting me to be gone. He wouldn't make that mistake again, which was a shame because I'd missed my opportunity to punch his face in.

Other than the snake, there was nothing of value in the property, so it wasn't as if I could sell some of his possessions to recoup my loss. Instead, I smashed the TV on the floor and searched the place from top to bottom. I found a load of stolen giros and ripped them up. Then I slung Mousey's best clothes and a pair of half-decent trainers into a mummy-style sleeping bag, hoiked it over my shoulder and left to catch the bus.

The journey was as horrendous as my comedown. A woman with learning disability insisted on leaving the bus for a cigarette every time it stopped, triggering an enormous argument with the driver. When we finally pulled into Helmstone, a torturous hour behind schedule, I decided to visit my old man as I needed some company.

'Oh ... hi, Chris.' Dad's face said it all. 'We were just going up the pub.'

'Okay, cool.' I felt fifty shades of shit but always enjoyed a pint with him.

'No-no, you ... *stay* here and relax.'

My father's insistence wasn't out of concern for my welfare, but because I was an embarrassment to him in front of his drinking buddies. I didn't argue. Alcohol had long ceased to be my thing and my old man had 9% homebrew on tap under the stairs anyway. No, I needed a hit, so I raided Dad's medicine cabinet for sleeping pills and whacked three tiny yellow ones in my arm ...

Stung

'Here you are, son.' Dad placed a cup of tea – an *actual* cup, with *two* sugars, not a pint glass with *twenty-two* – on the bedside table and threw open the curtains.

Dazed and dazzled would be my words of choice – plus plain exhausted.

'You were out for the count.' He frowned. 'I had to carry you upstairs.'

Maybe I should have felt guilty for getting screwed up on drugs and stealing his pills. Well, I did, but the fact he'd been ashamed to be seen with me took the sting out of my remorse. *I* had feelings too. How about simply being proud of me and telling the alconauts up the pub and his stroppy wife to go fuck themselves?

And why didn't my old man take any responsibility for *his* part in all of this? What with my smudged upbringing, I was hardly likely to make it to middle age unscathed. Yet he acted as if *everything* was my fault, while attempting to distance himself from the situation – or at least that's how it seemed.

Christmas approached and the neighbours went bananas putting up trees and lights. Many had joined the growing trend of decorating *outside* the house – so homeless people can enjoy the festive season too. I swear Carroll Road had turned into a polar paradise and I needed to keep reminding myself I wasn't an elf and I didn't live in Lapland.

As the big day drew closer, my doorbell rang. It was an anorak with a clipboard. 'Do you own a television, sir?' she asked.

'Yes, ma'am, but only for Armageddon.'

'I'm sorry?' She gave me a sideways look.

'Armageddon,' I clarified. 'It's my civic duty to own a TV – for the four-minute warning, I mean.'

'Four ... minute ... warning ...' She scanned her clipboard for a tick box covering the Apocalypse.

'Yeah, you know, the Red Peril, Stranger Danger, *When the Whale Blows*. Got to get everyone into the shelter pronto, hey?'

'Right ...'

'Nuclear *bloody* fallout!' I raised my eyes. 'Gets everywhere, doesn't it?'

'So, you ... *don't* actually watch any television?'

'Only immediately prior to an all-out atomic launch. There hasn't been one, has there?' I scanned the horizon for mushroom clouds.

She glanced around. '*N-not* that I know of.'

'Jolly good. But if there ever *is* a full-on attack, I'll be sure to spin by the post office and fill in the form. Need to keep on the good side of the law – *and* Moscow.'

The next day the bell rang again. Clutching a pint of pasta and porridge, I opened the door to find my GP standing there with two associates. 'Hello, Doctor.' I smiled and invited them in.

The doc introduced his fellow professionals, only exhausted from my latest binge I didn't pay much attention. Perhaps I should have been ashamed of the mess, but at least it evidenced my lack of motivation and need for a prescription from the drug service.

'So, Chris, when I saw you in the surgery, you said you had a problem with amphetamine,' my GP began.

'Not so much the amphetamine, Doctor. It's trying to function without it that's the issue.' I stubbed my cigarette out in a plant pot and gave the porridge and pasta a stir.

The professionals appeared mesmerised by the live spoon action – although more likely it was the contents of the pint glass capturing their attention.

'I'm sorry.' The doctor lifted his glasses. 'But ... *what* is it that?'

'Pasta and porridge with sugar and milk – *and* a sheet of lasagne verde.' I tilted the glass towards them.

No one responded. I guess cooking wasn't their thing.

'I spend most of my money on speed.' I shrugged. 'So I don't have much left for food.'

'Can we get you some support?' asked my GP.

'I think I'm okay, Doctor, thanks.'

I didn't wish to sound rude, only I couldn't think of anything. Taking speed to help you function seemed a perfectly normal practice to me. But when my guests flashed each other looks of concern, 'Can you put me on a prescription of Dexedrine?' I asked. 'That *would* really help.'

Dr Adams glanced at his colleagues. 'Speaking as a general practitioner, I'm afraid it falls outside of clinical guidelines, unless you're in treatment with the drug service.'

I told him I was on the waiting list and we exchanged thank-yous and goodbyes. I think the visit had been an education for them and rewarding for me. I felt touched the doctor had acted in my best interests, but how could I explain to these straight-laced live-by-numbers cats there was nothing wrong with me?

When the bell rang a third time, I began to worry it might wear out. I opened the door to find a closing-down sale at Oxfam had been handing out hallucinogens. Chunks sported an enormous black fedora and yellow paisley cravat, an orange-and-red-striped boating blazer, a loud dragon-print shirt and tracksuit bottoms bunched into cowboy boots.

Fuck me – Pierre Cardin!

'Christy Crinkleton the Third!' he chortled, his pink passion wagon crashed on the curb, blocking the street. *'Mission* Siborg.'

He barged past me clutching a bag full of beer. I was about to make excuses for the dirty carpet and chopped-in-half sofa bed only the Chunkbuster either hadn't noticed or didn't care.

'Think dental floss.' He cracked open a can.

I thought about it … but nothing happened.

'Siborg has handed himself in to the flip-flops. He's currently on demand at Hermaphrodite's Schism, Exeter. Ten strands of dental floss woven together should safely support his weight so he can abseil to freedom.'

'But …' – Maths never my strong point – 'if a packet of floss contains five metres and remand prisoners are on the third floor, he'll need at least thirty packets.'

Chinkity Changlebang pursed his lips and looked at the ceiling.

'Then what?' I continued.

'Then we smuggle him over to Switzerland on a fishing boat and he can lie low in the capital, *Copenhagen,* for a while. The Mafia will provide him with a fake identity and he can start a new life in Tripoli.'

'Mafia big in Libya are they?'

'Libya?' Chunks frowned. 'Who said anything about *Portugal?'*

'Never mind. But bearing in mind dental floss can be used to hang yourself – *or* someone else – prisoners won't be allowed more than two or three packets a year.'

'Two or three it is then.' Chunkleton beamed.

'But that'll take *ten* years and he's only gonna be in for *two!'*

My mother called to say I was welcome to join the family at Christmas but they didn't want any of 'that nonsense' ruining their special day. I had no idea what 'that nonsense' they imagined me getting up to – perhaps injecting gravy into my siblings with the turkey baster or snorting icing sugar off Grandma's nipples while dressed as Batman – but it was a hurtful thing to say nonetheless. Life would be a lot less painful if people accepted others for who they are, so out of principal I declined. Two days later, Mum turned up with a big bag of food, a kind gesture, but a simple 'sorry' would have done.

Following nineteen thousand interviews and advances in DNA profiling, the police charged a twenty-four-year-old male office worker with Josie's murder. With Damo and Simon also on the guest list at the Big House, Steve introduced me to another dealer, Sammy, the manager of a building firm.

Twenty stone of steroidal rage, Sammy was the original urban psycho, his narrow eyes, torn ears and Neanderthal jaw setting off a cleft snout, the latter courtesy of a Backward Parrot pint glass. Suffice to say, he was the sort of guy it's best to keep away from –

unless you needed an extension built or someone to knock out a bear. Sammy delivered gear to your door in a white Mercedes but had no qualms telling you not to pester him when he had none.

Prior to the Christmas fortnight my electricity and phone bill arrived, so I had no money to buy drugs. Dad had extended a dinner invite too, but I was happy to spend the festive season cocooned in Mousey's sleeping bag, watching TV and eating the snacks my mum had dropped off.

The variety in my diet improved when I began shoplifting in the supermarket. In an ideal world, I wouldn't have stolen anything from anyone, but as opposed to the time I let myself down in the car park, I couldn't care less about a greedy corporation's multimillion-pound profits. These plastic-spewing dolphin-slaughtering monsters had no reservations when it came to destroying local businesses, community spirit and a beautiful planet, so I'm sure they could take a hit on a jar of Bovril and a value-range chocolate bar every fortnight – although why I pocketed the cheaper supermarket brand, I have no idea.

Naturally, I yearned for the empowerment of speed, but lying in a warm sleeping bag, munching chocolate and watching *Raiders of the Lost Arc* came a close second. I shied away from all the Christmas fodder – *Fern's Festive Gobble, Wogan's Massive Craic, Blobby's Boxing Day Log* – because as someone far removed from society I didn't need the reminder.

In the build up to New Year, the phone rang and after a fortnight without amphetamine I felt grounded enough to answer it. My brother had recently moved to Plymouth, so hearing his old housemate's voice surprised me. 'I've got a big landscape-gardening project on,' said Raynes. 'Any chance you can help me for two weeks, cash-in-hand?'

Knowing thirty quid a day was the going rate for labour, I ran the all-important figures through my lightning-fast mind ... *McDonald's open a branch on Jupiter ... a boy is born with wings ... virtual pet dinosaur funerals ... invisible swimwear ...* and came up with £420.

Ker-ching! Pound signs popped up in my eyes like a cartoon duck. I'd be able to buy enough speed to last me for *months* and what a great opportunity to ease myself back into employment.

'You can stay with me and my girlfriend,' he continued. 'As long as you don't mind chipping in for logs and coal.'

Cornish cottages are Baltic beyond belief in wintertime, so this was understandable. However, rumour had it Raynes could be a little laid-back when it came to paying wages. He seemed okay with me, though, and I gladly accepted his offer. Besides, he'd have a job sticking one past this battle-wary call sign.

On our first evening together, Raynes drove us to see a guy named Grouch to score a teenth of hash. 'Grouch is a bit different,' said Raynes, parking in a patch of wasteland by a row of cottages. 'But harmless enough.'

This difference became apparent as we entered a six-foot-high maze, its walls formed by stacks of clear-glass bottles illuminated at intervals by coloured bulbs. 'This way,' said Raynes, leading me down a crystal corridor. 'Errh ... no, this way.'

I'd never seen anything like it. This Groucho character was obviously a rebel, and I liked him already. Further into the labyrinth, we came across a cut-down door from a red telephone box. Without knocking, Raynes pulled it open. *'Grouch?'*

Silence for a moment and then a reply floated from the dim interior in a soft Cornish burr. 'Come in you must.'

'Yikes, Scooby, it's *Yoda!*' I whispered, following Raynes inside.

'Grouch, this is Chris. He's doing a bit of work for me.'

'Make yourself at home you should,' said the mysterious voice.

At first, I could only make out the flame from a candle, but as my eyes got used to the dark, I saw our host, a squat chap with olive skin, fiery eyes and a shock of black hair like a Mexican bandit. His place was something to behold, about the size of a small shipping container and constructed from scrap wood like the rooftop dwellers' shacks in Hong Kong. We appeared to be in the living area, which comprised of the bucket seats from a rally car and hefty pink and yellow foam blocks tiered back against a wall to create a sofa. Cramped would be the word, with audio equipment and other techno-clutter stacked floor to ceiling.

'Some warmth that's kicking out,' said Raynes, nodding to a small wood burner.

'Got candles inside it has,' said Grouch in his back-to-front purr, opening the grate door to reveal twenty or more burning away.

I placed my hand over the hotplate, surprised to feel heat belting off it.

'Remould them with new wicks when they melt I do.'

'Good idea,' I said, not knowing you could reuse candle wax. 'But don't the lights in the bottle maze burn through electric?'

'A fair bit they can, but supplied by my neighbour the power is. He likes them you see.'

As my new employer rolled a courtesy smoke, I marvelled at Grouch's individuality and enterprising nature. Live this life myself I could.

That evening, Raynes sat in an armchair in front of the fire and I took the couch. We shared a couple of spliffs, while his girlfriend, Leaf, completed college work in their bedroom. 'I heard you do a bit of speed, Chris,' said Raynes, blowing out a smoke ring.

'Yes, mate. Helps me function.'

'Leaf was addicted to speed.' Raynes glanced at me. 'And I used to do a lot too.'

'Why did you stop?' I found it strange he spoke in past tense.

'I couldn't get anything done.' Raynes casually inspected the bifta, giving the impression he knew something I didn't.

I was confused – surely speed *helped* you get things done. But as my host chose not to elaborate, I didn't ask.

When Raynes went to bed, I curled up under a blanket on the soot-stained sofa and, mindful of the pricey fuel, shivered all night by the dying embers.

Morning gave me an excuse to build up the fire and as we

smoked a joint over a cup of coffee my speed-wrecked blood supply gorged on the heavenly heat. Paradoxically, if there was ever a return-to-work program designed to put you off returning to work, then this was most certainly it. For as it grew toastier inside, facing the *bitter* cold outside became an ever more daunting prospect. With hash-induced lethargy amplifying this feeling of dread, I'd willingly have forfeited a day's pay to remain under the blanket by the flames.

British Leyland would have made a fortune if they'd produced freezers instead of grandad cars. Huddled in the passenger seat of Raynes' Austin Maestro, I chilled, quite literally, as we set off in stoned silence down the country lanes. In the next village along, we stopped to pick up our co-worker Pat, a dope-dealing dole-squatting waif with a blond Mohican.

'Come in, boys?' he said. 'Let's pull a shotty and then blitz this thing.'

'A shotty?' My drug radar blipped.

'Shotgun,' Pat clarified. 'It's the best way to smoke hash.'

'Here we go ...' Raynes looked to the ceiling, his sarcasm acknowledging our shared powerlessness to say no.

The notion that smoking a bong would somehow help us to 'blitz this thing' sat somewhere between naive and utterly delusional. Yet despite already suffering from the activity's demotivating effect, I welcomed the chance to delay working outside in this temperature and joined my fellow shirkers on the couch.

Pat lived in a bedsit in his parents' lavish country home, so I was surprised to see so much drug paraphernalia, especially a mirror glued to the coffee table. Our host inserted a pencil butt-first into a chrome barrel swiped from a tyre-pressure gauge. He thumbed a pinch of Golden Virginia into the open end and tamped it down using the pencil as a miniature ramrod. Taking up a razorblade, Pat then chopped a nugget of hashish into fine particles and racked them into a neat flat square on the mirror. He pressed the wad of tobacco down onto this layer several times, clamping the tube and protruding pencil tip between his thumb and forefinger to hold the makeshift plug in place. This resulted in a tightly packed puck of hash nestled in the tip of the chrome barrel. The other end he slid into a Coke-bottle bong, which had the usual inch of water in the bottom but no air hole.

'Watch ...' Pat held a lighter to his preparation and inhaled.

A fiery orange burn swept across the bed of cheap 'soap bar' hashish, summoning a dope genie into the bottle. *Hooph!* He sucked the unburnt tobacco plug down into the water, extinguishing the glowing embers and shooting the swirling grey fumes into his lungs.

Jeeze, it's eight in the morning!

Pat blew out a hearty plume and set a shotty up for Raynes. When my turn came, I hooped too early, only partially cremating the hash yet coughing like a forty-a-day smoker all the same.

Cor-blinking-blimey! If I hadn't wanted to leave Raynes' ice rink of a cottage, I certainly didn't want to leave this place. I hoped Raynes would declare a public holiday, but after another round of shotties he stood up, suggesting it was time to go to work.

Pat, the 'Shotgun Kid', passed out on the ten-mile commute but I kept it together to show Raynes this lean not-so-mean ex-fighting machine was up to the job. In truth, I wished we could drive along listening to the radio forever and never have to work again. Queuing to overtake a tractor, 'I've got a theory,' said Raynes. 'You only have a certain amount of heartbeats in your lifetime. So when you take amphetamine, it's like you're speeding towards your death.'

Killer heartbeats – *bummer.*

'Here we are.' Raynes pulled up outside a smart bungalow in a Cornish hamlet. 'The owner wants us to level the ground and block-pave the driveway. There's the bricks and sand I ordered.' He nodded to eight enormous pallets at the roadside.

'You've done this before?' I said.

'Nah.' He shook his head. 'Can't be hard, can it?'

Inspecting the veritable forest and mountainous slabs of granite that needed clearing before we could lay a single brick, *and* seeing the Boy Wonder stoned off his box and asleep on the back seat, 'No, it can't be hard,' I lied, knowing it would be the toughest labour I'd faced since leaving the Corps. *Still, in two weeks' time I'll have four hundred and twenty quid in my pocket.*

'Fancy a joint before we start?' Raynes shrugged. 'I've got a blim left from last night.'

'Rude not to, mate.'

In all honesty, a joint was the last thing any of us needed. They always seem a good idea but make manual tasks appear ten times harder. When you consider most workers would have been on site three hours earlier, we were skinning up a disaster. Raynes and I finished the spliff and listened to Radio 1's methadone for the masses a while longer. Then he shook Sleeping Beauty, who awoke in a hash-induced panic. *'W-w-wha ...?'*

I would love to have seen Pat's face when he clocked our Herculean task only I'd already begun heaving boulders into a skip. Despite my best efforts, two hours later the ground still looked like the Rockery from Hell.

Dad once told me middleclass folk were the worst when it came to making labourers feel at home. He should know, having fitted thousands of carpets over the years. This landscape-gardening job proved his point to a tee. The homeowners didn't even come out to say hello, let alone boil a kettle. Every so often, the curtains twitched and the non-thinking pen-pushing desk drovers peeked out at us as if we were an alien lifeform. Our welcome came from a neighbour, a wonderful old girl who brought out steaming mugs of whiskey coffee.

'Look, Chris.' Raynes nudged me and grinned.

Pat had planted his spade in the ground, wrapped himself around the shaft and gone back to sleep.

By the end of the year, we'd rid the ground of scrub and rocks and levelled the earth ready to flatten with a plate compactor. Our final task on New Year's Day was to move a ten-foot-high fir tree the homeowners wanted to keep. I don't know how they'd passed this information to Raynes – maybe smoke signals – as I hadn't seen them leave the house the whole time we'd been there. We dug out the tree's roots and I shoved my hand through the pine needles to grab the trunk.

'*Ouch!*'

Something had bitten me. I let go of the tree to find a wasp with its arse stuck in my finger. It was New Year's Day for crying out loud – the air temperature was minus *six!*

With the ground compacted, we sprinkled on a layer of sand and began the block paving. The bricks came in red, brown and yellow and Raynes had agreed a set pattern with the homeowner – I'm guessing via jungle drums, carrier pigeon or the medium of telepathy.

Every evening after work, we visited Grouch to score a teenth. Raynes would share a joint with me before disappearing upstairs to smoke the rest with Leaf – in between bouts of ridiculously loud sex. With no TV, I'd curl up on the sofa and shiver the night through, the £420 my motivation not to freeze to death. Each morning, the *Ice Station Zebra* routine followed by shotties at Pat's Pot Emporium began all over again.

Everything was going well until our Sunday off. I'd been looking forward to lounging in front of Raynes' living room fire, only he had other ideas. 'Erh, Chris. Me and Leaf were wondering if you could score some speed.'

'Are you sure?' I asked. 'I thought Leaf had a problem with it.'

'She used to, but we have a dabble every now and then.'

I drove Raynes' Maestro to the Backward Parrot and picked up three grams of base, alarmed to feel the car playing up on the return journey. I think the distributor cap needed replacing because the engine wouldn't fire on four cylinders – at least not in the right order.

When at last I arrived back at Metherton, Raynes and Leaf did their drugs in the bedroom and I worked on a Manga collage in the living room. However, life took a step sideways on the Monday and our usual round of shotties at Pat's on top of no sleep probably didn't help.

Raynes had tasked me with the final stretch of paving leading up to the house. Like a true pro, I cleared small stones and levelled the sand, while trying to work out a unique pattern to greet the front door, something to complement the driveway's existing one.

Before I knew it, three hours had passed and I still hadn't made any progress. The harder I concentrated, the more confused I got, to the point where it became embarrassing. This was a customer's home and Jens was paying me handsomely.

As I swapped the coloured bricks around for the umpteenth time, not daring to dive in with the lump hammer and cold chisel, Raynes loomed over me, tutting and shaking his head. 'That speed doesn't do *you* any favours.'

I wanted to argue, but ...

Payday arrived and Raynes drove me back to Plymouth. I couldn't wait to receive my bounty and despite the hard work and harsh conditions had made up my mind to accept the next job he put my way.

'So ...' Raynes pulled to a stop in Carroll Road. 'We better talk money.'

Forget the talking, amigo, and let's see some pesos!

I'd expected this, a bit of haggling bollocks, Raynes pleading poverty and offering a flat £400.

'Twelve days' work at a tenner a day,' he continued, 'is ... *one* hundred and twenty quid.'

Huh ...?

'Minus, say, *forty* for coal is eighty.'

I couldn't believe his mouth or my ears. Had I not been in shock I would have strangled the fucking chancer.

'Then there's the problem with the car.' He made an expense-laden shruggy face. 'That's gonna cost sixty.'

But –!

Oh, and we finished early twice ...' He pulled out a wad of cash and peeled off my retirement fund. 'So let's just call it a tenner.'

Sound Factory

A new club opened in town, the Dance Academy, in a wonderfully decadent venue, originally the New Palace Theatre in its turn-of-the-century heyday. Flemish Renaissance in style with an Art Nouveau interior and nautical-themed design, this rundown delight featured a cream ceramic-tiled exterior along with miniature domes, steeples and balustrades, like something from a Terry Gilliam film. Exquisite twin murals made for an impressive façade, depictions of the Spanish Armada before and after Sir Francis Drake got his cannonballs out for the lads.

As for the inside of this palatial Plymordial cave, we're talking an enormous stage with a proscenium opening of *twenty-nine* feet! We're beholding mock ships' transoms, clinker planks and lanterns, while prancing like princes in a two-tiered auditorium surrounded by lavish panelled walls, plush carpet and a Sistineesque ceiling. Consider curved balconies, slender cast-iron columns and military motifs. Picture an exquisite foyer built from exotic polished stone, rich carved wood and endangered animal parts.

Then unshackle your mind to envisage a Sicilian-marble staircase leading to a first-floor saloon decorated with nereids, dolphins and cherubs. Let's talk Cinquecento style, coffered ceilings, enriched spandrels, Ionic capitals and marble pilasters. And did I mention three impressive round-arched windows?

On Saturday, I decided to check it out, looking forward to boogying all night like in the Big Apple. In the afternoon, I cycled to the Backward Parrot to meet Sammy, who'd only been able to sell me a gram of base the previous Thursday. With the new packet tucked in my boot, I approached the bar to order my half of lager.

As 'Roll with It' played on the jukebox, Steve and I got chatting, the topic soon turning to sport. I liked sport – *all* sport – I just didn't know much about it. To get around this, I'd talk about the discipline itself, in broad terms as opposed to specifics such as matches and players. If someone asked me how Shearer would get on at Newcastle, I'd say, 'Hard to tell, mate. The game's changed a lot. So many foreign players.'

On this occasion, I was in the middle of telling Steve how boxing is a game of two halves and anything can happen in extra time when something pinged from my scalp. A flake of amphetamine-powered dandruff shot skyward, executing a graceful arc before landing on the bar. You find yourself in a lot of cringeworthy situations on drugs, but Steve's surprise as his wide eyes followed the particle's flightpath was a real embarrasser. Fortunately, a customer approached the pumps, giving me an excuse to slip away. But cycling home, I realised the alien bugs were back.

Early that evening, I decided to spruce up my appearance with a short back and sides. The problem was I only had a thinning-out comb bought from the car boot sale. The blade was as blunt as Cheddar cheese, so I swapped it for a Wilkinson Sword and scraped above an ear –

Noooo...!

It took *everything* off, leaving a big white swathe of baldness, like I should be playing a ukulele by a river.

Attempting to even things up only made it worse, so I opted to shave right the way around. The wickedly sharp razorblade was far from ideal. It kept digging into my skin, sending a river of blood streaming down my neck. What should have been a straightforward haircut turned into death by a thousand knives. My scrapes grew ever higher, until I ended up six hours later with stupid fucking wings sticking out of my swede like some mythological Greek figure.

By now, it was approaching midnight, a little over two hours before the Dance Academy shut. As if this wasn't bad enough, the alien mites had returned mob-handed along with the fear and panic. Thousands of red-hot needles jabbed my pale spotty skin.

Damn! I'd been through all this before. My house appeared to be a spawning ground for the demonic swine. Conscious of getting to the club, I tried to stay calm and annihilate the infiltrators in a logical fashion. I flushed my shorn hair down the toilet, wiped the surfaces and climbed into a cold bath containing a good amount of bleach. While drying myself off, I eyed the blackened sealant below the tiles. *Ahhh!*

Water dripping down the back of the bath must have created the perfect dark and humid environment for the conniving alien scum. Mould covered the bath panel too, but removing its rusting screws wasn't happening, so I smashed the wretched thing to pieces with a hammer. I chucked the soggy rotten wood in the tub and got down on all fours to peer beneath it.

Holy smoke ...!

An enormous alien colony sprouted from the unsealed plasterboard, *dense* black hubs hatching minute spider-like larvae, like something from a science-fiction film. It was all getting too much. I wanted to be in a bloody dance club not the shit sequel to *ET*. How could this be fair on top of every other indignity I'd suffered?

With no other option, I began to smack out the manky egg-riddled plasterboard and place it in the bath, my designated quarantine for the Martian menace. I would incinerate the lot, invaders an' all, in the back garden later. But it was no easy task, for as I hammered away my skin crawled and I could sense the bastards burrowing into my bleeding scalp.

The clock ticked. I had an hour to square things away and cycle into town to catch the Dance Academy before it shut. As if the itches weren't bad enough, the smell reappeared, the ever-changing duplicitous whiff. *Could it be coming from the aliens?* I wondered.

Patrolling from room to room, sniffing like a bloodhound with two colds in a pepper factory, I added Cornish pasties to the list of strange aromas. Even my *pee* stunk of them!

Once again, alien life pervaded my house and body and an inspection of my forearm only served to confirm this. It was *alive* with the damn things! What initially appeared to be freckles were in reality wiggling maggots. I began carving the evidence out with my Swiss army knife and arranging it on a mirror, something to show my GP to prove I wasn't imagining this stuff.

After another hit, I dressed in jeans, T-shirt and the waist-length denim coat and Nike Airs Mousey kindly 'gave' me. Then I smoothed down the albatross on my head and biked the four miles into town.

I arrived at the Dance Academy *off* my box to find it shutting. Many of the clubbers were heading to an all-night venue called the Sound Factory, which sat above an open-fronted newsagent at the other end of Union Street. Flanked by a motley parade of really good binge drinkers, I pedalled down the chaotic strip, past emptying clubs, puke-splashed taxi ranks and packed kebab joints. Like a paperboy on Ritalin, I shot straight up the shop's centre aisle, coming to a balancing stop with my front wheel nudging up against the counter.

'Hello, sir,' said the Pakistani proprietor.

'Hi.' I smiled. 'Drinks?'

'Over there.' He nodded to the fridge.

Ridiculously dehydrated, I wheeled my bike over and selected a carton of Ribena.

'Are you okay, sir?'

'Yeah, I'm off to the Sound Factory, but I need somewhere to leave my bike.'

'No problem, sir. You can put it out the back here.'

Music to my ears, I propped my trusty steed against the wall in the passageway. 'I'm Chris.' I offered him a sweaty hand.

'Mustafa,' replied Mustafa. 'I'm here all night. So when you want your bike, it's no problem.'

I downed the blackcurrant beverage and skipped up the steps to the Sound Factory, an all-comers dusk-til-dawn affair with no entrance fee. Small clubs that play quality old-school house music until the wee hours are usually a great find. I wasn't disappointed and walking into a familiar, thumping atmosphere felt amazing.

Scanning around, I saw a bar running down one side of the club, the dance floor along the other, with various seating arrangements in between. The DJ platform sat atop a six-foot-high scaffold against the dance floor's back wall. I recognised several friendly faces from the Warehouse days, but unlike the original dance club scene, there were a fair few inebriants staggering around looking well out of place. Many of them were members of the local football gang, The Central Element, taking a well-earned break from their appreciation of Italian Renaissance art, neoclassical literature and kicking people's heads in on the terraces.

As I danced to Liquid's 'Sweet Harmony', many of the drinkers stood and stared. One chap gave me the evils for so long, I went over and asked if he was okay. He nodded and mumbled something with a look of surprise. I don't think he and his fellow lager lovers had experienced the dance scene before, where music is king, clubbers drink water, and testosterone and prejudice are overrated.

At a lull in the set, I wandered over to the chill-out area, delighted to find soft lighting, a cushioned horseshoe bench and trance music providing a welcome breather from the fast-paced beats. Folks sat giving each other shoulder rubs, chatting and passing joints, a far more relaxing atmosphere than the adjacent drink stands where the Lost Boys lurched around looking for blood.

The student-type sat on my right broke from preparing a spliff. 'Jenson, mate.'

'Chris.' I met his elevated palm for the esoteric Ravy Davy handshake.

'Supposed to be in the second year of History, but *fucked* it right off!' he said, chewing gum for every figure *in* history. 'Been dealing gear instead.'

'Be careful, mate,' the protective me kicked in. 'Drugs are alright, but you need an education at the end of the day.'

'Nah.' Jenson passed the bifta. 'I was only doing it to keep my old man happy.'

This was understandable and went some way to explain the Mockney accent. How this impressionable young lad thought dealing drugs was the way forward, though, I hesitated to ask. As we swapped phone numbers, the South West's top DJ, Lee Mavers, interrupted a crescendo in the music. 'Party people, can we please sing happy birthday to the Wizard. He's *fifty* today!'

Everyone turned their attention to the red-faced crusader on my left, who had to be Plymouth's oldest raver, and a chorus of happy birthday rang out.

'Hello, mate,' I said. 'Are you really a wizard?'

'A white one,' he replied. 'So don't worry, I won't turn you into a toadstool.'

'Thank *fuck* for that!'

The Wizard told me he'd only got into the dance scene a year ago and absolutely loved it. He had a quality source for party pills and powders and seemed a man to know – even more so when offering me a lift home. We agreed to meet out front at 7am.

When the club finally did shut its doors, the dance crowd mingled outside on the pavement, chatting and deciding which after-party to attend. Ordinarily, I'd be eager to head off to someone's flat to smoke weed and listen to Goa trance, but this time it was different. I felt self-conscious in my baggy laddish clothes and floppy trainers. My shaved hair and wounds from the thinning comb were embarrassing and I was acutely aware of being *off* my bonce and having pupils the size of lawn bowls.

'Hi, Kierra,' I said, recognising a friend of Sarah's little sister, whom I'd met a couple of years ago. Back then, she'd been a student with a bit of a thing for me, the 'big tough' marine. How the tables had turned. No longer an awkward young woman finding her way in the world, Kierra was in with the in-crowd, her confidence boosted by drugs, her outlook altered but not in a good way. Throwing me a caustic look, 'What the *fuck* have you done to your hair?' she sneered.

In that instant, I sensed the thirty-strong crowd leering at me with unbridled disdain. Perhaps it was paranoia, but as a shoplifting car-stealing drug-addicted unemployed under-achiever wearing Shaun Ryder cast-offs and a Stan Laurel haircut, it wasn't as if I didn't have good reason to be.

'*Fuck me,* mate! How much *speed* have you done?' asked Lee Mavers, the South West's top DJ.

As Lee looked in my eyes and chuckled, my opinion of him and my remaining self-esteem went down a notch. I was glad when the Wizard chucked my bike in the boot of his car and drove me home.

I went out dancing less and less. Every time I attempted to hit the Dance Academy's majestic tiers of hedonism, I left it too late and ended up cycling like a lunatic to the Sound Factory. I enjoyed sharing a joint with Jenson and the Wizard, but our shaking a groove attracted the unwanted attention of the thugs, who stood there bemused while trying to appear hard. The loved-up non-violent dance scene that brought millions of people together and awakened a shared spiritual consciousness had gone and it was never coming back.

One morning after the club, I lassoed some company in the form of a chap named Craig, a transport manager, who accepted my offer to come back and chill at mine. But when I interrupted him staring at my mural and asked, 'Craig, do you want some of this?' and held out my bag of speed, 'No, mate, I did my drugs last night,' he replied and made an excuse to leave.

On another occasion, I bumped into a clubber I'd known for years. Short of stature and with unmissable prematurely white hair, Gavin was your typically friendly 'cheesy quaver'. He also sold extremely good base. 'Could you get me a quarter?' I asked.

'No worries, Chris,' he said. 'Guess you'll be needing a few vallies too?'

'How come?' I replied, surprised by the idea of taking tranquilisers. Why would anyone want to mix a super-strong upper like base with a potent downer? It seemed counterintuitive.

'Shuteye, mate,' said Gavin. 'How else you gonna get any sleep?'

Well, this was a new one on me. It made complete sense, though. If I could snatch a few hours' kip a night, I'd function better *and* the gear would last a lot longer.

Gavin dropped off my quarter and gave me two double-strength blue pills free of charge. I waited until my eyelids dragged along the floor before popping one. He was right. I had a solid and much-needed nap. Typical of my luck, the drug squad busted Gavin a week later. He got a suspended sentence and stopped dealing and I never took Valium again.

Unlike in Wan Chai, where I used to enjoy nipping down town at all hours to see who was misbehaving, I stopped seeking other people's company. On the rare occasion I went to the Sound Factory, I'd leave Mustafa's shop the next morning and cycle to the car boot sale, getting far more of a buzz rummaging through junk than a twenty-seven-year-old probably should.

One day whilst browsing the stalls, I began to experience the panicky self-conscious sensation I had in Happy Valley that time. A weird nervousness washed over me, my heart fluttering like a caffeinated moth. 'How much for this?' is what I'd wanted to ask the boot seller, pointing to a ten-metre coil of prime extension lead. But as I choked on idiot dust, 'Hu mu ... *muurr... siss?* drooled from my mouth instead. I panicked and began waving the cable in the air in the hope the guy would come to my rescue. In the end, to lessen my embarrassment, I broke a major rule of the Boot by paying *full* price for the *World's Biggest Book of Sharks.*

Shotgun

'So our next guest recently found out her boyfriend of eight years – wait for it – is a horse!'

'Whoop-whoop!' Clap-clap-clap ...! 'Yeah-yeah!'

'So let's meet Tanya ... and Neddy!'

'Whoop-whoop!' Clap-clap-clap ...! 'Yeah-yeah!'

'Tanya, Ned, welcome.'

'Hay-lo, Jair-ray.'

'Neighhhhh!'

'So, Tanya, when did you find out your partner was a horse?'

'Way-yel, Jair-ray, it all started when we was watchin the Ken-tuc-kay Dar-bay on the Tay Vay. Chester – I mean Nair-day – began scrapin his foot – erh, his hoof – on the flaaw. Then hey jumped over the couch and ate all ma cair-rots.'

The Jerry Springer Show. *'My Boyfriend's a Horse'*

After my last trip to the skip behind Furniture World, I came home with a green-plastic fish box, a pair of autumn-pattern curtains, two half-used cans of Spraytack and four round plastic feet from an ex-display sofa. The autumn-pattern curtains I hung across my open stairway, preventing the precious warmth from disappearing upstairs. I hoped this would put a stop to the out-of-control shivers, which I experienced far too often now.

As an added precaution, I kept the hairdryer handy to avoid the godawful scenario of being so bitterly cold I couldn't move towards the Economy-7 radiator. Now whenever my blood pressure plummeted, triggering the onset of hypothermia, I'd shove the hairdryer inside my shirt and give it a good long blast.

Shutting the door to the hall and the curtains over the stairs kept the front room habitable, allowing me to store up enough body heat to nip to the frozen wasteland upstairs if need be. When I showered – usually fortnightly after buying speed – I would dash up to the bathroom and yank the pull-cord on the wall heater and then retreat to the lounge while it warmed the room up. I used the same system if I had to spend more than a minute in the kitchen.

Upon arriving home from the boot sale one Sunday, I closed the blinds so the kids wouldn't knock on the door and ask me to play footy. I hung my bike on the hooks above the stairs, redrew the autumn-pattern curtains and set about having a hit. Although I only had a gram of gear left and five days until payday, my mind always believed the bag of powder would last forever, so I tapped a load into the spoon.

I'd also bought a teenth of soap bar from the Wizard for £7.50, hoping to relive my amazing coughing experience with the Shotgun Kid. I rooted around in the carrier bag from the boot sale, looking for a four-inch-long metal tube bought from a guy selling garage tools and related bric-a-brac. Using a soldering iron, I poked a pencil-sized hole in an empty plastic 330ml Coca-Cola bottle, easing the tube into the opening at a forty-five-degree angle so as the plastic hardened it would create an airtight seal.

I fetched a Stanley blade from my tool kit and prepared the little block of hash the way Pat had done. The only difference was I used a chopstick as a ramrod and a plate instead of a mirror. I dabbed the tobacco-plugged end of the tube into the hash particles, punching out a neat hole, repeating this three times to ensure a strong enough hit.

The knack lay in withdrawing the chopstick and inserting the tube into the bong without disturbing the carefully packed mix. Holding a lit cigarette lighter over the layer of hash, I sucked on the neck of the Coke bottle. I had to draw quite forcefully at first because the plug did its job, reducing the inflow of air to a trickle. I couldn't suck too hard, though, or the set-up would shotgun prematurely – a negligent discharge, so to speak – and drown the unburned Moroccan export.

The particles of soap bar ignited like a wildfire sweeping across a field of dry grass, a brown-and-yellow whirlwind eddying in the bottle. With a succinct pull, I sucked the fiery plug down the metal tube and into the water, releasing the hash smoke into my lungs. I held the breath for as long as I could before blowing out trace fumes.

Boy did it hit me! An instant reminder of why my career as a landscape gardener hadn't got off to the best of starts. The combination of pure dope on top of a copious amount of amphetamine was intense and much more effective than smoking a spliff. I stashed the bong by the side of the dilapidated sofa in case anyone came to visit me – no one ever came to visit me – and sat there enjoying the feeling of being higher than high.

It was a slight itch on the back of my neck initially. When I scraped a fingernail over the spot, my hair came alive and then my *bloody* eyebrows! I began systematically scratching my face, scalp and neck and collecting whatever I picked from my skin on the mirror.

Adding to the tiny alien foetuses I'd dug out of my arms was a pile of skin flakes, dandruff and tiny white powdery snakes that I took to be amphetamine. I inspected the accumulated body matter with the magnifying glass on my knife, but nothing moved. *Damn!*

At the very least, I'd hoped to see an alien pulling a mooney, perhaps a couple of dust mites playing hopscotch or a flea snorting dandruff whilst giving it the big one with his mates. Everything appeared inanimate, though. My desire to get to the bottom of this went banzai, anxiety at DEFCON 3 and rising. My entire body *crawled* with bugs. I dug fingernails into my ears, scraping out the larvae and depositing it on the shiny glass.

Fucking shit badger! Now that *bloody* awful smell had returned. What the hell was it ... *burnt toast ... porridge oats ... washing-up liquid ... or maybe those black bin liners?* Yet again, my poor house was up Crap Creek with calamity for a paddle and in serious need of delousing, only I had no idea where to start.

I wandered around inspecting the carpets, walls and furniture as well as the food in the kitchen cupboards. Somehow, those sneaky little squatters had infiltrated the porridge oats, so I poured the flakes into a Pyrex dish, removed the infected candidates and placed them on the mirror. The rest of the Scottish staple went in the bin – *27p* down the swanny and my meal planner screwed up indefinitely.

Upon spotting the same infestation in the bread, I picked the little deviants out and added them to my growing body of evidence, gutted to throw away half a loaf, knowing I had no money to buy another.

Now I had to disinfect myself, only the bath was full of damp rotting wood and plasterboard, all incubating Martian spore. I neutralised the lot with bleach and threw it out of the bedroom window and into the garden. Albeit indoors, a cold winter dip in my emaciated state was not a particularly pleasant prospect. I dumped a quarter of a bottle of bleach into the icy water, followed by my hideously prickling self.

'Brrrhuhuuhrur!'

Shaking uncontrollably, I forced my head and shoulders below the frigid surface, a reminder of tackling the Royal Marines' endurance course in February. I used to think wading up to your neck while breaking a thick layer of ice to cross the infamous Peter's Pool was the ultimate torture, particularly injured, exhausted and carrying a rifle and heavy equipment. When viewed from the harsh landscape of addiction, though, the notion that such a fun teenage jaunt was ever in any way hard now seemed laughable.

I stood under the fan heater towelling off, unable to stop spouting gibberish, my mind's way of fending off the demons attacking me inside and out. Words could never do justice to the amount of pain, cold and loneliness I felt, except to say I would willingly have given up my house and everything I owned if it meant never having to live through this hell again.

I huddled next to the Economy-7 heater in the front room, dressed in the only clean clothes I possessed – a black 'I Love Egypt'

T-shirt, fake Adidas bottoms with anorexic stripes, chunky leather cross-country ski boots and a baggy blue-and-red quilted lumberjack shirt that used to be way too small for me. When I finally felt warm enough, I fetched the telephone directory.

My GP surgery shut on a weekend, but I didn't want to put my health in the hands of the NHS anyway. No, I needed the loyalty and professionalism of the British Royal Navy, *my* family, *my* comrades, people I could *trust* with my life. Me being a civilian now was irrelevant. My brothers and sisters in the world's finest fleet would set fire to the rulebook and kick it along the plank if it meant supporting a shipmate.

I called the nearest base, HMS Drake, and asked the operator for the sickbay, my seven years of service seeming only yesterday when a Wren medical assistant answered. 'Oh hi, M.A. Sleaman. My name's Chris, a former marine. I know I'm no longer in the Corps, but I desperately need to speak to a doctor.'

'If you've gone outside, Chris, you'll have to contact your local surgery.'

'I know, but they're useless and it's an emergency.'

M.A. Sleaman covered the phone and conferred with the duty doctor. A moment later, 'Erh, what is the emergency?' she asked.

'I've got like these weird *alien* grubs in my ears. It's driving me crazy and my GP doesn't understand.'

'Ah, hah –!'

Her laughter cut off as she smothered the mouthpiece, but I could still hear the conversation. *'He says he's got aliens in his ears – ah ha-hah! He says his GP doesn't understand – ah ha-hah!'*

M.A. Sleaman came back on the line. 'Hello, Chris? The doctor says go to your GP.'

Humiliated, I hung up. Fucking *useless* matelots. I'd only wanted some guidance. Don't former service personnel deserve that? No wonder so many veterans end up homeless and suicidal.

I thumbed through the book and found a number for medical emergencies. Surely, aliens in your orifices are an emergency, so I gave it a call and got told to attend a clinic at the Cumberland

Centre. Exhausted in mind, body and drugs, I couldn't face cycling the five miles there. My nerves were so completely exposed I couldn't see how I'd make it home again. I called Chunks and got his answer machine. I tried my old man, but Ellen said he wasn't home. I didn't have my brother's new number and so the only option was my mum.

'*Chris,* you always call at *inappropriate* times,' she said – as if I called every day as opposed to twice a year. 'I'm baking a cake and David wanted to tidy the garage.'

'Mum, for *fu* – this is *urgent!* I'm crawling with bloody mites and I need to get to hospital.'

'Can't it wait until Tuesday? We're free Tuesday morning.'

'Mum, that's *two* days away. I've got to get there *now!*'

'Okay, we'll try and pop over around five-ish.'

'Oh … *Mum.* Can't you come now? *Please.* I'm in agony.'

My mother muttered something about my teenage sister having to come home to an empty house, but finally acquiesced.

Jeeze, people are strange! So much for the Good Samaritan. I'm surprised he found anyone benevolent enough to answer his phone line.

Mum was still going on about the inconvenience I'd caused when my wonderful stepdad, Dave, stopped the car at the Cumberland Centre. It was okay, though, because these bloody bugs had put me through such out-and-out horror it was simply comforting to have my parents' love and much-needed support when I met the doctor.

'Right, we're off to do a food shop,' my mother announced, dragging Dave off to Somerfield.

The doctor I saw must have had lots of practice at being utterly useless. I poured my battle-weary heart out, explaining how these weird little mites had taken over my home, my body, my mind and my senses. I told him I was beyond miserable, that I couldn't go on *any* longer and needed to know what the hell they were in order to annihilate them.

He prescribed me a cream.

Great! Now I had to wait God knows how long for my folks to return and then find a chemist open on a Sunday.

'Oh, *Chris!*' Mum was not a happy bunny. 'You only asked for a lift to the *hospital.*'

Buying into the nigh-on-moronic notion that this cream would somehow fix the alien apocalypse which had eaten my bathroom, I appealed to my stepfather's placid nature. 'Dave, I need a chemist.'

'Erh ...' His eyes flicked sheepishly to the Mafia don.

Christ on a bike – you'd think I'd asked for a lift to *fucking* Mars!

'There's a chemist on the *way* to my house, mum!' I attempted to introduce an element of logic.

'But it's *not* on the way to *our* house!' Mum fought to bolster her non-existent argument.

'It *is* on the way to your house!' A mix of panic, frustration and anger twisted me up. 'It's *exactly* on the way to your house. It's the *quickest* route!'

'But it's *not* the route we take.' Mum looked as if she would burst into tears.

A smarter person than me would say there was something else going on here, but hell be damned if I knew what it was. As far as I was concerned, it was simply a continuation of years of anxiety-inducing irrationality, so I got out of the car and walked off.

The Eclipse

On Monday, I made an emergency appointment at Parkside Surgery. I arrived carrying a jam jar – a *specimen* jar – containing the weird larvae I'd dug out of my skin. I figured if I placed the evidence directly in front of Dr Adams, he would have no choice but to take my concerns seriously.

'For the laboratory, Doctor. So they can analyse it.'

Dr Adams glanced at the jar, threw it in the bin and prescribed me a cream.

Why would no one take me seriously? I needed an answer. My skin prickled all over and every so often a bug would burrow into my heel, causing such agony I had to remove a trainer and massage my foot.

Although high as a kite, I felt determined to challenge the medical profession. I marched back into the practice and up to the reception desk ... *but everything blurred like a dream sequence in a film ...*

'I'm *not* happy!' I told the receptionist.

She put down the latest edition of *Thin Celebrities* and looked confused.

'I've got bugs *digging* into my skin and I need more than a bloody *cream!*'

'I'll ... *call* Doctor Singh,' she replied.

I'd heard about the surgery's Indian director from the lads at the Backward Parrot. Apparently, Singh was brilliant at being a complete prat. He insisted his secretary stood to attention by his parking space every morning, umbrella in hand – even in the height of summer – ready to escort him into the building. When he approached me at the front desk, I sensed a waste of time.

'Mister Christopher, are you hearing voices from the television?' He gave me the annoying beady-eyed-sceptic look Gabriel used to in our flat in Wan Chai.

'Yes, Doctor, I hear lots of voices,' I played along with the idiot.
Singh's eyes widened. 'Go on?'

'Well, it depends what I'm watching. I quite like medical documentaries. You should check one out – you might *learn* something.'

I awoke with toothache in one of my molars. Bar a capped incisor and a couple of fillings, I'd had no real problems with my gnashers, so this was a disappointment. I had to find a dentist and began calling around, but none of the regular practices had room for NHS patients. One receptionist suggested I attend Scott Hospital's emergency drop-in. I cycled there expecting the usual drilling and filling, but the dentist took a look in my North and South, prodded the offending tusk and said, 'It's got to come out.'

'Sorry?'

'It's completely rotted.' He shrugged. 'I've got no choice.'

He began giving his assistant instructions in dentist-speak. As she prepared the sterilised instruments, I lay in the chair coming to terms with the fact I'd screwed up my body so much on drugs that part of it was being removed. The dentist said to rinse my mouth regularly with saltwater and not eat anything for twenty-four hours. However, recovering from a speed binge my body craved calories. So off I went to the Co-op with a dream shopping list in my mind and a nightmare in my wallet.

Having pinched enough Bovril these past few months to supply an Everest expedition, I'd come to the conclusion this shoplifting malarkey must be risk free. *Why not get a load of good grub?* I rationalised, thinking a tin of ham would go down well. I placed one in the basket, intending to transfer it to my pocket when no one was looking.

A guy further down the aisle happened to glance in my direction, so I moved to a different part of the shop and stashed the ham in my jacket. After doing the same with some chocolate bars and a Turkish Delight, I meandered towards the meat department, checking the odd price here and there while projecting a benign smile.

I passed the same guy as he stood at the deli counter and by strange coincidence we made eye contact again. The thought struck me this average Joe might be a store detective. *But why would he take a ticket and stand in line and have awkwardly shaped, freshly baked sticks of French bread in his basket?*

Something bugged me, but I continued on to the bacon shelves and tucked a pack of smoked rashers into my waistband. Then I joined a checkout queue behind a chap with a ruddy complexion, crew-cut hair and a Freddie Mercury tache. He had to be a marine or a soldier as he epitomised a good percentage of the blokes I'd served with.

As I placed a packet of porridge oats and a cheap loaf on the conveyor belt, the military man turned around. 'Mate, that bloke there's been following you.'

I followed his finger ... to see *Mr Bread Sticks* duck back into an aisle.

'Thanks, bud.' I patted the player on the arm.

'I'll be right back.' I threw a bluffing nod to the checkout girl. 'If that guy's been following me, I want to know why.'

It all fell into place. The store detective must have flagged me immediately in my Oasis-meets-Oxfam clothes and Goofy-length shoes. He couldn't apprehend me until I attempted to leave the shop with the goods, though. Fortunately, the lead singer of Queen had come to my rescue, for reasons I could only hazard a guess at.

My heart pumped fear into my head. I had to get rid of the evidence. Like a reverse game of *Supermarket Sweep,* the ham landed on a beer shelf, the chocolate bars got intimate with joints of lamb in a chest freezer, the pack of bacon rolled off the yoghurts and fell on the floor. I returned to the till knowing the jobsworth had nothing on me.

'Sorry about that.' I smiled at the checkout girl and got my wallet out.

'*Oy!*' The deli dick grabbed my shoulder. 'Follow me.'

I should have told the creep to take a running jump as I hadn't broken any law.

Once outside, 'Listen, you *cunt.* I know you shoved that stuff back on the shelves. So fuck off. You're banned for life.'

'Okay ...' I replied, knowing Bread Sticks would be on his merry way next week when the Co-op's Easter security stood down.

I cut through the woods and arrived home in shock, vowing never to humiliate myself in this way again. I was exhausted and confused. My life didn't seem real – and not in a good way. I felt like an imposter, as if wearing a mask and gatecrashing someone else's gig. I'd strived to achieve, to *get* somewhere, by earning a green beret. I'd attempted to further myself in business and invested thousands of hours to make it work ... and yet none of it seemed *me.*

Nothing made sense. How come my company had turned over a hundred thousand dollars a month and yet now I was reduced to thieving a seventy-pence packet of bacon from a poxy Co-op? How come six months ago I'd lived in the Orient and worked in a nightclub full of dragon-tattooed thugs – and yet was now walking through the door of a twee house in the arse end of England as if nothing had happened?

Then there was the weird Foreign Triad and that nonsense with puppets on strings. Why did this shit only happen to *me?* My life was always challenging and surreal and I simply accepted it, blundering forth with my *Snakes and Ladders* map and Mickey Mouse compass.

And who was I supposed to talk to about this? I had no one, no family, no friends and certainly no therapy. Who would understand anyway? Who knew how it felt to have an enormous black leech sucking the marrow from your very existence?

That substance misuse specialist, Julian, thought I was clinically depressed and suffering PTSD, I guess from Hong Kong, my childhood and Christ knows what else. But what was I supposed to do? I'd seen all those professed specialists waving clipboards and palming me off with happy medicine. I'd signed on the waiting list for the drug service. I'd *pleaded* with them to prescribe me amphetamine so I could function and wouldn't have to give all my money to criminals and demean myself by shoplifting.

If that store detective knew my *real* story, had lived *my* life, understood about the itches, the starvation, the hypothermia, the loneliness, the filth, the dark memories, the confusion, the trauma, the ostracism *and* the addiction, he'd have turned a blind eye to my chocolate-coated heist. Hell, he would probably have ordered me a hamper from Fortnum and Mason.

I'd always faced the music, ducked the punches and hit back as hard. I never stopped believing in myself through the difficult times and kept the fire in my heart alive. I hadn't committed suicide or let an institution take control of my life. Yet despite my core belief that there was *nothing* wrong with me … I felt ashamed.

Chunkenhoffen Doogleblaster rang my doorbell, cheering me up immediately. He stood on the front step wearing an Aussie cork-dangling hat, an iridescent-purple rave jacket, brown jumbo cords and yellow flip-flops. Clutching a six-pack of Strongbow and a book on astrology, 'Chrissy, my twizzled pistonburger. How's it hanging on the Polaroid Peninsula?'

'It's groovy, mate,' I lied.

I hadn't told Chunks the depths to which I'd sunk both mentally and physically. He treated me as a friend, never probing below the surface or asking why I lived in a pigsty.

First off, we discussed Siborg's situation. I hadn't been aware of my friend's court appearance, not until a letter dropped through the door the other day. Writing on daffodil-yellow legal paper from the comfort of one of HMP Exeter's eight-by-twelve-foot holiday cottages, Simon told me he'd received a two year sentence but expected to be out in twelve months.

Making a mental note to write to my old mate, I listened to Chunks' latest get-rich-quick scheme – and *boy* it was a belter!

'The *Eclipse!*' He beamed – the way Galileo must have done when theorising the Earth is round.

'Right-o.'

'Americans!'

I was none the wiser.

'Accommodation!'

I waited for an explanation as Chunky Changlebats polished off a second can of cider.

'The Yankee Doodles will cough up mega bucks to witness Saturn blocking out Jupiter,' he continued. 'So you rent your house out to our friends from across the ... *Adriatic* and sleep in a tent in the back garden. We'll make a fortune. Two thousand spondelemontes a day. *Three* if they want breakfast! I'll be your agent.'

'Chunks, the Eclipse came and went.'

'Oh ...' He pouted. 'Day trips to Stonehenge?'

When Chunks left, I called Plymouth Drug Service to find out when I would enter treatment and, more importantly, receive a prescription of Dexedrine. I'd dreamed of those little white pills ever since speaking to Julian. I wanted my life back. To wake up, pop a couple of dexys and go about my day like a regular person. No more selling my soul to drug dealers and spending every penny to feel normal and no more living in a filthy home without the motivation to tidy up. I wanted the security of picking up my little lifesavers from the pharmacy for the rest of my life.

'Mister Thrall, we took you off the waiting list,' the woman on the phone announced.

'W-w-what do you mean?'

'We sent you an appointment letter and you DNAd.'

'I did *what?*'

'DNAd – you "did not attend".'

Her use of in-house jargon and passive aggression spoke volumes.

'But I didn't *get* a letter.' I tried not to sound exasperated. 'I *swear.* I've been waiting months to get my life on track. *Why* would I not attend?'

'People DNA all the time,' she replied arrogantly, no doubt

pigeonholing me as the archetypal methadone merchant working the system – as opposed to a desperate human being. 'If you can't be bothered to turn up, you obviously don't want treatment.'

My blood boiled. If this thick fucking idiot fell under a bus, I'd high-five the driver and buy them a chicken dinner. 'So you think I can't be *bothered?*' I fumed. 'Can I speak with a manager, please?'

'Why do you need a manager?'

'To make a complaint.'

'You can put it in writing.'

'But why can't you send me another appointment letter?'

'I *can* send another one, Mister Thrall.'

I fucking hate it when obnoxious receptionists feign decorum with the repeated use of 'Mister'.

'You'll still have to wait a year, though,' she continued.

'Fine!' I slammed the roamer phone down ... *on* the sofa.

I'd so been looking forward to reclaiming my life, rekindling friendships and making my family proud of me. Everyone kept telling me I was ill, so where was the support? Surely, I shouldn't be doing *everything* on my own. Weren't professionals supposed to help you?

Rather than upset myself further, I set about writing to Simon. All I had in the way of stationary was a box of printer paper I'd retrieved from a skip, the type with sprocket holes along both sides. Its continuous zigzag arrangement meant that at the end of each page of cod-eyed claptrap, I could continue seamlessly onto the next.

> *To: Senator Simon 'I Didn't Do It So You Can Let Me Go Now' Preece. C/O Her Majesty's Pleasure Palace (the one fit for a king ... so long as he's a criminal).*

> *Hello Brother*

> *Apologies if I've been slack in writing to you. If it wasn't for the fact I'm a compulsive liar / gambler / archaeologist / porn star / bounty hunter (delete as*

appropriate), I would say I've been meaning to for a while, but that would be a lie as I don't usually enter into one-on-one communications with villainous scum.

Talking of circles, I ran in one yesterday for two hours and thirty-seven minutes before throwing up the four litres of Vimto I'd downed on top of forty-eight Alka-Seltzers and a bottle of Fairy Liquid. As I span around spewing out sugar-laden E-numbered bubbles, I looked like a rubbish Catherine wheel – but with a settled stomach and soft hands.

Back to what I was saying. Sorry for not writing sooner but I've had busloads of Scandinavian nurses knocking at my door asking for 'Butch'. Not wishing to disappoint these nymphos from the North, I've been inviting them in to practice bed baths, mouth-to-mouth and hospital corners. However, it's been completing my 'Sleepy Harbour' jigsaw puzzle with Ulrika that has taken up most of the time, despite the fact it's my 48th attempt and I've numbered all 3000 pieces.

Anyhow, what with packing them off up the A38 with a red warning triangle, a flask of tea and directions for Stockholm, you can see I've been very busy. In fact, I'm rubbed raw – in places you're not meant to be rubbed or raw. On the bright side, my Swedish is now 'mycket bra' and once you've had pickled herring you can never go back.

I hope by now you have asserted your position as 'Daddy' of the joint, but not in the sense of carrying Big Ron around on your shoulders or helping Jimmy the Snitch with his homework. How you broach the birds and the bees with Bareback Bob is your business (although I know someone who will buy the negatives).

You will be pleased to hear I have been making plans for your release. I think it is important to go straight and set your sights high, so I have bought you a compass and a hot air balloon. Seriously, I have been putting some thought into a trip to the North Pole – going via Leicester to cheer up my Great Aunt Dave. Sadly, she's had to surrender her driving licence, as it was surrounded and had run out of ammo (it's the way you tell 'em). No, even more seriously-er, due to her failing eyesight and dodgy hip, she reversed all the way to Scunthorpe, before crashing into Cost Savers with four policemen on the boot. It worked out quite well, though, as the coppers apprehended three shoplifters while waiting for the ambulance to arrive.

Right, where was I? Oh, yes, the North Pole. Other than going via Ulrika's place in Gothenburg (I'm missing three pieces from 'Children and a Kitten'), I'm open to ideas. To speed things up, I suggest you write to Father Christmas. Don't forget to ask him for a grappling hook and a nail file. If the screws ask you what they're for, say you're taking up shark fishing and from now on you want to be called Loretta.

You should also ask Santa for a copy of 'Husky for Beginners'. I don't bark the language myself, but I recommend at least learning 'Stop', 'Go', 'Left', 'Right' and 'Which one of you furry fucks ate my skis?'

Talking of skis, could you let me know how many you think you'll need? The general consensus among polar explorers appears to be two, but I didn't reach the dizzy heights of sixer in the Cub Scouts by not being prepared.

That's it from Planet Plymouth. See you on the flipside and don't drop the soap.

Love you brother,
Chrissy
PS. I did all your drugs.

Female Company

'Quiet in the courtroom, all rise. Call Chisholm versus Spender.

'So Missus Chisholm, you two are divorced. Can you tell me in your own words why you are here?'

'Well, Judge Judy, I had my bike since high school. But the day after the divorce, he drove off with it in the back of his pick-up. Two days later he mails me the bell.'

Judge Judy turns to the defendant. 'Is this true, Mister Spender?'

'Yes, your honor, but –'

'Stop! If I want you to explain, sir, I will ask. Do you understand?'

'Yes, ma'am.'

'Explain.'

Subdued laughter ripples through the audience.

'Well, ma'am, over the years, I replaced the frame, the forks, the wheels, the handlebars, the brakes, the cranks, the pedals, everything except the bell –'

'Ahh!' Judge Judy slaps her forehead. 'Why do I get the feeling you two are here to pee on my leg and tell me it's raining?'

Judge Judy. *Season 18, episode 215*

Still in the manic stage of my fortnightly speed binge, I decided to turn the green plastic fish box I'd salvaged into a designer coffee table with storage space beneath for magazines. I spray-tacked rectangles of my offcut black cord carpet into the box's four recessed side panels and screwed on the plastic casters to raise it off the floor.

A side panel from the redundant hi-fi cabinet provided a base for the coffee table's lid. Around this, I built a rectangular frame using a length of skirting board found in the attic, which I varnished in teak. I removed twenty-or-so redundant pine slats from the bottom of my venetian blinds, cut these to size and laid them in a parquet pattern inside my chunky wooden surround.

Having unscrewed the hi-fi cabinet's glass door, I prised off the hinges and laid it on top. Perfectly proportioned, the pane protected the slats from dust and spillage, its polished edges overlapping the teak-glossed border by an inch all the way around. *Result!*

I secured the see-through top in place with two carpet tacks at each corner, careful not to clip the glass with the hammer for obvious reasons. In my growing collection of fixings, I had a pair of brass hinges, ideal for attaching the lid, and a length of brass chain to prevent it wrenching itself off.

The result was a sturdy little coffee table like a flat-topped pagoda. Maybe, subconsciously, I'd replicated the ornate mother-of-pearl-inlaid black-lacquered box I'd smashed up in my flat in Wan Chai.

Unusually, the project went to plan and didn't leave me in a drug-zapped sleep-deprived mess. Only, the front room now looked like the backdrop for a humanitarian crisis. As I pondered how to put the place back together, the phone rang.

'Krisstofenheim!' Chunks bellowed. 'How's the pingly shinglewinger, me old custard?'

'It's ... It's ...' I gave up trying to be clever. 'It's fine, Chunks.'

'I have our *first* client!'

Pound – or dollar – signs kerchinged in my eyes as I pictured the gullible American willing to rent a child-sized bedroom at an overly inflated price – to witness an interstellar extravaganza that had already taken place. Then I remembered this was Chunkfest talking, the pioneering proponent of hotfooting up erupting volcanos in the name of ornamental garden art.

'Go on.'

'My niece. Just split with her chap and needs somewhere to stay.

I'll bring her up tonight for a viewing.'

'Okay, I'll start cleaning.'

Whizzing off my head, I focused on tidying up, using a systematic approach. I didn't want to let Chunks down or embarrass myself in front of this girl. Besides, I could do with the extra cash as well as the company.

I began by shovelling the mountain of bits and bobs into my military suitcase and stashing it under the bed. Then I pushed the two halves of sofa together, propping up the reunion with some discreetly placed house bricks, and hoovered the dirt-blackened carpet. Washing the dishes came next, after which I took three and a half showers and splashed on some smellies. Fortunately, my eagle-wing haircut had grown out a little, so I no longer resembled Asterix the Gaul – more like Peter Andre's unspoken-about twin.

Chunks arrived with his niece, Jeanette. I set mugs of tea down on my smart new coffee table and told them to have a look around and shoot me any questions. Then, with the tenacity of a champion rodeo rider, I balanced on one half of my temperamental seating arrangement, projecting the image of a carefree bachelor with the world at his feet.

'I'll take the room, Chris, please,' said Jeanette.

Jackpot!

'I'll bring my stuff over tomorrow, if that's okay?'

'Absolutely, fine,' I replied.

'Oh ...' she added. 'Can I get a TV signal in the room?'

'You can with a portable aerial,' I assured her. 'But I'll put a proper socket in anyway.'

Banking on the additional income, I tapped a ridiculous amount of speed into the spoon, picturing myself hobnobbing with the stars, taking on servants and buying a holiday home in Torpoint. I already had an aerial socket for the spare bedroom, so I was faced with the straightforward task of chiselling a hole in the wall, locating the coaxial cable dropping down to the lounge and splicing in a spur.

Sadly, modern life is rarely simple, harder still when you're straining like a cup-winning horse. The existing cable, which turned out to be telephone wire and not proper coax, ran down the centimetre gap behind the plasterboard as opposed to dangling freely inside the blockwork cavity. Attempting to fish it out with a bent coat hanger took me so long I worried TVs had become obsolete. The rungs on the loft ladder almost wore through due to the amount of times I ran up and down them.

When Jeanette returned the next day, I helped bring in her belongings and packed my tools away so she could have some privacy. As I fixed up a hit in my bedroom – one I'd have to sleep in now – I reflected briefly on my secretive druggy lifestyle, wondering how she would feel if she knew.

The following afternoon, I tried to finish the aerial job but allowed meaningless undertakings to sidetrack me. I managed to fit the socket, but the trip upstairs to test the signal proved too much for my aging gogglebox, which now gave off an incredible-hulk-coloured hue. To complete the installation, I'd had to remove the faceplate from the socket in the front room and was now too tired and uncoordinated to screw it back on.

Jeanette told me she worked in a call centre. About a year older than me, she had frizzy red hair, a slim figure and pleasant personality. That evening, as I fidgeted in front of the telly, she came downstairs wearing a nightie and clutching a CD. 'Mind if I put some music on?'

'Sure, no problem,' I replied. On my fifth day without sleep, I wasn't really watching the program anyway – I just didn't know where to put myself now I had company.

My new housemate made a play of bending over to put the disc in the player, making the length her already short nightie redundant. My mind flashed back to the time I'd visited the beautiful Kerry at her home on the Peak – the difference being I was infatuated with Kerry but felt no attraction to Jeanette. I wondered how come whatever state I got myself into, girls – *and* boys – seemed to take a shine to me? Perhaps I needed to believe in myself more – easier said than done when you're preoccupied with something society hates.

On my sixth day without zeds, I sat in the lounge staring at the unscrewed aerial socket, trying to get my mind together to finish what I started. Yawns rocked my fragile existence. The dreaded itches plagued me. With no gear left, I felt sketchy at the thought of having to tell Jeanette my place crawled with spec-sized space invaders immune to every chemical the Co-op had to offer.

In an inane attempt to invigorate myself, I decided to make a pint of strong tea, but while willing my body to stand up I spotted an orange syringe cap on the carpet. *You idiot!* I cursed, imagining the embarrassing repercussions had Jeanette found it.

I climbed the stairs, intending to put the cap in the Perspex dish under my bed, but paused for ages on each step because my exhausted mind couldn't remember what I was doing. Hours later, when I finally made it to the kitchen, I had the same problem boiling the kettle. I leant against the sideboard, gibbering to myself like a shaman in trance and nodding like an agreeable donkey. Every time I came around, the water in the kettle had cooled, meaning I had to flick the switch once more.

Three more hours passed. I was still trying to make a cup of Rosy Lee when the front door crashed open and Jeanette stepped over the threshold with a random in tandem. 'Chris, this is Carlito.' She raised their clasped hands. 'He started at the call centre today and I've decided to move in with him.'

Along with skin-tight black jeans, a leather jacket with the collar turned up and cowboy boots, Carlito wore Buddy Holly glasses, their pebbled lenses thick enough to resist armour-piercing rounds, and gold studs to let you know he was up for it. Upon hearing my name, he grinned at the fridge-freezer, gave it a Mexican finger wave and winked – with *both* eyes.

Jeanette beamed – the way a women does when she's bagged a guy named Carlito in under eight hours and decided to spend the rest of her life pumping out little Litos to the sound of Bon Jovi with him. You notice such things when your parents have notched up five marriages between them.

Attempting to get a grip, I stepped forward and put my hand out. Carlito grinned and began fanning the air like he'd farted. I thought he was having a seizure or perhaps showing off his disco moves, but realised he was trying to locate my palm. When at last we connected, Plymouth's answer to Billy Idol levered it up into the 'Right on, brother!' handclasp made popular by the Harlem Globe Trotters and cast of *Top Gun*.

We mumbled pleasantries, but I was glad when the front door slammed and Carlito lovingly crammed Jeanette and her bulging black bin bags in his Fiat Panda and roared off into the sunset above Whitleigh's council flats. I chopped up my last blim of hash for a super-quick shotty ... sucking the smoke into my lungs two hours later.

Stumbling about the house, trying to concentrate on at least *one* of my projects, I was in such a mess I wouldn't have been able to focus on an eighty-foot-tall Pot Noodle if it covered itself in baby oil and sang Right Said Fred's back album in Urdu. A shuddering yawn rocked my body and reluctantly I decided to crash. I laid the sleeping bag on one half of the sofa bed's extending cushions and stripped to my boxers. But then remembering the loose faceplate on the aerial socket, I grabbed a screwdriver and crawled under the TV ...

Be Somebody

Upon opening my eyes, I saw the screwdriver lying near my hand. *What the ...?*

I raised myself off the floor and – *'Ouch!'* – banged my head on the television table, payback for dodging the licence fee perhaps. Sitting there in my boxers, exhausted and famished, I tried to recall what I'd done to deserve such dishonour. *Flathead screwdriver... TV... sleeping bag...?* It was like an episode of *Columbo*. 'Erh, just one more question, sir. Why did you saw the sofa in half?'

The screwdriver was the smoking gun, cracking the case wide open as everything came flooding back. I checked the Casio to find I'd been comatose beneath a television set for twelve hours. This wasn't a new scenario. You get used to opening your eyes and wondering who the fuck you are when you have a problem with amphetamine.

As I shivered on the filthy carpet, knees pulled up to my chest, something felt distinctly different this time. Sunlight filtering through the blinds reminded me there was a world out there I no longer was a part of. Intense hunger demanded I walk to the corner shop and spend the few remaining coins in my wallet on a Cornish pasty.

Only, I hesitated ...

I could hear the kids playing football outside my door, their chosen spot because I'd never tell them to get lost. I thought about how they always accepted me – unlike grownups with their cruel judgements. I thought about my own messed-up childhood and getting thrown on the street at fifteen. I thought about my fear and distrust of adults and how I'd made a promise growing up to be one kids weren't afraid of, someone who would treat them as equals and always listen. I thought about all the times they'd called to ask me for advice – not a parent, a teacher or a family member, but *me,* the person they trusted.

How could I go outside, though? My jeans were dirty and ripped, my shabby trainers too big, my hair a mess. I'd lost a third of my bodyweight and had caves instead of cheeks – not to mention the horrifying track marks on my arms.

Is hiding behind closed curtains, shunning the company of friends in favour of punching a blunt needle into your fragile veins normal? Is it worth destroying your life, your health, your finances to make some drug dealer rich?

There was no way I could let the kids see me in this state, and not only that but I knew their parents and pretty much everyone else in the street. What if someone stopped to talk to me? How would I explain the mess I was in? I couldn't even get my words out properly. I wasn't a good example – to *anyone.*

What happened to you, Chris?

I'd been a big tough commando, chiselled, shaven and shorn, the *most* handsome marine in the history of the Corps – according to my mum. My passion had been going for a five-mile run, changing into a fresh set of neatly ironed clothes, slapping on a decent aftershave and going about the day with a spring in my step. I'd awake after a night on the town to find slithers of paper in my pockets with girls' phone numbers on them. Sure, it sounds vain, but at least I had the option of vanity back then.

I would park my BMW outside the house I'd bought when most of my mates still lived with their parents. I'd deliver snappy business presentations in Europe's top hotels, one time giving a conference speech to a three-thousand-strong admiring crowd. Many of the audience came and shook my hand afterwards, congratulating me on my success in Hong Kong and achieving financial freedom for life.

I remembered flying out to the Orient with British Airways to run my company, the Max*Tech* Group, the fastest-growing network-marketing operation in the Asia Pacific, one *I'd* built from scratch, a smartly dressed, self-sufficient, quick-minded entrepreneur on target to achieve ... but I also recalled the empty sensation in my stomach as the train had left Plymouth, my demons letting me know I still had to pay the universe.

Taking crystal meth the first time. How *brilliant* did that make me feel. As if I could achieve *anything*. I learned *so* much through taking drugs, especially about myself.

But they're not helping you anymore, are they?

I thought about Sarah leaving me and how I'd let Vance, my Hong Kong brother, down. *I'm sorry, Vance. I'll call you. I promise.*

How awful it had been, *beyond* awful, hearing those scathing Cantonese voices, right before he kicked me out of the flat. Wandering the streets homeless, forced to sell my Rolex, renting that crummy top-floor apartment in Wan Chai where my life descended into further chaos.

And how close had I come to dying whilst working for the 14K? I'd only ever tried to do a good job for them, because for the first time in my life I felt I belonged. Then there was the Foreign Triad, those cliquey cowards who'd laughed at me and pretended I was going to be murdered.

Thinking the whole of Hong Kong, possibly the world, was one enormous puppet show …

I'd felt certain there was some kind of global conspiracy going on. Hadn't I scanned instructions on food packets and scoured books in an attempt to crack the code?

Fuck, I'd been unwell!

I remembered the disgusting mess I'd lived in, so screwed up on drugs I couldn't even tidy up. How I hoarded stuff like a mad person, and everything I touched, including that bloody air conditioner, ended up in pieces.

Let's face it. You've never completed anything important when you're off your head.

I'd decided to stop taking amphetamine on more than one occasion, knowing I had to prevent my life sliding further downhill. And what had happened? I'd *kidded* myself the drug would help me build a future in the UK. But I had to get *real*. I'd been back from Hong Kong a year and *nothing* had improved – just the *opposite!* Each day was one hulking great calamitous farce. I needed to accept amphetamine wasn't getting me where I wanted to go. It simply wasn't working anymore.

And another thing, I had to stop attempting to elicit the magic answers from those around me, especially my parents, who only saw it as blame. I would forgive the past and accept their shortcomings. My folks had come good when I'd needed it the most, and I knew enough about life now to see beyond their emotional outbursts, irrational actions and inconsistent behaviour. Reading between the lines, I sensed things might well have been awry in their own childhoods, they'd just never had the means or opportunity to heal from it.

Finally, I needed to stop putting my Hong Kong experience on a pedestal and start seeing it for what it was – awesome in some ways and awful in others. No different to Plymouth in that respect. It had been a laugh and an eye-opener. I'd got to live a hedonistic lifestyle and sample a unique culture. I was one of the few westerners who'd worked for the Hong Kong triads. But I'd had incredible adventures in many far-flung locations around this beautiful blue planet, so why stack all my chips on one square when there were plenty more on offer?

I cringed at my shitty wardrobe, my track-marked arms and shambles of a house. I could hear those wonderful kids passing the ball to one another, knowing they'd come running the second I stepped out of the door because they appreciated their friend Chris. As I reflected on the extra mile I always went for them, moreover *why,* my emotions welled up.

I thought about that innocent little boy who cried when his beloved tortoise died, his best friend through years of uncertainty. And for the first time since smoking crystal meth in the toilet cubicle in Gung Wan Hong, I realised what the hell I'd put that kid through – put *myself* through – and I burst into tears.

I sobbed for an age … I sobbed for the *state* I'd allowed myself to get into … I sobbed for letting my *family* down … my *friends* down … those *kids* down … but most of all I sobbed for *me,* that timid little boy who'd been subjected to so much pain and confusion.

Adults let you down when they should have protected you. But you're the grown-up now and you have to look after that little boy. Do you get it, Chris? Only you can look after you!

I did get it. That damaged little tot had become a man and it was up to me to take care of him. Who else would?

Everything seemed so clear. I'd been lost and the drugs helped me find my direction. However, they were only a stepping-stone, one I'd continued to try and use when the river was deep in flood. I needed to make some serious changes in my life, to start prioritising my needs and not substances.

I wouldn't be rushing to any Narcotics Anonymous meetings or throwing my hands up to the Lord and confessing my supposed mistakes. I hadn't made any mistakes – unless life experience is a sin. Nor would I charge around the house binning all my drug paraphernalia. I enjoyed taking drugs and it would be a lie to say otherwise – not to mention that speed had allowed me to engage my brain, step outside the matrix and question the status quo.

No, I wouldn't stop taking amphetamine, at least not for the foreseeable future, but I'd stop taking so much of the bloody stuff. With the money I'd save, I could fix up my home and buy a bit of food for the cupboards. I would embrace the life my parents had created and Mother Nature blessed. I would force myself out of bed every morning and *smile* at the sun – even when it was behind the clouds. I would crack at least *one* task a day – which might only be the washing-up – and then kick back on the sofa and relax *without* the constant need to get high.

For the first time in years, I felt excited, *enormously* excited. I placed the original seventies illuminating world globe on the floor, grabbed a red marker and began circling places ... *Vietnam ... Colombia ... Honduras ... Philippines ... Australia ... Japan ... Israel ...*

One day at a time, I would rebuild my life. No matter how I felt, I'd tell myself I was happy. I could buy new clothes and get out and about more ... *Bolivia ... Venezuela ... Costa Rica ... Malaysia ...*

South Africa ... Brazil ...

If I cut down the drugs, I wouldn't be tired all the time and sleeping the week away. I'd get up early and make the most of my day. I'd be able to concentrate more, maybe write that CV and get a job ... *New Zealand ... Belize ... Mexico ... India ... Panama ... Singapore ... Russia ... Iran ... Iceland ...*

Eventually, I would visit all the places I'd dreamed of. I'd dive off the cliff in Acapulco like Elvis did in that film I loved as a kid and camp out in the jungle like my hero, Tarzan. I could do some adventure sports, maybe learn to fly, the sky really was the limit. And what about writing that book Richard always mentioned?

From now on, I would never spend more than ten pounds on amphetamine. I would buy one gram, have my buzz and then crash. *But* when I awoke, I'd make a delicious cup of tea, roll a ciggie, throw open the curtains, *smile* at the sun and shout to the world, 'I'M GONNA BE SOMEBODY!' and then I would go about my day.

Out of the Ashes

'*Be* somebody!' I greeted the morning rays, awaking two days after my recent spiritual awakening. I felt the usual grogginess from a weeklong speed binge, but that weird black cloud shit had begun to thin. Deep in my soul, a tiny flame flickered, dissipating the dark mists of doom and exposing a golden corridor to a brilliant future. I'd arrived at a crossroads. I could tell life to fuck off and crawl back into bed – I'd *finally* made it to bed – or I could fuel that miniscule burn and rise from my pitiful mess to *be* someone.

I put the kettle on and sipped a humble yet motivating cup of tea while doing the dishes. The simple act of washing up with a smile – as opposed to seeing it as a chore – bolstered my determination to continue with this positive mindset. So much so, I blitzed the whole house, adopting a mercenary approach to the accumulated junk, throwing anything with no foreseeable use onto the rubbish pile in the back garden. After a quick hoover up, I felt remarkably good about the world. It was a turning point in my journey and there was no going back.

It was probably a good thing I still felt a bit rough, because I had a medical assessment that afternoon with the Department of Social Security. I'd heard horror stories about the doctors there. Apparently, they were under strict instructions to turf claimants off their sickness benefits if there was even the slightest suggestion of them swinging the lead. To say I felt nervous would be an understatement. With my confidence in tatters, I wasn't ready to return to full-time employment.

I arrived at the appointment on time but was only halfway through explaining about the drugs, the itches, the starvation and so forth, when the grey-haired quack raised his hand. '*Okay* ... okay!'

Damn! I should have prepared a proper speech. He thinks I'm fit for work.

'I've ...' The doctor took a deep breath and looked strangely distraught. 'I've heard enough. I'm signing you off indefinitely.'

As he completed the paperwork, I sat there in surprise. Did I really seem *that* unwell?

A letter dropped through the door. Rather than put it to one side, worrying it might be a bill, I opened it on the spot. *Wow!* The Halifax Building Society was in the process of demutualising and had made me a stakeholder. Apparently, the estimated value of my shares would be £1500, so I ticked the box indicating I wished to sell them immediately.

That evening, rather than sit in my manky sleeping bag scoffing toast, I walked the mile and a half to my brother's new place. He'd bunked in with Mike, a buddy from the precision engineering company in Cornwall. Mike and I had attended two of my six schools together but had only really got to know each other recently. This didn't stop him treating me like a long-time friend, and as the three of us settled down to smoke the first of many joints, life felt a whole lot better.

I admired Mike and Ben's lifestyle. They got up at 6am, five days a week without fail, and after a smoke and a coffee drove an hour into Cornwall to graft all day in the workshop. Back home, while Mike rolled yet another happy stick, Ben would chuck a pie and chips in the oven and they would sit down to eat in front of *Coronation Street.* Working hard and relaxing in their spare time, the boys had balance and discipline. Moreover, they had a *routine* and stuck to it no matter what mood they were in.

One evening, as the three of us witnessed some despicable goings-on in the Rover's Return, there was a knock at the door. In walked one of my brother's friends carrying a large holdall. Charlie was his name, a thickset lad with short bleached-blonde hair, freckles and total control over one of his blue eyes. Fancying himself as a hip-hop gangster, Charlie had an attitude as cocky – or cocksure – as his designer sports clothes. After introductions, he opened the bag and began counting out packs of Golden Virginia.

As my brother stacked them in piles of ten on the carpet, I watched intrigued.

'Baccy, from Belgium,' Charlie explained. 'My stepdad is Shotgun Freddy' – he alluded to Plymouth's best psychopathic gangster. 'Fred came across a tobacco warehouse while driving back from the Dam last year, so he bought a few hundred packs and sold 'em for triple the money.'

'Wow!' I'd seen Chunks smoking this imported stuff and had always wondered where it came from.

'He got rid of 'em so quick, he went back the next day and filled the car up. Now I'm his wheelman. Grand a week for three days' work.'

When my money came through on Thursday, I stuck to the plan and only bought a gram from the whizz wizard – although a real wizard would have waved his wand and turned it into a kilo, surely? *When it's gone, it's gone!* I reminded myself, visualising my spiral into the gutter to bolster this resolve.

In the manic phase of my binge, I made a midnight trip to Furniture World, promising to only scavenge stuff I could put to good use. In the rusting yellow skip was a brand-new quilted spread with a sturdy elasticated drawcord and eye-catching turquoise-and-cream-chequered pattern. I'm not sure what the cover had come off, but being the same size and shape of a fitted double-bed sheet it would look great on my trashed sofa.

I was in a far better place now. As such, I chatted with neighbours and made more time for the kids, playing footy, invented silly spur-of-the-moment games or simply sitting on the front step to chat about life. I gained a fascinating insight into their view of the world and the – often-unapproachable – adults inhabiting it. The council had bought a number of houses on the estate and let them to single mothers. When a little one began a question with *'Chris...'* and had a certain look in their eye, I knew what followed would be something they wanted to ask an absent father.

The following afternoon, Jolene and five of her height-restricted homies rang the bell. I yanked the door open and looked over their heads to scan the street. *'Hellooo!* Who knocked on my door, *please?'*

'We did!' the kids chorused.

'Who said that?' I checked all around – with the exception of down.

'We did? came the pantomime refrain.

'Okay, listen.' I squinted at the guttering above. 'I'm sure your all very nice grown-up adults and you've got *cars* and *jobs* and *money,* but I *can't* even *see* you. You're *invisible!'*

'We're down *here* and we're *not* adults we're *children!'* one of the half-pints replied.

'Right, right, I got it.' I inspected my neighbour's roof. 'So you're *up* there and you're *not* even children, you're *adults.* Yeah-yeah!'

Amid the giggles, *'No!'* Jolene's girl friend insisted. 'We're down *here* and we're *children!'*

'Okay, I *got* it! You're great *big* adults about ... *erm* ... *thirty*-six-years old and you *don't* even go to school anymore *and* you're invisible, so you're probably all ghosts and you're gonna try and *scare* me!' I checked the airspace above Plymouth for condors.

'We're *not* ghosts, we're just *kids!'* screamed the spokeskid.

'Yeah-yeah! So you're not even *kids* you're just *ghosts!'*

As her friend ran out of ideas, Jolene punched me on the thigh.

I dropped to the hallway floor, clutching what might well have been a broken femur and severed artery. *'Arrrhhhhh!'*

'But you're *not* even hurt!' she scoffed.

Only then did I spot my five assailants.

'Whaaahhh!' I skedaddled backwards like a victim in a slasher film. *'Take* anything you want, but *don't* hurt me!'

'We're not even gonna take *anything.* We're just *kids,'* said another of the mini-monsters.

'Well ... that's okay then.' I stood up and brushed myself down.

'Where's *Bird?'* demanded Jolene.

'Oh, Bird's flown down the shops at the minute to get a

cuttlefish and a new mirror.'

'No he *hasn't!*' Amber looked unconvinced.

'He *has!* He broke his old mirror and got seven years bad luck.'

'I bet he's in the airing cupboard,' said Jolene.

'Nah, he'll be back in a minute.' I craned at the sky. 'He's probably stopped to chat to Big Bird.'

'Coming out on your bike?' asked Toby, a lad who lived opposite.

'All right, but wait a minute ...' I clicked the door shut.

In the attic, I began rifling through the duffel bag of fancy dress costumes ... *a fez bought in Turkey ... a Middle-Eastern get-up from Cairo ... a Blues Brothers suit picked up in a charity shop.* However, my favourite had to be the gorilla costume I'd made out of an Arctic camouflage net sprayed brown. I clambered into the suit and pulled on the accompanying hairy mask and gloves and then wheeled my bike outside.

The children's reaction was priceless, an uproar of screams and laughs. How ironic I understood these youngsters' needs but society didn't understand people like me. 'Let's go biking *now!* Everybody's learning *how!*' I shrieked and pedalled off up the street. 'Catch me if you can, you *big* old ... you *big* old ... *kids!*'

Later in the week, while perusing *Plymouth Extra*'s completely *free* pages of furniture adverts, property sales and charity bike rides, I came across a lonely heart for none other than Jesus himself. Clearly, hero in the biggest-selling book of all time had failed as a chat-up line.

> *Single Jewish male (Capricorn) with GSOH and own donkey, bunking with parents but seeking to inherit the Earth. Currently a chippie in family business, Joseph & Not So Sure If He's My Son, but looking to branch into event catering, after-dinner speaking and ophthalmology. Likes winemaking and wild camping. Dislikes stonings, leprosy and the Roman Occupation.*

Good listener, keen angler, allergic to lions. WLTM someone for walks on the sea and dinner with friends. Own chainsaw an advantage.

In reality, a local church had run a small boxed advert in an attempt to bolster its congregation with Plymouth's dispossessed.

He never owned property
He never had savings
He never wrote a book
He never held office
He never taught in school
He never went far from home
He never wore fancy clothes
He never sought friends in high places
Yet he is the most celebrated figure of all time
He is Jesus Christ

Strewth ...!

As kids we had to attend church and I don't think I've ever wished for two hours of primetime weekend to fly by faster. I doubt any of the devil dodgers in that spiritless tomb – and certainly not the vicar – had even the slightest clue as to how to decipher the pearls of ancient Eastern wisdom enshrouded in the Scriptures' esoteric prose. Ironically, what with the religious community attempting to have the film banned, I'd gained a more convincing picture of who Jesus might have been from watching *Life of Brian*.

And yet the advert's simple but hard-hitting juxtapose knocked my parrot clean off its perch. Not that I'd be getting all religioned-up or anything – I valued freethinking too much – but right *here,* right *now,* I experienced an intense secular connection with this enigmatic character.

Here was a guy born into humble, challenging and questionable circumstances during a callous, pious and benighted age, a time when anyone of difference would have been bullied mercilessly. Yet

Jesus rose above the detractors and affirmed his equality through a process of existential study, introspection and reflection. In doing so, he uncovered alternative knowledge, developing the progressive mindset essential to living in harmony with the universe – a way of being he freely taught others.

An exponent of peace, a master of physical and mental health, Jesus was a revolutionary visionary who viewed the world through altruistic eyes. He referred to the nature of being as 'his father', perhaps to replace one he'd never known. He loved all people, even the haters and particularly children, and spent his time among society's downtrodden, guiding the lost, healing the sick and enriching the poor. Moreover, he despised false authority and the crime of usury, having the foresight to realise these evils would eventually enslave us all.

And what happened? After being mocked, spat on and flogged, he was paraded past baying crowds and put to a barbaric death. Yet this kind, principled and courageous man still forgave his tormenters and maintained integrity and dignity until the end.

I thought about my own rocky start in life and the sense of apartness often accompanying me like an invisible hound. I recalled the soul-searching I'd done in the wilderness of addiction and how whilst working for the triads I could have sold that soul to the Devil and my financial troubles would have been over. People had shunned me, ridiculed me and ganged up against me, when all I'd wanted to do was connect with them, irrespective of difference, as I had done with Johnny Horsepower and the old man who lived on the stairs.

Putting allegory, religion and the historical record aside, in *this* moment, my sixth sense told me Jesus had existed. In the same way a racing driver *feels* a car around the track as opposed to bullying it, I just knew, and ten thousand words couldn't explain how. In a society full of cowards, here was an unselfish man prepared to stand by what's right, even if it meant making the ultimate sacrifice ... and surely the world's allowed one fucking hero.

I sat on the doorstep, enjoying the sunshine dancing on my face. Two lads in white shirts with plastic nametags came walking down the street, kicking a ball between them. I gave them a friendly wave.

'Hey!' one greeted me in an American accent.

'You guys from the Church?' I asked.

'Yeah!' they choroused.

'We're missionaries,' said one.

'Come in.'

Over a cup of tea, Bill and Ken told me about the Church of Latter-day Saints, explaining how young male 'Mormons' like themselves spent two years ministering abroad, 'saving people', as they put it. I asked how many people the boys had saved.

'Hah!' Bill chuckled. 'We've been here six months and it's only you and one other person that's invited us in.'

'Yeah, a woman in Whitleigh,' Ken chipped in. 'She lives on her own.'

'And self-harms,' Bill added thoughtfully.

I felt a little proud of my openness and independent thought. Like a lot of people who grew up in Seventies Britain, I was still affected by those hard-to-shift traces of prejudice deeply ingrained in us by the nation's complex cultural norms, but wanting to suck up life's richness and be available to all, I would never allow them to control me.

The boys and I struck up an easy friendship. As with most Americans I'd been lucky enough to meet, they were brilliant fun, open-minded and generous of heart. I appreciated their subsequent visits, looking at them as a part of my regeneration. Not once did they suggest I enter their fold. They accepted my philosophy of believing in yourself, not sweating the unknown and letting Mother Nature take care of the rest. We even prayed together – although I did feel a bit of a fraud.

As the postman disappeared, I opened a letter from the Halifax and found a cheque for £1,533, the proceeds from the sale of my shares. Things were certainly looking up.

'Chrisington Christley-Chrisstler!' Chunks boomed down the phone. 'Remember you said you were gonna buy a speedingly speedy speedster with your windingly windy windfall?'

'Yes, mate.'

My brother-in-law, Marlon, deals cars to the stars. You know, top-end motors – Rollers, Porsches, Ferraris.'

'Chunks, I'm looking at spending five hundred not fifty thousand.'

'Don't worry. He'll do you a cheesy. Take down this number and give him a racquet.'

'Brother-in-law', 'cars to the stars', 'top-end motors' – had I been a rationale human being, I would have heard someone smashing me over the head with an alarm bell or, better still, have bitten my arm off and beaten myself to death with it. But me being me, I gave Marlon a call and later that day found myself standing next to him and Chunks on a pavement in a sink estate staring at a Fiesta Supersport with 118,000 miles on the clock.

I couldn't help glancing at Marlon, moreover the guy's self-inked tattoos, unsure if the one on his forehead was a cross or an unfinished swastika. What with the dodgy teardrop running down his cheek, he looked like an emotional Nazi.

'Got a *little* bit of rust on her ...' Marlon gave the driver's-side front tyre a gentle kick.

Seems reasonable, I thought – as the passenger door dropped off.

'Just cosmetic,' said Marlon, as Chunks helped him manhandle it back into place. 'Bit of WD40 should sort that out.'

And so it continued, Chunks yepping in agreement as Marlon attempted to sell me on the aging rust bucket's up-to-the-minute sixteen-year-old technology and state-of-the-art vintage extras while slugging Tennent's Super.

I gave the car a *thorough* going-over, checking the eject button on the cassette player and the wear in the ashtray, letting out audible tuts and shaking my head as I did. With a robust list of haggle points, I put my concerns to Marlon, stressing the roundness of the steering wheel and arguing the fog lights might well place a strain on the carburettor.

He batted them back to me, the way people who sell shit second-hand cars do, the kind of responses that convince pensioners to buy a timeshare in Albert Square. 'Well, you need rust holes in the floor to let the rainwater out.' He shrugged.

That figures.

'A bit of play in the steering allows for a relaxed driving style.'

Hadn't thought of that.

'Seat belts aren't meant to be tight in case you have an accident.'

Stupid me.

I asked Marlon for a moment alone with Chunks to discuss the finer points of purchasing a piece of fucking junk. 'I thought you said he deals in *sports cars!*' I hissed, crouching to check the driver's door alignment and wondering if this particular door had ever actually belonged to a Ford.

'He *does!*' Chunks snapped. 'Look, it's got *sport* written on it.' He pointed to a badge declaring 'Fiesta Supersport'.

With his manliness in question, Chunkfest attempted to demonstrate his knowledge of the second-hand car market by testing the dilapidated run-around's non-existent suspension – but in his bright yellow dungarees, basketball boots and backwards-facing baseball cap, he looked like a children's television presenter trying to have sex with a hatchback.

At this point, I should have jumped in the Supersport, swerved around Chunks and disappeared. There's no way Marlon would report the theft to the police as the calories needed to make the phone call were worth more than the car. Yet despite the thug bug's shortcomings, it was the closest thing I'd get to sporty with five-hundred quid and I was desperate to get back on the road.

Mr Cars for the Stars reappeared. 'And *check* this out!' He winked, plugging a cable into the cigarette lighter socket.

A neon purple bulb inside the Fiesta's see-through-plastic gear knob lit up.

Oh, do concentrate, 007!

'If you think that's good, watch *this!*' He flicked a switch and it started flashing.

'I'll buy it,' I told him, ignoring all the warning signs to become the proud owner of half a ton of rust with a fly-zapping gear stick.

I parked the Supersport on one of my two off-road spaces and began fixing the flashing-neon gear knob – the one that came off in my hand on the journey home. Then I phoned an insurance company and gave them the car's particulars. 'Has it been modified at all?' the female agent inquired.

'Just a flashing-neon gear knob,' I replied, figuring honesty was the best policy.

'And is that a permanent fixture in the car?'

'Sometimes ...'

'And was it fitted by a recognised auto electrician?'

'It was fitted by my local sports car dealership,' I assured her.

'But are they *recognised?*'

I thought of Marlon with his crappy facial tattoos. 'Yeah, pretty recognisable.'

After agreeing to forward a cheque for an extortionate amount of money to the company, I taxed the car at the post office and filled it with petrol. Paying off my unauthorised overdraft left me with three hundred pounds but determined to maintain my upward trajectory I drove into town and spent another two hundred on clothes and a duvet. My updated wardrobe consisted of a blue short-sleeved polo shirt, two T-shirts, a pair of Levis 501s, Nike tracksuit bottoms, black skate shoes, boxer shorts and socks.

Back home, I symbolically snipped off my unruly umbrella-shaped fringe and went for a short back and sides using clippers I'd bought at the boot sale. I tried my new clothes on in front of the mirror and couldn't believe how much a fresh set of threads and a no-nonsense trim complemented my new mindset. The old Chris was emerging in mind, body *and* appearance, and I felt *good.* Not born again or any of that jazz and far from the kudos you experience as a young marine with a Lenor halo, snazzy Reeboks and a Phil Collins album, but I felt *something* and it made me happy.

I screwed the sofa back together and covered the folded-away cushions with the blue-and-cream-chequered throw from the skip. After a bit of stretching and smoothing, I pulled the elastic drawstring tight to secure the fabric in place. It was a vast improvement on a pipe-dream of a corner suite and the fabric's gorgeous colour matched my mural. Now to get a job, sort the rest of the house and rekindle some relationships.

The Duel

SMASH! A rock flew through the front window, sending shards of glass everywhere. I jumped up to see the kids attempting to distance themselves from an older lad who stood in the road sporting an imbecilic grin. As I left the house, I could hear Jolene's gang tearing a strip off him.

'Chris, we told him *not* to do it!' Jolene looked worried.

'It's okay. Go ride your bikes.'

I turned to the lad and his smirk waned. 'Mate, why did you smash my window?'

'Dunno ...' He stared at the ground.

Luke ... this lad's missing something from his life. He wants attention but has gone about it the wrong way. Use the Force, Skywalker ...

'What's your name, bud?' I asked.

'Danny.'

'Danny, see all these houses ...' I pointed up and down the street.

'Uh-huh.'

'Do you think any of the owners would let you break their window and not march you straight home to your dad?'

We both knew it to be true. Everyone else in the street would have chucked a police-flavoured wobbler.

Danny's bottom lip trembled.

'You ... don't live with your dad, do you?'

'No,' he replied, confirming the obvious.

'Okay, can you shake my hand and say sorry.'

'Sorry.'

'Right, let's forget about it – and *I'll* pay for the repair.'

As I was measuring up for a new pane, Danny rang the doorbell. 'Chris, I'm really sorry. I don't know why I did it. My nan would kill me.'

'Nan?'

We sat down on the step.

'Uh-huh. I stay with her at weekends – to give my mum a break.'

'Do you see your dad at all?'

'Nah.' Danny blushed. 'He's got a girlfriend and a new baby.'

'That's tough.'

We were silent for a while.

'Dan, adults don't always behave the way they should.'

'I know ...'

'It's not your fault, mate, but you can't take it out on other people, huh? You've got to keep yourself happy, concentrate at school and everything will work out in the end.'

'Thanks, Chris.'

The next day, I stood on the thin strip of front lawn, chiselling glass from the window frame. I heard a bizarre screech and turned to see a young lad of four or five riding a mini BMX along the pavement.

'Alright, wee man?' I wondered what gave.

'What ya doing?' He dropped his bike on my grass.

'Household repairs.'

'Hug-gug-gug-gug!' he chuckled, sounding like Honey Monster and Popeye's lovechild.

I watched as the little lad picked up my brush and attempted to sweep the redbrick sill. Now it was my turn to laugh. 'Erh ... you need to point the bristles down.'

'Hug-gug-gug-gug!' He proceeded to brush more glass into the house than out.

The following afternoon, as I attempted to fix my flashing-neon gear knob – which had ceased to flash neon or change gear – the little chap cycled past. *'Ahhhhhhh!'* he screamed like a banshee again.

The kid appeared to crave attention but lacked even the basic age-appropriate skills to interact with others. 'Alright, mate?' I called after him.

'Hug-gug-gug-gug!'

'So what's your name?'

'Alan.' He clicked an empty cap gun in the air.

'Okay, Alan, Fancy a duel?'

'What's a duel?'

It wasn't the first time I'd answered this question. 'It's how cowboys settle arguments in the Wild-Wild West.'

We went back to back, Alan clutching his toy Colt 45 and me an invisible Howitzer I'd smuggled out of Wan Chai along with a box of see-through shells. I conducted the customary count – *eight... nine... TEN!* – and spun around faster than the Lone Ranger in ballet slippers –

Alan stood on the same spot still facing the other way.

'You gotta *turn* around, Alan!' I twirled my finger.

'Hug-gug-gug-gug!'

'No, not *all* the way.'

'Hug-gug-gug-gug!'

'That's it.' I took a backward stride. 'Now *fire!'*

'Hug-gug-gug-gug!'

He didn't move, so – *'Ack!'* – I shot him, *twice,* although the number of times you shoot someone with invisible ammunition is somewhat irrelevant.

'Found a friend, Alan?' a female voice asked.

I looked up to see a smiling young woman in a doorway across the street. 'Hi!' I grinned and walked over. 'I'm Chris.'

'I'm Emily.' She chuckled. 'That duel was *so* funny!'

Emily's outgoing persona made a refreshing change in this typically reserved city. 'I run the office for a plant-hire firm,' she said. 'I took advantage of the government's rent-to-buy scheme to get this place.'

Since arriving back from Hong Kong, I hadn't met an attractive and unattached female – who I sensed liked me, that is. It was a confidence boost for this box of broken biscuits, a step back to my heady pre-Hong Kong days. The longer our easy conversation flowed, the more I weighed up the state of my house. It wasn't *too* bad now, albeit the floor could pass for an aerial shot of Flanders Fields on Armistice Day. So, 'Fancy a cup of tea?' I tendered.

'Yeah, that would be nice.'

Yes!

While Emily told me more about herself over a cuppa, I remained mindful of my own disclosures. Folks fall into two camps with respect to the devil-feared drugs. Either they're in the know or they're not, and it's best to keep schtum until you ascertain which and establish common ground. A little way into our chat, 'My family are all Witnesses,' she announced, face noticeably tense.

'Okay.'

Only knowing these cats from their door-to-door gig, I was under the impression they didn't associate with infidels.

'But I left the Church to get away from them.'

'Why?'

'They wanted me to abort Alan – my family, I mean – because I wasn't married.'

'Sounds like it was best you left.' I glanced at the awesome little fella pedalling his bike up and down the pavement out front. 'So where's his old man?'

'He lives in Plymouth but wouldn't have anything to do with Alan for years. I begged him to have contact and now they see each other once a week.'

Nob!

You don't need to be a fucking mastermind to know rejection screws kids up. No wonder the lad screamed for attention but lacked the wherewithal to befriend others his age.

Emily was gorgeous and I didn't want our meeting to end. When she asked, 'Do you fancy pizza and wine later?' I let my heart answer for me. To be completely honest, after two years of isolation, I let it shout from the rooftops. I skipped across the road that evening like Fred Astaire on a Connect Four date with Ginger.

Alan was a chubby little chap and the funniest kid I'd ever met. When Emily placed a bottle of Liebfraumilch on the coffee table and returned to the kitchen to check on our food, he picked it up and took a *huge* slug!

Emily reappeared, frowned and took the bottle from him.

'Is that ... *okay?*' I pulled the question-mark face.

'I don't encourage it, Chris, but my upbringing was so strict, I don't mind him having the odd sip.'

The odd sip! I mused, as the wee man roly-polied around the front room pissed. *'Hug-gug-gug-gug!'*

When Alan went to bed, Emily and I chatted on the couch. She told me his old man only saw him for two hours a week and *that* was under duress. How sad when there must be so many non-parents in society willing to act as guardians for neglected kids, folks who appreciate young people and understand their developmental needs.

Emily slid Alan's favourite DVD, *Men in Black*, into the player, but too smitten by her effervescent persona, pixie features and sexy geometry, I didn't pay the film much attention. What I did notice, though, were the three glasses of wine she'd downed before I'd finished my first. *Is this because she's hurting?* I wondered, recalling our conversation of earlier. I don't remember much else, for my aching atoms screamed at me to put my arm around Emily and kiss her ... so I did.

When Emily wasn't working, the three of us spent a lot of time together, visiting the sights around Plymouth and taking trips over the moor to enjoy pub lunches. I'd let Alan steer the car along the quieter country roads and Emily would get in a flap, punching me on my non-feeling arm and screaming in my deaf ear. I met her two brothers, who weren't in the Church, and they treated me like family.

On Thursday evenings, Alan's dad would arrive in the street beeping his horn. The spanner didn't even bother getting out of the car to knock on his son's door. Watching my little friend scurry from the house like a timid animal, I felt like going over and having a word. Not a euphemism, but the throbber obviously didn't understand the damaging effect his insensitivity was having on the boy.

Weekdays after school, Alan would stop at mine until his mum got home. I'd pour him a glass of orange squash and make Bovril on toast – with *brown* bread and *paid-for* spread now that I'd gone up in the world – and we'd watch his favourite TV programs.

One day, Alan arrived on roller skates, legs jiving and pelvis gyrating like an incontinent Elvis. There was an abandoned shopping trolley down the road, so we went to fetch it. I chopped the basket off with an angle grinder and streamed the chassis on a rope behind my bike. It created the perfect stabilised yet mobile environment for the novice skater, Alan holding onto it like a Zimmer frame and not falling over once as I pedalled around the street.

During one of our orange squash and beef-flavoured blowouts, I asked Al what he did with his dad.

'We go in the loft,' he replied.

This was a first. *'Why?'*

'His train set's up there.'

'You go in the loft for *two* hours?'

'Uh-huh.'

'You must like playing with trains.' I smiled.

'I don't play with them.' He frowned. 'My dad don't let me.'

'How come?'

'Because I'm a *stupid* idiot.'

'No, you're *not!*' I squeezed his shoulder.

He shrugged.

'Why don't you say, "Hey Dad, can I have a go?"'

'I don't call him Dad.' Alan shook his head. 'I just say, "Can I do this?" or "Can I do that?"'

After a silence, he looked up. 'Chris … you're more like a dad to me.'

Although I still lacked the confidence to re-enter the workplace, my life had come somewhat back on track. I saw my parents more often and dad no longer called me a dropout now I'd cut my hair. Since our drive from Heathrow, I hadn't mentioned Hong Kong to him – or anyone else. Where would I begin? 'Well, my buddy got hacked up by a vanload of triads wielding meat cleavers. I worked with this *six*-foot-*six* assassin and – *oh!* – did I tell you they wanted me to smuggle gold out of Nepal?'

No, I kept what happened in Asia to myself and stopped opening up to my parents about my substance use because it only upset them. 'You're looking a *lot* better!' they'd say, fishing for a definitive, 'Yeah, I've put that shit behind me.'

'Well …' I'd remain indifferent. 'Not a lot's changed.'

Drugs had played an important role in my development and I wasn't about to stop taking them. My goal was moderation and balancing my inner seesaw. It hurt that my family accepted me now based on false assumptions but hadn't when I'd needed it the most. I continued to reflect on my folks' upbringings in an attempt to understand their worldviews and actions over the years. Not to cast judgement – moving forward was about embracing knowledge, understanding and acceptance – but to make sense of my own struggles and become a better human being.

Sure enough, Marlon had ripped me off with the car. The head gasket blew, so I bought a replacement and a torque wrench and paid one of Ben's workmates a tenner to skim the cylinder head. For the time being, the not-so-Supersport rusted away on my parking space.

'I've been thinking about the Church,' said Emily, as we sat chatting on her stairs. 'You know, I think they might be right about a few things.'

'Go on,' I said, recognising a wobble when I saw one.

'Well, if man evolved from monkeys, how come there are *still* monkeys?'

I should have twigged the Jehovah's Witnesses in her family had got to Emily. They were undermining the girl's newfound happiness by exploiting her vulnerability. Why else would she start spouting the creationist dogma of an organisation whose members had blackballed her? I might not have had all the answers in life but felt sure blind faith wasn't one of them.

Drawing upon my limited knowledge of Darwinian Theory, I explained humans didn't evolve from apes but that we share a common ancestor, adding, 'It's easy to fool someone by employing false logic.' But when Emily immediately regurgitated the straw-chimp argument, I could see she sought acceptance at the expense of enlightenment, a sign we were travelling on different paths in opposite directions.

The following evening, my XXL blinkers firmly on, I crossed the road, looking forward to spending more quality time with my girlfriend and her son. Emily remained cold and indifferent and wasn't the person I'd fallen in love with. 'Things have progressed too fast,' she said. 'It's confusing and best if we split up.'

'I know,' I replied, shrugging my acceptance and heading for the door.

Emily grabbed my arm and looked me in the eyes.

I saw her own were full of tears.

'But you can still see Alan,' she said.

I was glad her child's needs came before those of the Church.

Backwards to go forwards

Derek popped over to ask if I could labour for him on a construction site in Ivybridge. 'Going rate's thirty quid a day,' he said. 'Come over to mine for seven Monday morning.'

I turned up in my military fatigues and leather ski boots, carrying camouflage Gortex waterproofs, a flask of tea and a wrap of sandwiches. Derek seemed pleased I was on time and we hopped in his van for the twenty-minute drive up the A38. En route, he explained that Best Properties, the company responsible for our estate, had contracted him to build two starter homes on a large new development.

I was familiar with labouring work, having mixed 'compo' and shifted breezeblocks on site as a teenager. A major difference now, though, was the weather. It was a wonderfully warm August, whereas before I'd slogged through a bitter winter. In fact, it was so cold the frozen blocks needed prying apart. After a ten-hour day, I'd come home *knackered* and fall asleep in the bath.

Right from the start with Derek, I got stuck in, climbing ladders with a huge hod of bricks on my shoulder and firing up the diesel mixer to keep up the supply of compo. I made it my goal to remain a step ahead of Del at all times so as not to interrupt his wage-earning masonry work. On the Wednesday, as I hosed down our tools, my brilliant boss said, 'Here Chris,' and handed me ninety quid.

'Oh, thanks very much!' I was delighted, happier still to have slotted back into employment so easily.

It was two weeks since I'd binged on speed. *Give it a miss until the weekend, Chrissy. This behaviour always ends in tears.*

But despite my positive self-talk, the ten-pound notes in my pocket wouldn't shut up. *Come on, you deserve a treat and one gram won't hurt.*

On the drive back to Plymouth, I tried to dismiss the idea, only it kept repeating. *Imagine scoring from the Wizard, preparing the spoon, whacking the needle in your arm and feeling sheer bliss.*

Stop! I told myself, but as we pulled into Carroll Road I couldn't think of anything else. I *had* to score to silence my unrelenting anxious internal dialogue.

I felt fine in the morning, considering I'd stayed awake all night painting the mural, adding a gun-toting Hong Kong detective and a sour-faced Chinese villain who looked like Homer Simpson's evil twin.

The Wizard's base was strong old stuff, so I loaded a syringe for my lunchbreak and left the rest at home. Energy abound, I enjoyed every moment on site, shifting more blocks than a high score on *Tetris* and enough sand to recreate the Sahara.

After work, I showered and cycled to Morris's place. I took pride in my relationship with Moz, always seeing the person and never his disability. Back in the day, after spilling out of the Warehouse at 3am, us sweaty wide-eyed clubbers would gather in Toy 'R' Us car park to discuss which after-party to attend. I'd stop Mozzy as he wheeled away to go home alone and persuade him to chuck his chair in the boot of my car and hit a chillout together. If our host had limited space, I'd carry Moz inside and set him down on the sofa.

'Hello, Chris.' He grinned and held up a palm for our Dave-loves-to-rave handclasp.

'Alright, Mozzy?' I reciprocated and then waited for him to wheel his chair backwards down the hall so I could enter the bungalow.

Morris's décor was sparse, his appliances functional yet dated, the kind of living standard popular with Moroccan drug lords – moreover their accountants. At odds with this frugality was a futuristic water-cooled PC, the size of a small horse, super powerful and no doubt the most expensive in town.

While Moz rolled a joint, I tapped my feet to K Klass's floor-stomping classic 'Let Me Show You' and mused on the sole picture hanging on his wall. In watercolour, the painter had attempted to capture the allure of an attractive young woman lying on her stomach, Internet-bride style, a hint of sultry in her otherwise shy eyes.

Sadly, the ill-proportioned Jimmy Hill chin didn't do her any favours, nor the ladyboy hands it rested on. As for the goo-goo eyes, I think one of them had dropped MDMA. Although not a bad effort, 'Lisa' was clearly the work of an amateur – *or* a professional who didn't like her very much. In this instance, it was the former artist, one currently known as Morris.

Having spent most of his life in the shelter of the care system, Morris was vulnerable and susceptible to abuse. At the height of the rave era, Lisa had exploited this innocence, latching onto Moz and fooling him into believing they were an item. Spurred on by her hyaenic mates, the devious witch syphoned off his disability benefit and savings. Fifteen grand went on drugs and they made the poor chap chauffeur them around in his mobility car to buy them. When Morris declared himself bankrupt, she told him straight, 'Fuck *off,* you sad *cunt!* I'm *not* your girlfriend.'

Yet, in denial, my besotted buddy *still* referred to Lisa as his 'missus', and what with my bull-headed views on such deluded practices as ex-partner worship, I found it hard not to get angry.

As Moz passed me the bifta, 'I've been cutting down on the speed,' I told him.

'Hmm ...' He tilted his head and squinted. 'You should cut down a little each day.'

'Nah, that wouldn't work, mate,' I dismissed his jejune reduction of what for me was a complex historical issue.

'If you take *three* grams a day,' Moz went on in his deaf monotone, 'cut down to *two* ... and then *one* – '

'But I don't *take* it every day,' I snapped, wishing he'd stop pulling the rug from under my battered ego.

'Then *don't* ask me for fucking help!' he hoarsed.

'I *didn't* ask you for help, Moz.' I felt exasperated. 'I just wanted you to say, "Well done."'

'*You* need to sort your life out.' He scowled, completely missing the point.

'Oh, and *you* don't!' I nodded at the picture.

'Leave my girlfriend *out* of this.'

'She's *not* your girlfriend, Moz. She *took* you for a ride!'

'Fuck off, *drug* addict.'

Whoa ... steady, tiger! I could handle Morris's limited outlook on life but humiliating me was out of order. 'Moz, you have *no* idea why I'm like this,' I fumed. 'And if you *ever* call me a drug addict again ...'

'Fucking *drug* addict,' he sneered – and *punched* me on the chin!

'Right, *that's* it!' I tipped the fucker's wheelchair over.

Rocky Balboa sprawled across the carpet – not exactly my best moment.

There, if you want to fight, you'll get *no* special treatment!' I collapsed on the sofa, massaging my jaw.

Morris lay motionless.

I honestly hadn't meant to hurt him. In truth, my 'real world' response had been purely tokenistic.

Slowly, he pushed up onto his arms, turned his head ... and grinned.

We burst out laughing.

'Spliff?' He shrugged.

'Why not.'

Having grabbed two hours' kip on Morris's sofa, I shot up the last of the gear in his bathroom, not worrying about the noise I made as my buddy slept soundo in a doped-up sans-hearing-aid stupor.

'Mate, got a different job for you today,' said Derek. 'The site manager needs someone to paint his portacabin.'

'No worries,' I replied, happy to avoid lugging heavy blocks around all day as the effect of the speed dwindled.

Following a recce of the portacabin and paint shed, I decided rainbow-coloured zebra stripes would be best for all concerned. Del reckoned the site manager was on Prozac, so with any luck this effect would cheer him up – even more so if he identified as a gay gold prospector with a penchant for exotic horses.

I filled a paint tray with orange emulsion and began rolling jagged lines a few width's apart on the caravan's flimsy walls. I continued with primrose yellow and lime green and was in the process of finishing sky blue when Derek appeared – and fell about laughing. 'Nice job, Chris. But I don't think the manager will appreciate it.'

'Leopard spots?' I shrugged.

I preserved my masterpiece under a coat of magnolia so future generations of fed-up forepersons could enjoy it. As I set the roller down in the tray, my shoulder blade itched. Giving it a rub, I felt an all-too familiar dot under my fingertip. *Fucking* aliens!

In seconds, I was prickling all over and scratching like a man possessed. I *was* possessed – my body at least. No sooner had I picked a parasite off my skin or spat one out than another emerged. The bloody hut was *full* of the damn things, like some sort of portal to a mother beast lurking on the dark side.

'*Ahh!*' I winced as a bug burrowed into my left heel. Cursing the medical profession, I ripped my boot and sock off and inspected the area of intense pain, but found nothing. I gave the foot a once over and – *Bingo!* – there they were, alien scum clustered in between my toes in some sort of breeding frenzy.

'Alright, Chris?' Derek stared down at me.

'No, mate. I've got these *bloody* flea things all over me.' I showed him the mites having a ging-gang-goolie between my little piggies.

'That's dead skin, mate.' He frowned. 'From wearing boots in this heat.'

Derek was a straight-up guy, only he didn't convince me. I was glad we finished early on a Friday, so I could get home and delouse everything. My problems didn't end there, though, as I opened the front door to that *awful* odour. Its elusive origin was still on the tip of my tongue – or should I say nose, for those pesky space critters were on my tongue. The constant dry spitting and cursing made me sound like a beatboxer with Tourette syndrome.

I inspected the carpets, couch, curtains and cupboards, anything that could possibly harbour the asylum-seeking sadists. I swear I saw tiny holes in all my coverings and furniture, but tiredness wouldn't allow me to concentrate long enough to be certain. *Are the bugs eating up my place and excreting the foul stink in return?* I wondered.

I phoned the council's pest-control unit, gutted to learn the exterminator wouldn't be available until Thursday. In a panic, I called the Wizard to check his 'stock' levels before cycling the two miles over there. I would be breaking my one gram a fortnight rule – *guideline* – but staying awake long enough to disinfect the house took priority.

The phone rang as I arrived home. 'Chris, it's Charlie, the tobacco guy.'

'Can't talk, mate. Can you pop round?'

'Sure.'

I gave Charlie the address and asked him to stop at the Co-op and pick up a large bottle of bleach and some flea powder. He arrived to find me in my boxers in the back garden. After a simplified explanation, 'What did you want to speak to me about?' I asked.

'I need a bod for a baccy run to Belgium, thirty quid cash.'

Ordinarily, I'd have leapt at the offer, but I had to defeat the infestation. 'Count me in for next time, Charlie, yeah?'

'Sure.'

'Right, now pour that bleach over me.'

'Why?' He looked at me askance.

'I've got to get rid of these fucking bugs. You might want to check yourself over when you get home.'

Charlie went into the kitchen and began inspecting the surfaces. 'Chris, there's *nothing* here!'

'There is, mate, but they're so tiny you can't see them. Anyhow, pass me the bottle.'

Charlie appeared hesitant, so having ushered him to the door, I watered the bleach down and splashed it over myself. Then I showered and began the rigmarole of washing clothes and ditching foodstuff. Bread, pasta, porridge and teabags all went in the rubbish. *Should I warn the dustbin men about the possibility of infection?* I wondered.

Determined to get the house ready for the exterminator's visit, I decided to go the whole hog. Anything that could possibly shield these horrible ticks and prevent the poisonous spray from working, I wanted out of the house. Wearing my naval overalls dusted with flea powder, I ripped up the carpets and dragged them in the back yard. Flannels, towels, dishcloths, rarely worn clothes and Mousey's sleeping bag went too. I refrained from torching the pile in case the smoke soiled neighbours' drying washing or spread the contamination in an airburst-like scenario. Instead, I fetched the red plastic can from the Supersport and doused the heap of rubbish with petrol to neutralise the threat.

Next, I brushed down the skirting boards, making sure to get the dirt out from under them. On my way around the lounge, I came up against the black-ash shelving unit. *Can bugs live in books?* I wondered. *Could the aging literature I pinched from the junk room in Wan Chai be harbouring these beastly prickers?* I pulled a Hong Kong guidebook from the shelf and stared at a page, shocked to see alien foetuses gestating in its yellowing pulp. *Fuck!*

Not wanting to throw my precious souvenirs away, I placed them in a bin bag along with an *un*-healthy dose of flea powder.

When high on speed, I chain-smoked roll-ups or at least had one resting in the ashtray – or as I moved about the house, the high-fi's metal casing, the sink or a similarly fireproof object. I built a smoke now, making sure to use a filter because the space squatters had infected my tobacco again. Every time I took a drag, the ciggie crackled and popped and smouldering aliens pinged through the air like fighter pilots ejecting from a burning jet.

This shit was *beaucoup* fucked up and I desperately needed a hit. I tapped some of the Wizard's gear into the spoon and – *piff-*

paff-puff! – sucked the magic potion into a syringe. But when I spiked a vein, the plunger wouldn't budge, no matter how hard I pressed. I inspected the barrel. *Hey…?*

The mix was *full* of frickin mites, like some kind of alien tapioca! The bastards had contaminated my stash. A check of the spoon confirmed this. It was *encrusted* with alien larvae suspended in a dried-up gloop.

Damn! I *needed* this speed. I had to prepare for the exterminator's visit and put this nightmare to bed. I snipped the needle off the syringe's barrel and squeezed the solidified hit into the spoon. I added water and heat and fortunately the sludge liquefied, allowing me to bang it into my arm, aliens an' all.

What was going on? Not content with ruining my home, my job, my tobacco *and* my gear, the space invaders had reduced me to smoking roman candles and injecting Clangers while itching for England. Why hadn't other drug users warned me about this shit? How come I'd never *heard* about it before? Why did everything I touch turn to supersized rat kak?

Unable to bear it in the house, I would decamp to the garden until the exterminator came on Thursday. With any luck, this would prevent the miserable mites burrowing into my bloodstream and working their way to my brain.

Under my bed, I kept an Israeli-made anti-aircraft ammunition trunk fabricated in industrial-grade Kevlar and balsawood. It had a diamond-impregnated carbon-hardened-chromium multi-point locking system originally designed by NASA to secure the snack cupboard on the Space Shuttle. Access to this impenetrable highly-classified chest required a four-dimensional six-pass cryptographic key and wireless intermetric protocol operated remotely from a new generation of 'smart' phones, utilising retinal technology on a virtual private network – *or* from the phone box next to the chippy (BT charges apply).

The trunk housed my extensive collection of leading-edge military hardware, which included a black flame-resistant jumpsuit, matching bandana and sweatbands, hypoallergenic camouflage cream and deep-water piranha repellent. For home defence, I'd opted for Claymores to secure the perimeter, an MP5 machine gun and thirty loaded mags, a low-fat rocket launcher and twenty-five stun grenades.

My weapon of choice was a *jolly* big knife, sharpened on a genuine Gurkha, which had a double-pointing compass secreted in its handle along with a *really* good sewing kit, an inflatable helicopter and map coordinates for all the top-secret NATO bunkers in Serbia, Ukraine, Tajikistan and the Isle of Wight ...

Actually, it was a pink-and-mauve flowery suitcase that had belonged to Sarah. It did contain bits and bobs from my time in the marines, all relatively harmless, like my ninja throwing socks and flameproof mess tins, but most of it was camping gear bought in Blacks.

I pulled a poncho from the case and built a shelter amongst the weeds in the back garden. Bar the flimsy tiger throw, I had no expendable bedding, so I retrieved the petrol-soaked sleeping bag from the rubbish pile. I spent the next three days living outside, eating Cornish pasties from the corner shop and not daring to use my head torch for fear of igniting the petrol or drawing attention to my embarrassing predicament and skinny haggard self.

On Wednesday night, the patch of Heaven above Carroll Road opened and God chucked all the water out. I prayed for the torrent to cease, but it only grew stronger, until the poncho collapsed and rain seeped through my unleaded sleeping bag.

In the morning, I left my overalls and ski boots outside the back door and went inside for a shower. My worldly hopes now rested on the exterminator's visit. When I looked back, *all* the speed I'd taken, *all* the money it had cost and *all* the time spent trying to rid the house of this insidious evil had been a complete *waste!* The only thing I'd achieved was a half-finished mural and a coffee table that stank of fish.

With the Supersport as much use as a tumble drier on the Titanic, I stuck a note to the front door telling the bug busters to let themselves in and then walked to the post office to get my money. The council had given me instructions to vacate the premises for several hours, so I took a bus into town to kill the time. I needed somewhere to sit anonymously and opted for a café upstairs in the pannier market.

As I approached the counter a surge of anxiety gripped my words. *'C-c-cup ... t-t-tea, plea ... se.'*

'Sugar, love?' the woman asked.

Fuck I was embarrassed. Rather than nod and hold two fingers up, I felt the need to explain my dishevelled demeanour so she wouldn't think I was one of those bloody druggies. *'Pr-r-roblem* in *ma ha ... ha ...'* I rasped, pointing a finger over my head in the direction of 'my house', as if this made things clearer.

The old girl squinted at my baseball cap. 'Problem in your ... *hat?'*

'Ma ... ha ...ha ...' I flicked a thumb over my shoulder.

'Problem in your ... *hump!'* Her face lit up like a contestant on *Give Us a Clue.*

'Nah ... nah.'

'... your harbour?'

What?

'... your hamster?'

'Ut ... huh.'

To her credit, she was persistent.

'Your *house!'* She beamed.

'Yeaaah ... the *exterminat ... exterminat ...'*

Oh, fuck it! I dropped the Dalek impression, waved a polite hand and carried my mug to a window seat.

Watching the pedestrians and drivers in the busy shopping street below, I mused on how they managed to go happily about their day without the need to be high on Class A drugs. I envied their levelheadedness and secure frameworks. Although maybe not leading thrilling paint-your-mural existences, these folks lived without constant fear, anxiety and paranoia, appreciating the roofs over their heads and enjoying relationships that didn't revolve around taking, bartering or scamming for drugs. I bet the good people of Plymouth accepted family difference and joined in Sunday lunch without feeling inadequate and awkward. I'd wager they listened with interest to friends' stories, indulging the mundane *and* the predictable, not simply paying lip service while figuring a way to slip off and stab a scabby needle in their arm.

Sure, Plymouth's up-and-at-'ems likely had their addictions too – tea, coffee, food, television, cigarettes, alcohol, gambling or sex – but they didn't allow these vices to derail their lives, a skill I'd yet to learn.

Sipping my cuppa to make the fifty-pence investment last, I felt lonely, empty and powerless. I had a bit part in my own life story and addiction was writing me out of the script. Isolation and emotional troughs I could handle, but *why* did I need to put myself through this and how *long* would it go on?

I pictured the exterminators zapping those bugs. What would they make of my house? Would they think me a weirdo who'd ripped up his carpets and painted strange pictures on the wall? And what if I'd left a syringe lying around? *Maybe they've already reported me to the police!*

I walked to Mutley Plain to see Jenson, the student I'd met in the Sound Factory.

'Yo, *Chris!'* He grinned, looking relieved to see me. 'Come in, man.'

I stepped through the door to find a shithole almost as shit as my shit one – no carpets, peeling paint and appliances handed down from Methuselah's great grandparents. *'Fuck me,* Jens! I thought you drug dealers made a fortune?'

'Erh …' He looked away.

'Go on.'

'Got busted, bro.'

'What!'

'Bouncers caught me in the Sound Factory with a wrap of speed. Got arrested and when the cops searched this place, they found ten more.'

'Just tell the judge it was for personal use.'

'Nah, I had a set of scales here. Proved I was dealing.'

'Oh ...' I frowned. 'What did your parents say?'

'Haven't told 'em. They think I'm still studying History.' Jenson began rolling a joint.

I did my best to console him, saying he'd get off lightly for a first offence, perhaps a fine or community service. While on the subject, 'Jenson, do you know where I can score?' the ton in my skyrocket asked.

'Let's go and see Duane,' were the lemon curds the bangers and mash wanted to hear.

With fair hair, a solid build and more ink than a biro factory, Duane was quite a character – a seriously hard character. He'd recently served three years for dealing and now faced another stretch, having taken the rap when the drug squad nabbed his girlfriend with a kilo of base. 'I don't care.' Duane shrugged his massive shoulders. 'I'll do the time again. How much gear you after?'

'I've got a head gasket to fit ... so say a quarter?' I replied – as if you need three and a half grams of strong amphetamine to fix a car.

Duane pulled a Tupperware box brimming with scorebags of various weight from the kitchen drawer and handed me a dice-sized nugget the texture of snooker cue chalk. Looking me in the eye, 'Chris-mate, this *ain't* your usual bullshit,' he said. 'It's *pure* base, so don't bang up more than a match head or you'll go over.'

'Got ya,' I replied, appreciating the macho man's straightforward approach.

'And if you're replacing a head gasket, I've got sucker cups and paste you can have to grind in the valves.'

'Cheers, bud.'

So that was it. I had the drugs. I had the tools. I had Duane's step-by-step instructions. What could possibly go wrong?

Supersport

When I got off the bus to walk the mile to Carroll Road, something frightening occurred. Crownhill's busy shopping parade began to swim from side to side, its traffic noise morphing into a haranguing hum of hate. All the pedestrians slowly turned and began staggering towards me like a scene from the Zombie Apocalypse.

My heart pounded.

A weird asthma-like sensation clogged my lungs.

Everyone knew I had a drug problem!

'You ...! You ...! You ...!' the encroaching rabble moaned, acid drooling from their cruel twisted fangs.

I froze ...

'Drugs ...! Drugs ...! Drugs ...!' my accusers continued, their carrier bags spilling putrid contempt.

I stood swaying back and forth, fearing collapse as the pavement rushed up at me. *Why are they so angry?* I wondered. *What have I done to them?*

Unless they drove a crappy Ford Escort with a missing window rubber or were passionate about paying for Bovril, the answer was not an awful lot. Okay, so I had an issue with amphetamine, but addiction was hard, *harder* than earning a green beret. You battle through each day in a confused attempt to understand yourself in a world that patently doesn't. It's not exactly the easy option.

Standing on the tube platform in Tsim Sha Tsui that time, I knew drugs would take me to the Edge, most likely over it, and yet I was *still* powerless to resist. I'd accepted the hand of fate, never denying there was a problem. I'd had problems ever since I could remember and problems before that. At least when life chucked adversity my way, I had the balls to grasp it with both hands. Not doing so would be akin to avoiding the Fountain of Knowledge for fear your trousers might get wet.

What did these unhappy shoppers know about me anyway? Where were they when my nineteen-year-old life was on the line for the supposed security of this country? Did they honestly think they could intimidate me with their mob mentality? I was proud of who I was and had as much right to walk this planet as anybody else.

And with that my chest swelled, I *towered* over the shopping parade ... and the scene dissolved into calm normality.

Jeeze, Chris, you had a panic attack ...

As I walked down the road to home, putting the anxiety overload into context helped. It acted as a warning sign, highlighting the dangers of fucking with your mind so much you end up a prisoner of Prozac.

I stepped through the front door, expecting to detect signs of the exterminator's visit – a lingering chemical smell, a dusting of anti-bug powder, perhaps some furniture moved – but there was nothing. It was reassuring they had gone about their business without interfering with mine. Now I could start fixing the car, which would take a couple of hours, but first I needed to fix myself.

Jeeze ...! Before the needle slipped from my arm, I could tell Duane's gear was strong, almost *too* strong, as the industrial-grade grind it produced overrode the anticipated euphoria. With my mind running at warp-speed, I had to grab hold of the here-and-now and make the investment worth it.

The Supersport's cylinder head rested on the shopping trolley chassis in the kitchen. I wiped grinding paste around the fuel-mixture inlets and exhaust-gas outlets and slotted the valves back in by their stems. Sticking the sucker cup to the first valve, I had no idea how long or hard to grind, so I twizzled away for five minutes at each and then swapped to a lighter grade paste as Duane had instructed. I felt as if I was making progress, only I didn't know what constituted a ground-in valve and what didn't.

It had honestly seemed an easy job, yet falling darkness said otherwise. Believing I was almost finished, I ignored Mother

Nature's subtle hint and laboured through the evening.

The problem was I needed a proper clamp to compress the valve springs, but with no such luxury at hand, I resorted to using one of the slotted arms from the headboard on my bed. Placing the slot over the valve stem and spring and applying pressure with my knee worked well. However, the collets kept pinging out and what should have been a simple task rolled on for ages.

Finally, I had the cylinder head reassembled, only it was now 2am, pitch black outside and pouring with rain. Using all my strength, I pushed the Supersport off its parking space, rolling the car back and forth until the passenger side hugged the garden fence. Then I set up a poncho and spotlight, determined to persevere through the miserable wet night.

When daylight arrived, I had the head bolted down and the rocker cover filled with oil. I adjusted the tappets to the recommended settings in Haynes' *How to Fix Your Completely Shit Car While off Your Head on Mental-Strength Drugs* manual and reconnected the electrics and cooling system. With a sense of excitement and accomplishment, I turned the ignition key –

Nothing... except the starter motor coughing like a coal-mining dog. *Damn!*

Back to the *grinding* board. I knew the leads and hoses were good, so the problem had to be the valves. Obviously, I hadn't ground them in enough. Duane said you could save time by using an electric drill, which seemed a logical course of action. So off I went once more, removing the hoses, leads, rocker cover and cylinder head and fetching my Black and Decker.

Despite numerous attempts, I was still at it two days later. My journey out of addiction had taken a humongous U-turn and the house was once again an utter dump. The lack of flooring gave the place a derelict feel and the oil stains, greasy tools and cigarette butts strewn about the messy kitchen made it look like the sort of horror movie where people have body parts lopped off by toothless halfwits.

By the third evening, I was *hanging* out my arse – to use a marine's parlance. In the pouring rain, I huddled shivering under the poncho, attempting to bolt the bloody head block back on for the umpteenth time. Not having eaten for a week, I'd lost so much weight I was the lightest I'd ever been as an adult. My wizened cheeks sucked endlessly on roll-ups in a desperate bid to focus my mind and complete this troublesome endeavour. I glugged pint after pint of sugary sweet tea and injected countless syringes of the ridiculously strong amphetamine.

And then – no pun intended – it came to a head …

I turned the ignition key to hear the now familiar sound of the struggling starter motor but no combustion at the plugs. When the battery finally died, I stood leaning against, or *clinging* to, the engine bay like a drunk at the bar. I was hallucinating like Timothy Leary and had no idea how to proceed. At eleven o'clock that evening, I still clung to the car, still clung to the dream of fixing the thankless shitbox, still clung to the notion speed helps you achieve anything.

A neighbour's porch light flickered on. I looked over my shoulder to see a bloke in his dressing gown walking towards me. His name was Ian, but despite living in the same street for five years, we had never met formally. I knew he was a good man, because he'd knocked on the door one day to let me know I'd left my keys in the lock and another time having spotted Morris crawling from his car and struggling to reach the bell.

'You alright, Chris?' Ian's eyes wandered over the scene as if taking in the aftermath of a drone strike on a scrapyard following a tornado.

'Yeah, fine, mate.' I was pleasantly surprised he knew my name.

'So what's going on, then?'

'Oh, the head gasket's gone and –'

'Hah!' He turned to look me in my bloodshot eyes. 'Do you think I'm stupid?'

For some reason, I hoped he was.

'What are you on?' he continued.

'How do you mean?' I squirmed, wishing he'd borrow a cup of sugar and go away like a normal neighbour.

'You *know* what I mean. You've been out here for three nights now and haven't slept a wink. Look, I used to smoke a bit of weed and pop a few pills in the navy, so I know the score.'

Your heart drops heavily and often when you have a drug problem. Now was no different.

'W-w-why do you ask?' I glanced around. 'Have the neighbours been saying anything?' I began to worry the street might be forming some sort of witch-hunt.

'Chris ...' Ian's voice took on a gentle edge. 'If you must know, a couple of the neighbours have been gossiping, but you don't have to worry about them. They're petty-minded and could never understand a guy like you.'

'How do you mean?' I realised I was shaking.

'How many of them ever bother to kick a ball around with the kids? How many of them ever give the little ones their time? Those kids *fucking* idolise you, mate! They fucking *adore* you! I see them waiting on your doorstep when you're out, and they're saying, "Oh, we can ask *Chris* that" and *"Chris* will do that for us." Fucking *hell,* mate! It's fucking *special. You're* fucking special.'

Christ, I couldn't believe what I was hearing. I thought Ian was coming over to give me a lecture on Beelzebub's talcum powder, but for him to say *this.* It left me gobsmacked. Having spent the last two years keeping the faith in myself, everyday promising I would find my answers, well, I think I'd found them.

'Now' – Ian patted me on the arm – 'fuck off inside and get some sleep.'

When I looked up, he was gone.

Something inside me changed. Fixing this crap-ass car no longer seemed important. A simple meeting with a stranger had given me the direction I needed. Sure, there was still stuff I had to work on, but I felt like one of those Buddhist monks on the path to enlightenment, having gained enough understanding to see life for what it was and appreciate why people acted the way they did.

Struck by Ian's kindness, I walked into my front room. A shockwave of emotion hit me and my nose promptly exploded. Blood sprayed everywhere, all over my jazzy sofa cover and mural. I collapsed on the bare chipboard floor and the floodgates crashed open.

I cried for letting the drugs fool me *again.* I cried for having a brother I loved dearly but couldn't explain my feelings to. But most of all, I cried because a kind man thought enough of me to tell me I was okay ... and this meant I didn't have to fight anymore.

Wired on Duane's ultra-strong base, I couldn't sleep, so I called Elsie, hoping she might be awake.

'Hello lovey!' She sounded pleased to hear from me. 'Are you okay?'

'My nose just exploded,' I said through the tears.

'Oh *darling!* What happened?'

As I retold events, my sobs turned into a giggle, then a chuckle, and before I knew it Elsie and I were bellowing with laughter. As two years' worth of stress flowed out of me, it felt wonderfully therapeutic. I hadn't guffawed like this since Old Ron and I put Neil's poisonous viper in the bath!

In the morning, I went back out to my defunct Supersport. Logic told me I had no chance of fixing it. Addictive logic told me to shut up, inject some more of Duane's lethally strong speed and crack on.

It was no good. The wind blew right through my bloodied overalls, licking the warmth from my emaciated frame. I went inside to make a cup of tea but forgot what I was doing and ended up married to the kitchen counter for hours. As darkness fell, I replaced the block for the tenth, twelfth or perhaps fifteenth time ... with no success. I sighed and reached across the engine bay to grab my torque wrench, but found myself lying on the wing of the Fiesta staring into space.

A car pulled into the road. I didn't take much notice as I was in a trance, trying to sum up the will to remove the head yet again. The spotlight flickered and a familiar face appeared under the tarpaulin. 'Hello, mate,' its owner said softly.

My jaw dropped. *'Lloyd!'*

Lloyd was one of my oldest friends. We'd been to school together and joined the military within weeks of each other. Although far from an angel, Lloyd was one of life's good fellas, a real solid character. He'd left the army about the same time I did the Royal Marines, yet we hadn't caught up until now.

'What's up with this, then?' He browsed under the bonnet.

'Head gasket's gone.' I waved a screwdriver at nothing in particular. 'Been at it a few days now.'

'I can see that.'

His kind but concerned tone told me this wasn't about head gaskets or screwdrivers. It was time to fess up. 'I've developed a bit of a drug problem, mate.'

'I know ...'

I stood there trembling with exhaustion, unable to look my old friend in the eye.

'We *all* know,' he said, referring to the guys we'd grown up with. 'But no one wants to barge in and upset ...'

As Lloyd's words tailed off, I saw he was fighting back tears. I might have been on wake-up call number fifty-seven, but this was the biggest shocker to date. I could see my dear mate was terribly upset, and not just to find me in this state, but upset for *me.*

It was the last straw. I was cold, hungry, tired, wet and miserable. I was jobless, penniless and lonely. I'd tried to do it my way and failed *miserably.* I'd done a good job of cutting down on the gear and life had certainly improved, but I was in danger of letting the ground I'd gained slide.

I might be stubborn. I might be willing to push the boundaries of acceptability to discover myself. But I wasn't stupid. It was now or never. I had to seize the offer of genuine friendship stood in front of me. I had to break the pattern. I needed to become *me* again. I had to leave my comfort zone and get the hell out of Dodge.

'Lloyd … can I come and stay?'

'Awwh, *mate!*' He made the hallelujah pose. 'Of *course* you can! I wanted to ask but … *you* know. I didn't want to upset you.'

I'd known Lloyd would say yes. He was nothing like the sketchy characters I'd surrounded myself with this last year. He was no-nonsense ex-military, but most of all he was my friend, the oldest one I had.

'Right, let's go,' he ordered. 'Leave all that shit.'

Not wishing to appear rude, I told Lloyd I couldn't rush out of the house. I needed to make sure Emu would be okay and all my trash secure. In my present state, I might forget to shut a window or lock a door. The last thing I wanted was to see someone cycling around town on a Raleigh Shopper next week dressed in a monkey costume.

But most important of all, I had to finish the last of the gear. Lloyd sat in silence, not judging as I prepared a syringe. I wasn't taking the piss. I wanted him to see how I'd been living my life, the depths to which I'd sunk, to understand what he was taking on. In short, I wanted him to accept *me* for who I was – no holds barred.

'Don't bother packing a bag,' said Lloyd. 'I've got loads of clothes.'

'Okay, let's go,' I replied, but climbing into Lloyd's convertible Beetle I couldn't remember if I'd locked the front door.

'Go and check,' Lloyd said patiently.

I made sure it was locked and got back in the car.

Lloyd went to pull away.

'Hang on!'

'What is it?'

'Sorry, mate, I can't remember if I locked it.'

'Okay, go and see.'

This happened three more times. I'd obviously locked the door. I just couldn't *remember* doing it. In the end, I told Lloyd to just drive, and as we headed for his quaint cottage overlooking the picturesque Barbican Quay, I felt I was coming home.

Oasis

Lloyd's cottage was an oasis of calm, like stepping from a shack in war-torn Mogadishu into the penthouse suite at the Ritz-Carlton, Beverly Hills. The place was immaculate and smelled fresh and homely. Even the troublesome seagulls, hated by local residents, added a holiday feel to the experience. It was definitely *not* Carroll Road. I'd left my home to *come* home and I could tell in my heart a new phase of my life had begun.

Lloyd ushered me into his smartly decorated spare room, its majestic sea view sandwiched between Laura Ashley curtains. The spotless duvet had a crisp new feel and was three times thicker than my thin clumpy rag. Beneath my socked feet, the pile on the sage-green carpet was deep enough to bounce on. Simple still-life prints decorated the walls, a hint the person who owned this house had nothing to prove. I already dreaded the day I'd have to go home.

Lloyd pulled open the shoe drawer on a distressed wardrobe. 'These are my spare clothes. Help yourself.'

Like a native of a recently discovered Amazonian tribe, I picked up a light-blue pair of Next cotton boxer shorts, put them to my nose and breathed in the luxurious fragrance of fabric conditioner. I felt a sudden urge to cleanse my filthy body and scrub my grease-blackened fingernails. 'Lloyd, can I have a shower?'

'Sure,' he replied, throwing a pair of jeans and a chunky leather belt at me.

Expensive toiletries filled Lloyd's jazzy bathroom. When I stepped back out, having used a reservoir's worth of steaming hot water and dried off with an elephant-sized soft towel, I wore the jeans with the belt pulled tight and turn-ups in the legs. I didn't care. I should have been experiencing a severe comedown and would ordinarily be chain-smoking marijuana, but instead I felt fresh, invigorated and a completely new man.

'Just do me one favour, Chris,' said Lloyd, seeing me eyeing the kitchen cupboards. 'That's *my* food in there.' He pulled the doors open to reveal an edible bonanza. '*I* bought it. *I* paid for it. Help yourself to *anything* you want – just *don't* fucking ask me, okay?'

This broke me. It was the kindest gesture I'd experienced in years. I put my arms around my buddy and hugged him.

Lloyd looked a little off-footed. I think like many blokes in Britain, he was still confused by society's outdated notions of masculinity, not to mention our macho military conditioning. Immerse yourself for a night in the dance scene's emancipating harmony and all that homophobic nonsense gets kicked right out of the window along with the horse it rode in on.

Despite the public's pigeonholing of drug users as evil losing wasters, I think Lloyd was finding my recently opened mind and independent thought something of an education, although this must have seemed an incongruity in view of my battered physical and mental state. Plus, now that I was in company, I'd developed a neurotic need to constantly explain myself, even stupid things like the reason I was going upstairs or why I tied my shoes the way I did.

Lloyd whacked a tray of battered cod and chips in the oven and a bowl of frozen peas in the microwave. Unquestionably, it was the most delicious meal I'd eaten since the business banquets in Hong Kong. Afterwards, he plucked a bottle of cognac from an array of spirits on the sideboard and poured us generous shots. Then he reached up to a shelf and grabbed a joint-making box.

'Here!' He tossed a blim of squidgy black to me.

Bonus!

While I rolled a doobydoo, Lloyd leant over and pulled a book from his white-glossed shelves. '*Mr Nice* by Howard Marks.' He flashed me the cover. 'He was Britain's biggest ever hash smuggler. It's an amazing read.'

Wow! The nineties sure had been a decade of openness with respect to substance use. Everyone seemed to be on drugs or singing or writing about them – or all three.

Leafing through the pages of Howard's memoir, I recalled Richard's suggestion I write a book. The thought definitely appealed to me, but I only had a GCSE in English, from a correspondence course taken in the Royal Marines. Besides, what the hell would I write about? I certainly couldn't imagine ever meeting Howard or ending up in his literary league.

Lloyd climbed the tiny staircase to go to bed, leaving me pleasantly tipsy and stoned. 'Can you square away the sofa before coming up?' he asked.

I took extra-special care to arrange the throw without a single crease and then hit the hay myself ... and slept like a baby.

In the morning, I watched in admiration as Lloyd washed and stowed every item of kitchenware before leaving for work. Having used his army experience to land a well-paid job operating cranes, Lloyd was making a real go of it. I envied the discipline he applied to his day, even the simple things like getting out of bed at six-thirty every morning.

As he went out the door, Lloyd paused. 'You're gonna get down the Job Centre today, yeah?'

Whoa! I wasn't expecting this. I mean, I was *ill*. How could I *possibly* work? I was getting over a *chronic* drug problem. I needed to *sort* my house out. I had to *write* a CV. I didn't have *any* skills. I had *no* experience to offer an employer. I *didn't* have a car ...

I *didn't* ...

I *didn't* ...

I *didn't* ...

Fuck ... I was making excuses, because in truth my confidence had taken a knock. When you've lived on a sofa bed for eighteen months, sticking illegal drugs in your arm, surviving on daytime TV and Bovril, you don't exactly feel prepared to go tell a potential employer how bloody awesome you are.

I could see what Lloyd was doing, though. He wasn't going to indulge my perceived barriers. He was taking the military 'no mess tins' approach and, irrespective of my flagging confidence, I appreciated it and would never let him down. 'Sure, Lloyd.' I smiled. 'I'll scoff some cereal, clean up and get myself over there.'

If you're sixteen and looking to join the British Army then the Job Centre is definitely the place for you. If you have the culinary skills to be a chef in the Scilly Isles (bed, board and weekday off), you're bang on the money. If you're a machine operator – apparently not the fruit, vending or washing type – you're onto a winner. If you're an uneducated ex-bootneck whose last employer was the Hong Kong triads *and* who even managed to fuck that up, then you may as well look for a job as a cross-dressing penguin translating Swahili into doughnuts on Mars.

Scanning the cards pinned to the boards in the Job Centre, I felt the way I had most of my adult life, *paralysed, helpless* and *lost.* I believed I had the potential for some sort of vocational accomplishment, but it was as if I kept missing the boat, taking the easy option or having bad luck. The lack of avenues in the employment exchange only served to confirm this, so dejected I trudged back to the cottage.

Later that evening, 'Well, there's a job going at South West Crane Hire,' Lloyd referred to his employer. 'You'd definitely get it as it's nothing to do with operating cranes.'

'Go on.'

'They've got a contract with the dockyard. You work in a chain gang loading food onto ships. It's hard – *really* hard. In fact' – Lloyd's chin tremored – 'they call it *Niggers,* because you work like a ...'

Lloyd wasn't condoning the racist workplace parlance. He was simply outlining the nature of the role and highlighting its thuggish environment. They could call the job what they liked, though, because I needed to get back into employment and couldn't care less about starting at the bottom of the shit pile.

'I'll speak to Pete, the team manager, and put a word in for you,' said Lloyd.

'Cheers, mate.'

'Most of the lads sign on the dole,' said Pete during my interview –

although it wasn't really an interview, more a formality for anyone desperate enough to be sat in front of him.

The poor guy looked uncomfortable throughout, probably because he had to refrain from swearing. The way he swallowed hard when referring to the 'contract' told me everyone in the workforce used the 'other' name.

'But you should tell the Dole you're working here,' Pete continued, 'because they ask us for a list of our employees.'

He swallowed hard again, a sign *none* of the benefit claimants in the chain gang informed the Department of Social Security, meaning the 'list' was obviously fudged to anonymise them.

Nonetheless, I figured South West Crane Hire must sacrifice the odd lamb to appease the DSS, so I decided to declare my employment. I'd read the rules about working while claiming Income Support and it appeared I could do sixteen hours a week without receiving a financial penalty. Besides, surely the DSS would be pleased I was easing back into employment having rehabilitated myself from chronic ill health. I said goodbye to Pete and left the portacabin to go and write them a letter.

Chain Gang

On Saturday, I moved back into my house. After a week of sheer extravagance and companionship with Lloyd, stepping over the threshold at Carroll Road wasn't exactly cheese on toast, but to keep my reformation on track I took it on the chin.

Without a pause and high on only life, I stowed the engine parts in the boot of the car and dumped the remaining junk in the garden. My actions were as much symbolic as they were for appearances and I would worry about what to do with it all later. After this, I washed and stowed a lifetime's worth of dishes – my old lifetime, that is – and scrubbed the blood off the sofa cover.

As the place took shape, Chunks stopped by with his Mad Max petrol strimmer. He annihilated the jungle, front and back, and took the rubbish to the tip. It was a hugely touching gesture, a seminal and deeply ratifying moment in my recovery, particularly as my 'true' friend had a banging beer head. He'd simply wanted to help me get my life together and I would never forget it.

Pete rocked up in a company van, saving me a four-mile cycle ride. He checked I'd sorted out my ID badge with the dockyard's security office and then drove to Camel's Head, one of four policed entrances in the yard's towering stone walls. It seemed strange going into a naval base as a civilian. The last time I passed through a dockyard's gates was while serving on HMS *Invincible*.

I wasn't here to reminisce about the past, though. I was here to load food onto ships and submarines and keep my mouth shut, then take my thirty quid, go home, put the telly on and smoke a joint. And that's what I did ... and I thoroughly enjoyed it.

My workmates were a right bunch of pirates – which is ironic because we were loading stores onto ships and not taking them off. Seriously, these guys were depriving a prison of inmates. All they talked about was drugs and football and every other word was fuck, fucking or cunt. Tattoos were in vogue – particularly self-inked ones – but dental hygiene was out. Puma did a roaring trade with the lads, as did Adidas, Nike and Golden Virginia. Spitting had evolved into a method of communication – especially when discussing our employer – and *everything* was 'shit'. The company was shit, the job was shit, the dockyard was shit, the ships were shit, the stores were shit, the dole was shit, even Plymouth was shit – which was a complete load of shit because none of these pretenders had ever been anywhere else.

I wasn't complaining, though. I'd narrowly escaped prison in the past and felt at home here. Despite my light-hearted observations, I didn't judge the boys and they didn't me. There was an unspoken understanding on the chain gang that you knew your place in society – at the bottom – which was fine by yours truly.

There was a lot of hanging around for lorries to arrive from food warehouses and ships late back to port. On standby too were the yard's tenacious little tugboats, moored in pairs along the granite-block wharf. Like orcas attacking a whale, they would bully the unwieldy war canoes into position alongside with their fat fish-lip bows. We would sit along the dock and crack out the roll-ups, chatting, joking and watching schools of mullet swimming lazily in the mucky water below.

When the gaffer gave the shout, we'd form a long snaking line from the supply wagon, up the gangway and down the ladders into the bowels of the ship, where the cold-storage rooms were located. Then it was a straightforward job of chucking the boxes of mostly frozen food to one another and making sure you weren't the one-handed juggler that fucked up the party. We were paid for an eight-hour day, starting at 7am, but usually finished by midmorning.

The submarines fascinated me. I'd never been on one while in the forces and yet here I was as a civilian inside an infamous, highly classified sea wolf and able to access every cabin and compartment. Other than the matelot chef coordinating the stores party, there was no one else around.

I couldn't believe how tiny they were. In films, submarines look like leviathans with operations rooms the size of dancehalls, the crew spread around having a banyan or doing a bit of clay pigeon shooting. In reality, the control centre on a modern hunter-killer consists of two dentist-like chairs facing a bank of electronics and a sophisticated digital periscope. There's just enough room for two hunger strikers and their vegan dog.

A small portacabin sat over the hatchway on deck, protecting it from the elements and providing a designated sentry point for the person on gangway duty. On the inside wall, someone had scrawled 'What's the similarity between HMS *Lunchard* and a stripper? ... They both wear fishnets.'

Typical of dark military humour, it was a reference to HMS *Lunchard* standing accused of dragging a fishing trawler, the *Hedero,* to the bottom of the ocean with all hands lost, a tragedy for Plymouth's close-knit seafaring community, one the MOD continued to deny.

Sadder still, following her recovery in a salvage operation, the *Hedero* sat not more than a hundred metres away along the wharf. A section of the boat's rusting barnacle-covered railing bent downwards, and you couldn't help but wonder if it was where the net pulled those brave men to their deaths.

Pete phoned me most nights to ask if I could work the following day. I accepted every shift without fail, grafting hard and getting to know the lads.

My workmates conversation usually centred on football. I had represented the Royal Marines against the Royal Navy while on ship, but never having supported a team, I knew little about the league. So when engaged in soccer banter, I stuck with my usual tactic of spouting irrefutable statements. '*Well,* the problem with Plymouth Argyle is there's *not* enough investment in the club.' I'd shake my head like an old boy on the terraces. '*Well,* the problem with the Premier League is there's *too* much money in the game.'

I soon made friends – and hooked up with an old one. Ollie was a drug dealer we used to score pills off back in the day. 'Trying to put all that behind me.' He gobbed into the dock. 'Just get pissed and stoned now.'

Over the coming weeks, I found myself musing on Ollie's statement. Getting pissed and stoned certainly seemed the lesser of the evils out there. Alcohol was legal and socially acceptable and marijuana paled into insignificance compared to chemicals.

Tito was the youngest lad in the gang. We hit it off immediately. Gentle and naïve, he'd been a professional footballer before a knee injury stopped his career. He was a bit slow, which came across as endearing. Every time I told him a rubbish joke, he would crease up. The others bullied Tito, so I buddied up with him and employed a bit of reverse psychology to bring him into the group and make anyone who tried to pick on him look a dick. The lads didn't want to bully him, but they were afraid of Malco, who'd make their lives a misery if they didn't.

Malco was a walking advert for why prison doesn't work. Built like the dockyard wall, he wore the most shit gold jewellery and had a flotilla's worth of wank tattoos. He did, however, hold three impressive world records – for using the words 'focking', 'cont' and 'focking cont' more than anyone else in history. Malco was commander-in-chief of Plymouth's vicious football gang, The Central Element, 'TCE', which when combined with his solid physique and mouthiness made him the alpha male. Cut Malco any slack and he would string you up with it like a verbal punch bag. I knew if this happened we'd end up at fighting stations.

Our working party spread along the dockside and up the gangway of a Type 22 Frigate.

'We have to take the stores down through this hatchway,' said the matelot chef, pointing at a big hole in the deck. 'I'll need someone strong on the ladder because it's near vertical.'

'I'll do the focker,' Malco grunted, seizing the chance to look hard.

I took up position below Malco and could see he was having trouble balancing on the rung. The golden rule of the gang was *never* slow down the chain, so when handed a box you shifted it to the next guy as fast as humanly possible. If you caused a logjam, you could expect the Chorus of Wrath and days or even weeks of pisstaking.

Malco only had one free hand as the other gripped the hatchway's combing. This meant he had to rest each box on his shoulder and slowly bend his knees until I could grab it. Rather than exercise initiative and tell the chain to ease up, Wayne, the numpty above, handed the boxes down ever faster.

'Ya fockin *cont!*' Malco spat his frustration, not wishing to lose face by asking everyone to slow down.

I fought not to smile.

'Fockin *bastard!*' His face flushed as a box of kippers slipped from his grasp.

I stopped the goods crashing on deck and then spun them like a rugby ball to Tito.

Tito received it like a pro and grinned.

'Conting, fockin ... *bastard!*' cursed Malco, increasingly embarrassed.

By now, he was sweating like a sex offender and still unable to tell Wayne to go steady. He began fishing around with his foot, looking for something to balance on and settling for a fire extinguisher bracket.

Oblivious to the poor bloke's struggles, Wayne shouted from above, *'Malc,* speed it up!'

The football thug's face took on the look of a sunburned volcano being squeezed by the coulees.

Rather than burst out laughing, 'Oy, *Weeyne!*' I yelled in a thick Plymouthian accent. 'Bloke's working his fockin *ass* off! E's got one foot on a *doobry,* the other on a *firkin* and 'e's oldin onto *thin* fockin air! And you, ya cheeky *cont,* is asking 'im to speed the *fock* up!'

As laughter roared through the compartments, Malco threw me an appreciative nod, and I knew we'd never have a problem.

Papa Smurf

Jenson rang. 'Chris, I need somewhere to stay.'

'Come on over.'

When Jenson arrived he was no longer the cocky young man I'd met a few months previous. After I'd dumped his bags in the spare room, he brought me up to speed. 'Court case is in two weeks, Chris. I'm *fucking* shitting myself.' He rocked back and forward on the sofa, clutching his knees and staring at my stained carpet.

'Remind me, what were you busted with?' I remained standing, casting half an eye over the mural.

'Only ten wraps of piss-weak speed.' Jenson's eyes flicked to my tobacco pouch on the fish-box table. 'But it's the scales and paper wraps they'll get me for.'

Passing him the baccy, 'Jenson, everyone's getting done for dealing,' I said. 'Ten wraps is nothing. Seriously, I reckon you'll get a slap on the wrist. Maybe a fine or community service.'

'I'm not so sure ...' Jenson shook as he rolled a smoke. 'The old bill are going after the dealers. What's the point if the judges aren't gonna bang 'em up?'

'Mate, you're *not* going to prison!' I chuckled. 'They haven't got room for small fry. What did your parents say?'

Jenson took a drag of his roll-up and blew out a silvery-brown plume. 'I haven't told 'em.'

'Oh ...'

'No point bringing them into it in case I do get off. My old man would go *fucking* mental and my old dear wouldn't know what hit her.'

You're brave going through this on your own, I thought.

'Do you need to earn some cash?' I asked. 'You don't have to pay anything to stay here, but it could come in handy if you get fined.'

'Not half, bud.' Jenson nodded. 'Spent me grant ages ago.'

I told him about the job with South West Crane Hire, saying

I'd have a chat with Pete.

I'd stuck to my original plan and only taken speed twice since staying with Lloyd – both times a gram when my benefits arrived. With my newly aligned mindset, it hadn't been difficult. My confidence and relationships had improved because I wasn't on a comedown most of the time. The house still bore the scars of someone who'd spent too long on the flipside, but it was in a much better state than before, plus I had food in the cupboards. My new clothes gave me a natural buzz, particularly when out and about, and I hadn't lifted up any shops since the time I'd narrowly avoided getting caught.

I saw my addiction for what it was – a learned-psychological condition, an ingrained pattern of behaviour, similar to Pavlov with his poodles. I understood that if I simply *considered* scoring amphetamine, chemicals in my brain would automatically convince me it was the answer to life's problems. This might well have been true in the early days of taking the drug, but now all the evidence pointed to the contrary.

I didn't have complete control over this false logic yet, but the improvement in my quality of life helped put things in perspective. To stop the endorphins in my brain from firing up in the first place, I mentally stamped on any thought of buying gear. I wouldn't even watch anything about drugs on TV. I'd swap the channel or hurl myself at the washing-up bowl. Slowly, I was reprogramming my mind to look beyond the instant gratification a hit of speed produced and consider the negative consequences.

My life fell into a pattern of one gram a fortnight – taking Pavlov's doggies for a walk, so to speak. It may have set my recovery back a day or two, but I could handle that. The downtime I spent crashed on the sofa simply bolstered my determination to keep on the up.

I was proud of myself. I'd managed to come through the hell of addiction on my own. *I'd* worked it out. Bar Lloyd, no one had gone out of their way to help me – no family, no friends, no medical professionals and no support groups. I was also pleased to have maintained a balanced perspective on drugs.

My childhood had been more complex than most people could ever understand. It set me on a naive trajectory guided by delusion and greed, along which I'd believed making a stupid fortune – zeroes in a bank account – would make me happy.

Having watched me travelling an ill-judged path, a slave to my insecurities, Mother Nature could see I needed taking down a peg or two. She'd sent her enforcer, 'Buster Addiction', around. He'd hauled me up by the shirttails, thrown me on the ground and while stomping on my macadamias shouted, 'Thrall, wake the *fuck* up, man!'

Well, I was up *and* a better, stronger and wiser man than the one that went down – or at least on the path to what a more educated individual would recognise as enlightenment. I may have taken the long way around – probably the only way you can – but it was better than stagnating in a boring career and never finding the real me. My motto became, 'Don't be an angel. Just get some balance back in your life'. And the great thing about having a stable life and a rational view on drugs ... is that you can do more of them.

'I think this is one, Jens!' I stood on a south-facing bank on Dartmoor holding up what I hoped was a liberty cap mushroom.

'Are you sure?' Jenson eyed it warily. 'It hasn't got the black ring around it.'

'It's got a bit of a ring.' I twisted the stalk in my fingers. 'It might be one.'

Why I was trying to convince myself, I don't know. If it was a magic mushroom the amount of psilocybin it contained wouldn't get an ant high and the wrong variety would likely kill us. After an hour of hunting, the word desperation came to mind.

One of the lads at work had told me it was magic mushroom season and a good place to find them was Cadover Bridge on Dartmoor. Having borrowed my brother's Austin Metro, Jenson and I stopped off at the library to find a book on fungi so we'd know what to look for. Everything had gone to plan, except we couldn't find a single psychedelic shroom.

Wandering along a bank of heathland sandwiched between an opencast China-clay mine and farmers' fields, we bumped into another hedonistic hunter, a middle-aged chap with an Asda tracksuit and gold earrings.

'Found any, bud?' I asked, knowing full well he wasn't out for a spot of fresh air.

A look of alarm came over him. 'Found any *w-w*hat?' he asked.

Inca gold ... the lost city of Atlantis ... two rhinos breakdancing – what the fuck do you think, you shaky dancer?

'Mushrooms,' I clarified.

'Yeah, I got these.' With a grin, the bloke reached into his plastic bag and held up two enormous white umbrellas – of the species *Breakfast.*

'Mate, I mean *magic* ones.' I cut through his sketchy bullshit.

'Oh!' He pulled out a smaller carrier.

Jenson and I peered into it, our faces lighting up like gold prospectors. There were three liberty caps – enough for an ant and two mates.

'You've got to get your eye in,' said the guy. 'Once you've seen one, you'll see 'em all!'

Yeah, all three of them, you fucking party animal!

We spent the next two hours scouring the hillside. It was true what our man had said. You first needed to spot a tiny lone butter-coloured umbrella in amongst the cattle-grazed grass for your brain to get a make on the rest. Having done that we found *shitloads* – about nine.

Downhearted, we trudged back to Ben's Metro, Jenson carrying our ennead of psilocybinic soldiers in a plastic four-litre milk container I'd cut the neck off. We had one of these handy carriers apiece – talk about optimistic.

I'd parked the car in the only available spot on the narrow country road, the entrance to a farmer's field. 'Just taking a piss, Jens.' I leant on the five-bar gate.

In mid-stream, I perused the constellations of bright-yellow buttercups sprouting from an acre of lush green grass. Tuned into the flower's alluring colour, my gaze hovered over a golden dot on a cowpat frisbee. *Could it be?*

I vaulted the rusty barrier, heading for the khaki splodge, delighted to find a mind-warping mushroom poking out of it. No sooner had it landed in the milk container than I spotted another ... *and* another ... *and* another ... until at a rough estimate, I'd say there were fifty party parasols in that patch alone.

'Jennns! Get over *here.'*

By the time Jenson joined me, I'd plucked them all. *'Look!'* I shook the container and immediately spotted a further cluster.

After an hour of combing, we must have picked every shroom in the field, our makeshift receptacles full to brimming. Gripped by gold-umbrella fever, we hopped over another gate. Once again, we were bang on the money and began cramming the little beauties into our already packed cartons. I had no intention of stopping, but a loud snort and the stamping of hooves soon changed my mind.

A huge black bull galloped towards us.

I looked to Jenson.

He looked to me.

'Run!'

Vaulting was something I did in school and again in the commandos, so I flew over the gate, giggling and expecting Jenson to do the same. When I looked back, though, sheer terror gripped the not-so-tough drug dealer's face.

The angry beast bore down on him.

Jenson hit the aging iron gate like a kamikaze jellyfish, his limp body clinging to the bars. *'Chris ... help!'*

I leapt up, grabbed his belt and hauled him over.

We collapsed in a heap as a ton of beef ground to a halt a metre away.

'Hah!' I prodded my dazed friend.

'Huh ...?' He still looked mortified.

'Hah!' I poked him again.

'Ha ...'
'Hah-hahh!'
'Ahhh-hah-hah-hah-hah ...!'

We were still laughing when I pulled into Carroll Road, hardly surprising as psilocybin had seeped through our fingertips and set us off tripping. I felt whooshy and the world was a fraction of a second slow. I couldn't wait to dig out my stainless-steel teapot and boil a load of the bad boys up.

While I rummaged in a kitchen cupboard, the doorbell rang. It was an anorak with a clipboard – actually a TV licence inspector in a crumpled shirt, tie and Barbour jacket. If there was ever a prize for the crappiest brown shoes, we had a clear winner.

'Excuse me, sir. But are you the owner of the propert –'

'Sssshh!' I put a finger to my lips and ran a cartoon eye over the victim. Then I motioned him to step closer. 'Have you *seen* our man?'

'Erh ... *who,* sorry?'

'The one we're staking out, the *target,* the *defector,* the *Scientist!'*

'I-I-I don't –'

'Listen!' You've breached national security – *MI6, CIA, MFI!'*

The TV guy began scanning his clipboard, seeking an excuse to getaway.

'We're talking *blueprints, microfiche, top-secret* data. *Capische?'*

The effect of the psilocybin grew stronger. I had to get out of this before things got even more random. After glimpsing the ID card hanging from his lanyard, 'Now, listen. Intelligence tells us you're *John* Taylor, aged *fifty ...'*

'Two.'

'Correct. And you're a TV *licence ...'*

'Enforcement officer.'

'Enforcement officer. Our sources tell us you're not entirely happy with your job?'

'No sir.'

'But *someone's* got to do it?'

'Yes sir.'

'And it *pays* the bills?'

'Yes, that's right, sir.'

'Now, it's imperative you keep our liaison a secret.'

'I won't tell a soul, sir.'

'And when you get to number seventy-two' – Derek's address – 'I want you to remain calm and professional.'

'Calm and professional.'

'We'll need details.'

'How do you mean, sir?'

'Reconnaissance – for the SAS. You know, height, weight, eye colour, nose hair. *Is* he carrying a concealed weapon? *Is* the place booby-trapped? *Is* there somewhere to plant a listening device?'

'Yes ... yes ...' John Taylor, licence to bill, lapped up his new role in international espionage. '*And* possible entry points?'

This guy was good.

'Sounds like you're a pro. You're not Mossad?'

'No, *Who Dares Wins* – on Channel Four last week.'

'It's probably best you put this address down as empty?'

'Better than that, sir, I'll mark it as derelict.'

'Excellent. Now don't break cover. *We'll* find *you*. And forget you ever came here.'

'Where, sir?' The mole grinned.

Back in the front room, I found Jenson sitting on the sofa, staring at the mural and grinning like a low IQ. 'How many of these things do you take?' I held up a mushroom container and the teapot.

'Yeah ...' He shook and nodded his head simultaneously.

Jens was even more mashed than I was, so I dropped fifty funsters into the pot and boiled the magic out of them and a teabag. Then I filled two mugs and added milk and sugar. The resulting brew tasted like an old man's trousers, but we downed it all the same. I returned to the kitchen to make a refill, this time adding a hundred to the pot.

Nothing came on hard or fast, so I brought round three to the boil and then sat next to Jenson on the sofa to roll a joint.

An hour passed.

'Did you see that, Jens?'

'Yeah ...' he replied with his eyes closed.

'Nah, Jens, I'm *serious*. Look at the mural. It's *moving!*'

My artwork had taken on a life of its own, the colours pixelating and swirling to form trippy patterns.

'*Duck!*' Jenson screamed and howled like a loon.

'What?'

'*Duck!*' He cackled and pointed at the mural.

'Oh, right.'

The evil Chinese guy had thick pouting lips which jumped off the wall, giving the impression of a duck's bill.

I looked down at the carpet and saw the oil and paint stains had turned into coalmines with shafts descending hundreds of feet into the ground. '*Stay* on the sofa, Jens.'

Talk about bad timing, the doorbell rang. With a look of helplessness, Jenson grabbed my arm. '*Don't* answer it, Chris!'

'What you on about, you nob? I've got to.'

Christ, he was acting strange.

'*Chris!*' he hissed.

'Yeah.'

'You've *got* to.'

'Got to what?'

'Answer the front door.'

'I know. I just said that.'

Feeling sure I was okay – in the way you couldn't be further from okay if you had tulips in your ears and pizzas for eyes – I opened the front door. A fat man with blue skin, a shock of white hair and cumulonimbus eyebrows stood on the step.

'Jens, did you order a smurf?'

As Jenson giggled, alarms bells rang. This sort of behaviour could only be followed by an episode of piss, shit or puke –

potentially all three – or some equally as heinous and regrettable action.

'Kristy-Kristenheiden!' said the smurf, his eyebrows growing bushier. 'How's it hanging on the intergalactic pinglesphere, me gurgly fergle-berger?'

'Yeah ... come in, man.'

The smurf entered the front room and almost stepped into a mineshaft.

'*Whoa!*' I shouted. 'Come this way.' I took his elbow and ushered him around the edge of the room.

'Oh ... okay.' He seemed lost for words.

'*Duck!*' screamed Jenson.

Papa Smurf and I ducked.

'Who's *he?*' The turquoise midget raised an eyebrow.

'Yes ...' I pondered the brilliance of this existential crisis. 'Who *is* he?'

'*Duck!*' screamed Jens.

Papa Smurf and I ducked – again.

'I've *got* it!' Our guest threw his hands up.

'Good.' I stared at him intently. 'I think we could do with some.'

'*Celebrity* answer machines!' He beamed.

More mineshafts appeared.

The abyss beckoned.

We were all in terrible danger.

Cursing the drunken bastards that built this house, I was glad Papa Smurf had perched on the windowsill. It seemed a sensible course of action – *if* he wanted to come through this thing unscathed.

With every shape, colour and pattern in the room not doing what it was supposed to, I struggled to concentrate on what the man with the weird blue tan was saying. Did he know his facial hair looked like candyfloss? 'But ... celebrities have probably *got* answer machines,' I whispered.

'You don't get it, Kristobell.'

Sitting there in ruby red dungarees, the smurf got all animated.

'We get celebrities to record answer machine messages for people and then *charge* them for it!'

Once again, I found myself staring at his eyebrows, only Papa Smurf took this as a sign I didn't understand his latest star-studded venture.

'Get this.' He made blade hands – things were getting serious. 'Someone has phoned your house, yeah?'

My eyes flicked to the telephone. It definitely hadn't rung. I'm not sure what this bloke was going on about – he might be a maniac.

'And,' he continued. 'You're not in.'

Shit! Now someone had phoned my house *and* I wasn't in. The guy needed help. Maybe he was on drugs.

'So they get the answer machine message from, let's say, Al Casino, and old Scarface says, 'Sorry, *Kreeeee*stoff can't come to da phone. He's saying *hellooo* to my *liddle* friend!'

The smurf grinned, awaiting my response. He seemed pleased with the gobbledygook coming out of his mouth.

'Liddle friend?' I clarified.

'Liddle *friend!*' He started spraying the front room with an imaginary machinegun.

'Duck!' Jenson yelled.

Papa Smurf and I ducked – *again*.

'Or,' he continued, 'it could be David Bowie asking them to leave *a mehh-saaage in-a baaaah-doll!'*

'So David Bowie is on my answerphone?' I looked for the little box's blinking red light.

'Not yet, but we'll make a list of people who want his celebrity spiel and then invite him around to their houses to record it. Before you know it, we'll be scoogle-booh, whizzbits and cheese, *bang,* shamoogli-dooh, money in the bank!'

Concentrating hard, I thought I understood what Papa Smurf was saying – but he was also shooting ducks and dodging mineshafts. 'We could ... just ... *post* Mister Knife a pack of answering machine tapes and a list of messages to record?' I suggested.

'Knife?'

'Bowie Knife.'

'Oh!' The smurf gave me a peculiar look. I think he'd sussed we were onto him.

'So who've you got lined up?' I sensed the effect of the shrooms levelling off.

'David Soul – from *Starsky and Hutch.*'

'He's on board, is he?'

'Not yet, but I saw a program about him the other day. He's living in a caravan in Gwent. He could probably do with the cash.'

'So ... your portfolio consists of no one, except, *perhaps,* a one-hit-wonder who hasn't been on TV since the seventies?'

'Just *think* about it, Kristaberg! You phone a friend and out of the blue you get David Soul singing down the phone. "Come on iron lady leave a message ..."'

Papa Smurf jumped up and began doing a Hutch impression, waving an imaginary pistol around as if looking for bad guys.

I put my hands up.

'What you doing?' he asked.

'Handing myself in.'

'Duck!' yelled Jenson.

Hutch and I ducked – *again.*

Tobacco

Following on from raging bulls, defecting scientists and celebrity answer machines, the week continued to throw curve balls. The next one came when I accompanied Jenson to court for his hearing. 'You'll be fine, mate.' I knotted his tie. 'They've got bigger fish to fry, believe me.'

Standing in the dock, Jenson didn't seem too reassured, even less so when the judge returned from chambers after the recess. Jens turned to me with a face like a stretched plank.

'You'll be cool,' I mouthed, giving him a snappy double-thumbs-up like Maverick would to Goose.

After the regulation lecture about the evils of drugs in society – the one that ensures their huge profits stay firmly in the hands of criminals – the judge lowered his spectacles and peered out from below his stupid wig. 'Therefore, I sentence you to two years confinement at Her Majesty's Prison, Exeter.'

That fucked up my theory.

As the security guard took Jenson down, I caught up with his barrister. 'Fuck me! *That* was a bit steep!'

'I-I-I'm *baffled,*' the chap replied, genuinely upset. *'No one* gets two years for a first offence, *not* with the amount he was arrested for.'

'Can I see him?' I figured Jenson would need me to make arrangements for him. He hadn't even brought a suitcase.

'I'll see what I can do,' said the brief, returning five minutes later with a security guard and giving me the nod.

It felt strange descending the naughty steps as a free man. In the corridor below, Jenson stood behind a plate glass window with a microphone and speaker set into it. He was grinning, which took the weight off my shoulders.

'Mate, I'm –'

'Don't worry,' he pre-empted me cheerfully. 'My brief reckons

I'll be out in twelve months with good behaviour.'

'Do you want me to call your mum?' I'd spoken to Margret on several occasions when she'd called to speak to Jens. His parents still didn't know he'd dropped out of university. I guess they were in for a double-whamburger.

'Nah, don't worry.' He shrugged. 'My brief will do all that.'

'That's good,' I replied, thinking no more of it.

With Jenson gone my mood dipped. Being Friday, I figured I could score a gram of base to take my mind off things. I'd stay up a couple of nights working on the mural and sleep through Sunday. Come Monday, I would have recovered enough to turn up for work. It seemed like a plan.

When Sunday night arrived, I still hadn't slept. My mural had hardly come on at all. I was way past the point of functioning properly and the house was an absolute pigsty. I hadn't eaten anything since Friday, nor drunk more than half a pint of water. I stared at the empty bag of amphetamine, knowing there was nothing left but determined to have one last hit.

Taking up a syringe, I filled the little Ziploc bag with water, massaged it to dilute the speed residue and poured it into my soot-blackened spoon. I sucked a tiny amount of water into each of my blunt syringes and then squirted it, blood and all, into the spoon's grungy bowl. Boiling it up, I bargained on a hit that would knock the socks off an elephant … only it was weaker than a cup of decaffeinated tea.

As the sun came up, I was in shit-state. What was supposed to be a cheeky hit on a Friday afternoon had turned into a weekend-long idiot fest and now anxiety plagued my exhausted mind. I hated to let Pete down, because I knew I was letting myself down, but I had to call in sick.

'Right-o,' he said.

I knew from Pete's tone I'd never hear from him again. In his mind, I was probably another wanker in a long line who'd let him down having overdone the booze the night before. I wished I could have explained this wasn't about not being arsed to get out of bed.

What was it with speed that always got the better of me? Why did it always seem like a good idea? Why did it always spiral out of control? When would I learn – or *how* could I learn – this behaviour wasn't doing me any favours? One look around my messed-up house reiterated that. Following on from Hong Kong, I'd lost *another* job, and life doesn't get much lower than fucking up passing cardboard boxes.

I awoke in bed on Tuesday afternoon, feeling shattered, lethargic and depressed. Not wishing to slide any further backwards, I forced myself to get up and make a cup of tea. Then I trudged to the corner shop to get a Cornish pasty, hoping not to bump into anyone because I felt as twisted as a pepper grinder. Back home, I sat on the sofa watching TV, miserable, lonely and wondering where my life was heading.

Now that the weird black feeling was gone, I didn't want to fester at home. I called Benny at his engineering firm. He and Mike left work around five and could pick me up on the way past. The thought of a few tokes in good company filled me with yearning.

Mike was a good man. He chain-smoked joints and had a well-earned reputation as a party animal. While Ben shoved chicken pies and chips in the oven, I told Mike I was feeling low following my recent binge. I wouldn't ever lie to my brother, who knew I still dabbled every now and then, it's just he was young and idealistic and I could do without a lecture.

People who haven't been through addiction don't understand that *true* recovery, and not the abstinence model you see in American films, can never be a straightforward process. It's a learning curve of trial and error, basically failing your way to success. Recovery always starts with one step forward and three back – absolutely the way it needs to be – but folks who haven't been there only perceive the physical act of you taking drugs and not the wider psychosocial picture, leading them to assume you're a lying loser who consistently lets everyone down.

'Ben, have we got any of those beers left?' Mike shouted through to the kitchen before turning to look me in the eye. 'Chris, I've been there, *yeah?*'

I nodded.

'Just *think* how far you've come,' he continued.

'How do you mean?'

'Mate, the change in you is *fucking* obvious! You've done well. Any time you need company, just come round here.'

Ben came in with cans of Fosters. I cracked one open, took a gulp and let Mike's kind words sunk in.

I always overthought things on a comedown. Attempting to put logic to your life while withdrawing from Class A drugs is a particularly futile undertaking. Everything, including your prospects, friendships, career and finances, seems below par with no hope of improving. But Mike was right. I had to congratulate myself on how far I'd come. I had to remember that desperate scenario of never leaving the house unless I was on drugs. I took another mouthful of beer, had a puff of Mike's joint and settled back on the sofa in a somewhat more blissful state.

On the subject of beer, I'd heard many long-term speed users end up swapping to cannabis and alcohol – getting 'pissed and stoned' as Ollie had referred to it that day. I was starting to see why. As opposed to smoking weed on its own, which mellows you to the point of demotivation, the combination of smoking and drinking invokes a gentle buzz that makes you want to do stuff.

Charlie dropped in with several packets of Golden Virginia and Cutter's Choice for Mike, Ben and their workmates. I'd always admired personal enterprise. It fascinated me when people step out of their comfort zone and do something different. Watching the young gangster dishing out contraband from Europe was far more interesting than the episode of *Coronation Street* flicking across the box of stolen dreams.

'I need someone in the car on Saturday, Chris, if you're up for it?' said Charlie.

Benny shot him the evils.

I knew my bro was trying to protect me. He thought I would spend the money I earned from the trip on drugs. I would have loved to be able to explain that addiction isn't down to whether you have cash in your wallet. In reality, you can argue the more dosh a person addicted to stimulants has the better. They will create more chaos in their lives and crash harder, thus arriving at turnaround point even quicker.

I wished my brother and everyone else would stop trying to dictate my life. It was belittling and futile. When a person sets their heart on a course of action, there's little you can say or do to stop them. It's simply best to extend unconditional love – sometimes from a distance – and help pick up the pieces if it all goes Pete Tong.

Besides, I was sticking to my one gram a fortnight limit and still had money in my wallet from the job with South West Crane Hire.

'Yeah, I'll go,' I told Charlie. 'Do I need to bring anything?'

'Toothbrush?' He shrugged. 'And a passport.'

On Saturday, I put on my best clothes and walked over to Mike and Ben's to meet Charlie. There was an off licence on the way, and still feeling out of sorts from the previous weekend's shenanigans, I figured a beer would go down nicely before leaving for Belgium.

The shop priced their cans individually, giving a clue as to the clientele buying them. I selected an 8% Tennent's Super, not giving a hoot if drinking beer in the morning was inappropriate behaviour. As far as this adventurer was concerned, I was young, I was a rogue, this was my outrageous life and I would live it as I saw fit.

I was smoking a joint with Mike when a car horn blared. I looked out of the window to see Charlie and another chap sitting in thirty grand's worth of convertible BMW, its roof down and Puff Daddy's 'I'll Be Missing You' deafening the neighbours.

It felt bad.

It felt good.

It felt *gangsta!*

Shame I couldn't get another blow on Mike's smoke, though.

As I hopped in the back seat, the passenger turned around and grinned. 'Alright, bey?' he said in 'Proper Cornish'. 'I'm Denton, but they call me Dents.'

Charlie roared off up the A38 in the direction of London, explaining we would skirt the M25 and then head for Dover to take the Channel Tunnel to Calais. He'd put the roof back up so we could talk, making me feel even more cramped on the token back seat.

'Dents is thick as pig shit, aren't you?' Charlie punched him on the arm. 'He don't work. He don't do *fuck* all. He's always pissed and stoned!'

'Hee-hee!' Dents turned to face me, grinning like a dedicated carrot-cruncher.

'And tell him about your missus, Dents?'

'*Hah!* My missus is fockin *mento!*' He beamed with pride at her extreme level of 'mentalness'. 'She's a fockin *big* ol' girl, and she'll give you a *big* ol' right hook if you fock with her!'

I made up my mind not to 'fock' with Dents' girlfriend.

'Tell Chris what you did last night, Dents,' Charlie continued, as if he was Dents' care worker.

'Got stoned as *fock – heeeeeee!*'

He seemed easily pleased.

'I got so *fockin* stoned' – he shook his head – 'I couldn't even *speak!*'

'Wow!' I smiled.

'And tell him what happened,' said Charlie.

'The missus had to pick me off the *fockin* carpet and put me in the *fockin* bed! I was fockin *wasted!*'

Dents pulled a six-pack of Carlsberg Special Brew from a carrier and offered me one.

Shit, this stuff had a reputation for sending people bonkers! At 9% and tasting like alcoholic glue, it was even stronger than the can of Tennent's I'd downed. Still feeling merry, I declined.

I was interested to know why Dents drank at this time of the day. I'd had many a daytime session, 'DTS', in the military, but they were in pubs. When I asked him, Dents shrugged and said, 'I like beer. I prefer it to Coke and coffee and stuff.'

I thought about the amount of sugar and chemicals in soft drinks and could see his point. Anyway, as far as I was concerned, when compared to crystal meth and base amphetamine, beer simply wasn't a problem, whatever time of day you drank it.

Dents downed his can and began rolling a spliff.

'*Dickhead,* I told you not to bring any hash!' Charlie attempted a reprimand.

''Tis only a blim, me bey.' Dents gave one of his village-idiot grins and continued the build.

Charlie didn't smoke He shook his head and muttered something about sniffer dogs at customs. Then he opened his window and turned up Tupac's 'Ain't Mad at Cha'.

A few pulls on the spliff went down well and before I knew it Charlie had pulled into the services at Reading. 'You coming, Dents?' he asked.

'I'm fine, bey. You go on,' Dents urged.

Charlie was either incredibly generous or had more money than sense, or both, because after we'd taken a leak, he bought us all a supersized Burger King meal to eat in the car. When he reversed out of the parking space, I spotted three empty beer cans on the tarmac and a fresh spliff in Dents' fingers. I could see why Charlie found him hard work.

'Passports, lads,' said Charlie, pulling up at an immigration kiosk on one of the Channel Tunnel's entrance lanes. I handed Charlie my new burgundy one, bought to replace the ten-year dark-blue one issued to us recruits in the first week of Royal Marines training. Dents pulled his from a back pocket and Charlie held all three up to the official, along with a Eurotunnel boarding pass.

When I reflected on our reason for entering France, my heartbeat picked up, but the immigration officer glanced at our documents and gave a dismissive wave.

'You *have* got rid of that shit, Dents?' asked Charlie as we headed towards the customs shed.

'Yes.' Dents tutted and gave Charlie an I'm-not-stupid scowl.

Knowing Dents hadn't got rid of his nugget, I felt a further pang of anxiety. It was obvious three hoods in an expensive car were entering mainland Europe to break some law or another.

'Don't worry, Chris,' said Charlie in the rear-view mirror. 'They're after the Mister Bigs.'

'How do you mean?'

'Guys bringing in gold from Amsters, or diamonds or kilos of coke. Besides, they're mainly concerned with people entering the UK.'

'I see ...'

Charlie was right. We breezed past the search bays, which were all empty except for two customs officers lounging in plastic chairs.

I thought we would drive straight into the tunnel, but Charlie parked up by some kind of supermarket. 'Duty Free,' he announced. 'Dents, where's the shopping list Shotgun gave us?'

Dents fished in the glove box and handed Charlie a scrap of paper.

'How it works, Chris,' said Charlie, 'is we each get our maximum allowance, basically a bottle of whiskey and two hundred fags. Then my stepdad sells them to pubs in Plymouth.'

'Can we get anything for ourselves, Chas?' I wasn't too bothered but thought I'd check.

'A pack of beers or perfume for the missus, just don't take the piss in case we get pulled.'

I felt lethargic from the hash, but not wishing to be seen slacking, I clambered out of the car.

'Zoomer!'

The shout came from across the car park. Zoomer, meaning 'bonkers', was my nickname on board ship. I turned to see a drunken Stretch staggering towards me.

'Hello, mate!' I grinned.

He gave me a beer-flavoured bear hug. 'Alright, Zooms. You're pissed as well, ain't cha?'

Stretch would go ashore and get shitfaced with Scooter every night when our ship was in port. I wondered if he had developed a problem with alcohol, as it seemed strange he automatically assumed I was drunk.

Since I last saw Stretch, Scooter had been killed in a road accident. I'd travelled to London for the funeral, but Stretch hadn't been able to make it as his unit was on exercise abroad. I would love to have gone for a catch-up with Stretch, but Charlie gave me strict instructions to be back at the car in ten minutes with the duty frees.

'Stretch, I gotta go, mate.' I raised my arms in a gesture of apology. 'But take care of yourself.' I loped off to the shop, feeling awful and wondering about the alcohol thing.

I climbed back in the car, clutching a four pack of Oranjeboom. Charlie drove to a tarmacked area the size of a football pitch, where we waited in line for an hour. Finally, the red light flicked to green and we followed the line of cars in front down a ramp and onto the ... *platform of a train station?*

'Hey?' I leant through the front seats. 'I thought we drove through the tunnel.'

Charlie and Dents laughed and explained how the vehicles boarded through the rear of a train and then drove forwards to fill up the carriages.

A guard waved us on.

Charlie squeezed the Beemer through a surprisingly narrow sliding doorway edged with chunky rubber lips to protect vehicles' bodywork. We travelled up a ramp to the top of two floors. Eight or nine carriages down, a guard stopped our car a foot from the one in front and said to leave the engine in gear and put the handbrake on.

'Proper job!' Dents gurned, pulling out his roll-up tin and the blim of hash.

'You fucking *nob!'* Charlie scowled. 'I told you to get rid of that shit.'

Charlie obviously didn't like having his authority challenged, but strictly speaking he wasn't the boss. It was Shotgun who was paying us. I was secretly pleased Dents kept hold of the gear and looked forward to a few puffs. Despite not smoking much these last two years, my relationship with Lucifer's lettuce went way back. And as any toker will tell you, it's as addictive as crack.

Upon our arrival in France, we opened the windows to get rid of the hash smoke, but immigration and customs in Calais couldn't care less and waved us through. I don't think they were bothered about illicit goods being smuggled out of Little Britain – English breakfast tea, jam and scones, red telephone boxes – only the drugs, bang sticks, gold and rocks coming in the other direction.

Belgium

It was an exciting moment when I roared the powerful BMW up the ramp into Europe and hit the immaculate dual carriageway towards Belgium.

However, as we drove across never-ending flatland dotted with agriculture and industrial plants, it soon became apparent French drivers were dangerous fucking morons. I liked to put my foot down but knew to keep a decent stopping distance from the car in front. These surrender monkeys would zoom up behind you at 120mph in their Renaults, indicator on in the *outside* lane, and then stick to your bumper as if this made the traffic in front disappear. *There really is no hope for le planet*, I thought, as another garlic muncher put all our lives in danger.

As always, I changed lanes to let Pierre go through. He drove past us laughing and making a very naughty sign. Twenty minutes later, we drove past Pierre. He was standing on the hard shoulder next to his upside-down Fuego.

We were still making Pierre jokes an hour down the road, having crossed the invisible border into Belgium. Charlie said to leave the main highway and gave me directions to a residential area of Ostend. In a quiet street sat a huge warehouse with a line of British cars and hire vans parked outside. 'EastEnders,' he announced.

In two years of selling tobacco at European prices to entrepreneurial Brits, the proprietor of EastEnders had made several million euros and retired. His nineteen-year-old daughter, Bianca, now ran the operation. 'Alright, Charlie?' she greeted him in a Cockney accent. 'See my new motor out front?'

'The SLK convertible?' Mr Materialistic replied, having clocked the forty-grand car right away.

'*Fackin* nice, innit?'

'Sweet,' said Charlie. 'Present from Dad?'

'Yeah, *fackin* should be. I've worked *every* night this month!'

Standing at the warehouse's long wooden service counter, beyond which lay hundreds of shelves holding tons of tobacco pouches, I wasn't the same person who had left the marines two short years ago. Back then, Charlie and Bianca's ensuing conversation about flashy cars, two-hundred-quid false-nail jobs and five-grand holidays would have piqued my interest. Now I saw it for what it was – an overly indulgent lifestyle impossible to appreciate without harder times to act as a yardstick and a well-rounded life experience to keep you grounded.

Bianca was pleasant enough, only she'd had this wealth handed to her as a teenager. I might well have been wrong, but had she ever gone without food to pay an electricity bill? Could she empathise with a homeless person's life story? Did she care that half of the world's population and a significant percentage of the UK lived in poverty? If Bianca was attuned to such issues or, better still, used some of her time or money to ameliorate them, now *that* would be impressive.

For all his riches, Charlie didn't even know how to fill up the windscreen-washer reservoir in the car. Before leaving Plymouth, he'd suggested calling the AA out to do it! If you've never owned a rusting banger and don't know what it's like to put two quid's worth of petrol in the tank at the end of the month or secure a dangling exhaust with a bent coat hanger whilst getting covered in soot and grease, how can you appreciate owning a *good* car?

I wasn't jealous, bitter or judgmental. I was merely observing that life experience allows us to cultivate our *own* understanding of the world. That way, we don't have to simply accept the dehumanising parameters force-fed to us by the media, an agenda that turns human beings into robot-like consumers who buy into all the superficial commercial bullshit without ever knowing why.

Sure, it would be nice to earn a few quid and get back on my feet, but I viewed my fortune-seeking business days differently now. I'd spent three years chasing the big bucks, thinking money would make me happy. Yet genuine contentment comes from mental and physical wellbeing, independent thought and ego-free actions, *purity,* the attainment of which requires a thirst for understanding. Until you make this connection with the universe, material goods act as a barrier, diverting you from the truth.

'How many, Charlie?' asked Bianca.

'Fifty green and twenty-five yellow, love,' Tupac replied, green being Golden Virginia and yellow Cutter's Choice.

Charlie had explained how this worked on the drive over here. Each of the paper wraps contained ten packets of baccy and cost twenty euros, about sixteen pounds, and so we had seven hundred and fifty packets. There was no specified legal limit as to how much tobacco you could take through customs as technically the duty had been paid in Belgium, but obviously us 'runners' couldn't take the piss because the cumulative effect would flood the British market and deny the tax man his easy-gotten gains.

Should customs pull us, so long as we declared our consignment was for personal use and weren't loaded to the gunwales they would turn a blind eye. At least that was the theory, but you'd have a hard time smoking two hundred and fifty packs any time soon, and so we were smuggling whichever way you looked at it.

'See those sketchy fuckers?' Charlie flicked an eye at two swarthy-looking players leaning against the counter.

'Uh-huh.'

'Scouse gangs. They use hire vans and don't give a *fuck* about personal use. They just stuff the fuckers to the roofs and take the risk.'

'What if they get pulled?' I whispered.

'Customs give them an ultimatum – either leave the van or we'll take you to court. Imagine explaining thirty thousand packs of baccy to a judge, especially if immigration knows you've done the trip twenty times that month.'

'So they walk away *scot-free?*'

'Not free.' Charlie shook his head. 'The gang bosses lose their gear and the hire company takes a hit on the vehicle. They have to go through such a long drawn-out process to get the vans back, most of 'em don't bother.'

'Shit ... These Scousers don't give a fuck, hey?'

'Hah!' Charlie glanced over his shoulder. 'You wait 'til we do the ferries. You'll see loads of 'em on there, scamming the duty free allowance, all fucked off their heads.'

Out on the pavement, we busied ourselves tearing open cardboard boxes, ripping off paper sleeves and emptying the loose packets into black bin liners to make our cargo less conspicuous. Before leaving, I bought a ten-pack of Old Holborn and nabbed a bottle of dark rum for three euros. I hadn't drunk much of the spirit before, but figured a pirate's drink suited my maverick nature.

Before I knew it, we were back in Calais and boarding the Chunnel train. I felt a sense of accomplishment. I had a job *and* it was a bit bad-boy. Thirty pounds wasn't a fortune, considering the long hours, but with the chance to do the trip up to three times a week it would be a welcome bonus, especially as the DSS didn't need to know. Upon our arrival in the UK, I saw signs for the M25, but Charlie drove past them.

'Mate, you missed the turning.' I shouted from the backseat.

Dents turned around. 'What *turr*ming?' he slurred.

'The one to go *home!*'

'Hah!' Charlie grinned in the mirror. 'We ain't *going* home, Chris. We've got another trip to do.'

'Eh?'

'We're *sss*topping at a B an' B to drop this lot off,' said Dents, passing me a spliff. 'Then we do it all agai*nnn.* '

Brilliant. It was approaching midnight – *and* I was knackered. My hopes of arriving home in four short hours went up in smoke, ironic considering what was in the boot. This would put half a day on the journey, making our thirty quid recompense a bloody joke.

Charlie pulled up on the pavement outside our digs in Dover. 'Right, sssh!' he whispered. 'The landlady left a key out, but don't wake the guests.'

This struck me as funny because coming from a loudmouthed family of scallywags, Charlie never gave a rat's arse about upsetting people. I guess he was under strict instructions from Shotgun, Plymouth's hardest man, not to fuck up the mission.

We found the key and hefted our black bags up the stairs to an immaculate room wallpapered in blue-and-cream marquee stripes. Charlie and I kept the noise down but Dents the dopey fuckhead bounced off the walls, giggling his straw-filled head off.

Upon seeing a kettle and teabags on the side and fluffy towels and soap laid out on the spotless white cotton duvet covers, I felt gutted we had to leave right away. I couldn't believe this holiday hedonism was paid for and yet we weren't going to enjoy it. We wouldn't even eat the breakfast as Charlie was under strict orders to haul the gear back to Plymouth pronto.

Waiting in line to board the cross-channel train had been a novelty the first time around, but now it was torture. Squeezed into the back of the car, it took me ages to drift off to sleep, and the moment I did, Charlie shook me to say the traffic lights were green.

In addition to the six-pack of Special Brew, Dents had downed half a dozen from the duty free shop and two cans of Belgian beer from EastEnders. As the lager lover levered the ring-pull on a fifteenth, I realised why he disappeared whenever the car stopped – he was busting for a leak.

As Charlie blitzed through France a second time, I tried to do the maths. One thousand five hundred packets of baccy sold for a fiver apiece meant Shotgun made five grand profit each trip, or *fifteen* large a week! Suddenly the thirty quid we earned felt even more of a pittance – or was it even *less* than a pittance? Well, whatever the shittier part of fuck all is.

Either way, the money definitely didn't compensate us for the punishing journey home. I'd lost count of the number of cans of super-strength lager Dents had gulped. On the M25, he began asking Charlie to stop at a service station so he could take a waz.

'In a bit,' the young gangster replied.

As we passed Bristol, 'Charlie, I need a *fockin* piss, man!' Dents groaned.

'I told you *not* to drink so fucking much, Dents!' Charlie

frowned.

Come Exeter, *'Chaaaarrrlieee!'* Dents begged and began bleating like a punctured goat.

'Bit longer, mate. Nearly home.' Charlie glanced nervously in his wing mirror as he nudged up the speed.

On the final mile of carriageway into Plymouth, Dents fell silent, making me wonder if he'd filled up and drowned. I twisted around in the front seat to conduct a welfare check. 'Are you alright, bud?'

'I'm fine, *bey...!'* A fat grin spread across Dent's pasty face, the wet patch on his jeans spreading too.

For the first time since Hong Kong, it felt *wonderful* to be home. I couldn't wait to draw the curtains and climb under the duvet, but before doing so there was something I had to do.

I poured a generous slug of rum into a tall glass, topped it up with milk and added a spoon of sugar. Not only was this Chunkfest's favourite cocktail, but it got around the issue of having no mixers in the fridge. Downing the tipple slowly, savouring its spicy, burnt-caramel flavour and the blissful sensation of the alcohol caressing my exhausted self, I could see why. Next stop was to build a spliff from a blim I'd sponged off Mike.

Yawning, I thought about my role as an international smuggler – or was I simply an unemployed bloke hopping the channel to support an out-of-control tobacco habit? *Hah!* I liked the former profile. Yet despite Charlie's belief that we operated between the lines of the law, surely something had to give eventually.

It Must Be Love

'Got another run on Wednesday, Chris, if you're up for it?' Charlie said down the phone.

'Belgium?' I replied, grateful for the offer.

'Nah, France. We're doing the ferries. Early start, five in the morning. I'll explain then.'

'Okay, me, you and Dents?'

'Yeah, and my dad, Big Charlie, and a girl called Jemma.'

Charlie turned up at mine in his mum's brand-new Escort Cabriolet, explaining Shotgun didn't want surveillance cameras at the port recording the same licence plate every time. I was under the assumption Chas meant a tobacco warehouse in Calais and a boat from Dover – as opposed to the Chunnel. However, as we travelled up the motorway, he unveiled a different plan.

'Whiskey and fags, Chris. The ferry line has a deal in the duty free shop, a bottle of Famous Grouse and two hundred Bensons for twenty quid. We board on foot and then run around the passenger decks asking people if they're using their duty free passes.'

'If not, we nab 'em,' said Big Charlie, also a former marine.

'One of the cashiers is on the take,' said Dents. 'So for a quid a pop, 'e lets you through as many times as you want. Then we do the same on the way back.'

'I thought you're only allowed one bottle of spirits and a carton of ciggies?' I was missing something.

'Hah!' Big Charlie turned to me from the passenger seat. 'The fat bastard in the customs hall doesn't give a shit. His brief is to stop illegal immigrants.'

So that was it. A shuttle bus picked us up from the ferry port car park for the midday departure. On the bus were a dozen or so Scouse gang members, all off their tits on coke or speed and passing joints around. With any luck, the dope would slow their reactions, allowing us to dash around the ship procuring the unused duty free passes before them.

Once on board, Charlie pointed out the bent cashier. 'Buy one deal at a time and don't forget to tip him a quid.'

I did as instructed, dropping the purchases off to Jemma, who waited in a seating area on the deck below. After my seventh trip, having bought as much contraband as I could carry off the ship without my crime looking obvious, I grabbed a chair next to the friendly and intelligent blonde. 'So how do you know Chas, Jemma?'

'We used to enter horse-riding shows together,' she replied in her sexy South-East accent. 'You know, gymkhanas' –

My image of 'gangster' Charlie dropped from Ice Cube ... *to* Vanilla Ice.

– 'and showjumping competitions.'

My image of 'wrangler' Charlie shot back up. I pictured Harvey Smith, the equestrian legend, who according to the makers of Victory V throat lozenges could jump a horse higher than a man – although their TV advert never specified how tall that man was or if he was lying down.

Jemma was always smiling, cool and relaxed. She had that attractive way about her women from Kent do, comfortably feminine, naturally maternal and not sketchy around men. Every time I spoke, her gorgeous blue eyes gave me their full attention, so much so I didn't want our conversation to end. When I told her a little about my Hong Kong experience, her perceptive replies pushed all the right buttons for a bloke rebuilding his confidence. 'You're such a nice guy,' she kept saying. 'Good things will happen to you.'

Big Charlie was right about the 'fat bastard' in UK customs. He let the smugglers straight through – despite some of us carrying so many duty free bags we had to walk a metre apart. Big Charlie and I packed fifty bottles of Scotch and the accompanying cigarettes into the cabriolet's boot and then we all squeezed in for the drive to the B&B.

Out of habit, I scanned the surroundings, looking for anything suspicious. 'Guys,' I hissed. 'We're being watched.'

'Where?' Big Charlie replied.

'Three o'clock, far distance, copse on the cliff,' I directed the veteran's gaze to the spotters high up on Dover's famous chalk backdrop. 'One finger left of the tall tree, glint from binoculars.'

'Seen,' Big Charlie confirmed.

'Old bill?' I asked.

'Nah,' said Little Charlie. 'Fucking Scousers.'

'Honestly?'

'Yeah,' said Dents. 'One of the conts sits up there watching the runners load up their cars, and when they leave on the next ferry, he radios his mates and *bam!* They break a fockin window and nick the fockin lot.'

'Hence why we're dropping this lot off at the B an' B, Chris,' said Little Charlie, pointing a thumb at the boot. 'It's not enough for these scummers to do the ferries – they have to rob everyone else's gear too. The *dense* bastards are drawing so much police attention, they're gonna *fuck* it up for everyone. Have a look at page six.'

He chucked me a copy of the *Sun,* which featured a two-page spread on the growing problem in Dover. The article centred on a notoriously sleazy hostel where a rival gang stabbed a fellow Liverpudlian to death four days ago.

By two in the morning, three trips later, we had enough whiskey and fags stored at the B&B to supply the Rat Pack during the Prohibition. While the boys got ready to hit the sack, I knocked on the adjacent door to say goodnight to Jemma.

She greeted me with a grin. 'Hello, sweetheart, come in.'

We chatted away like old friends, and I wondered if the attraction I felt was mutual – 'wonder' being the limit to which my fractured sense of worth would extend. My confidence took another hit when Jemma mentioned a husband.

'Oh, right.' I tried not to show my disappointment.

'But we've split up,' she added. 'We live in the same house but with separate living arrangements.'

'Really?' This sounded like a copout.

'It's my horses, Chris.' Tears welled in Jemma's eyes. 'I've got stables where I keep rescue ponies.'

'*Rescue* ponies?'

'Horses that were gonna be put down. I teach disabled kids to ride on them. If we get divorced, I don't mind losing the house, but no one would take the horses. Not at their age.'

'Right …' I suddenly appreciated my crappy uncomplicated life.

'He's a bully as well.' Jemma flicked her hair back. 'Calls me names.'

'But –'

Oh, fuck it!

I gave her a kiss.

I only got three hours' sleep, my *buzzing* mind waking me up. A part of me questioned my behaviour last night, but having not long got a grip on chronic addiction, sectionable mental health and those hideous mites, kissing a woman separated from an abusive husband wasn't a huge moral issue.

It wasn't just that Jemma *liked* me. It was that simply being back in this position represented a huge step forward. I was *me* again. I'd escaped a death sentence on Drug Row. I had my *life* back.

While the others slept, I put the TV on without volume. The screen was black bar a single white sentence in the middle.

Diana, Princess of Wales, and Dodi Al-Fayed have been killed in a car crash in Paris.

Although far from a royalist, I was gobsmacked. The media had forced this kind and attractive princess on the British public for seventeen years, making it impossible not to form a degree of attachment. '*Guys,* wake up!' I hissed.

'*Whaa* …?' Big Charlie lifted onto an elbow but Dents and Chas barely stirred.

'Diana and Dodi have been killed in a car crash!' I figured they'd want to know.

Dents groaned and Big Charlie shook his head. 'You got us up for *that?*' he frowned and went back to sleep.

Fucking tobacco-smuggling heathens!

I got more grief at breakfast, following complaints from the B&B's snooty guests. 'Please have consideration for others if you wake up early,' the landlady's note propped against the toast rack read.

I looked around the dining room, taking in a lost generation of spiritually-extinguished Rover chauffeurs and their passive-anonymous wives. Which one of these left-brainers had the small-mindedness to *moan* as the news of two shocking deaths and a bodyguard fighting for his life registered on the public? The irony that these union-flag-waving royal-arse lickers now sat guzzling the exact same toxic newspapers that reports were saying sent the girl to her death was not lost. I was glad to get back on the road.

'Hovercrafts,' Charlie announced as we neared the docks. 'They run more regularly than the ferries, so we can get back to Plymouth quicker.'

This was exciting. I was unaware such a craft existed – to take people to the Continent, I mean. In the departure lounge, the duty free shop's cashiers turned a blind eye as the five of us bought triple our allowance before boarding the Hoverspeed service on foot. The thing was bloody huge, weighing three-hundred tonnes and carrying four hundred people on the passenger deck and sixty cars in the hold.

Without warning, the sea beast's four Rolls-Royce turbines whined into life, its powerful fans inflating the sagging rubber skirt in seconds. A whirlwind of sand, spray and seaweed kicked up, blocking light from every window. Then, to a din louder than a pair of jumbo jets fighting in a cave, the aging monster lurched forward and charged at the Channel's formidable swell like an out-of-control floor sander.

Crossing the Dover Strait took thirty-five minutes, our pilot flying the air-cushioned vehicle at a hair-raising seventy knots whilst skilfully avoiding the other four hundred vessels navigating the world's busiest shipping lane this day. The hybrid machine roared up the concrete French beach and came to a sudden sinking stop.

Along with a handful of other baccy-and-booze bandits, we leapt out of our airline-style seats and disembarked *rapidement,* only to immediately emplane for the return leg. After dropping the goods off at the digs, we hopped aboard an ultramodern seacat, aptly named for the superfast feline landed us in Europe in a sleek snarling pounce.

As we trudged back to the car, following a fourth and final trip, a middle-aged man and woman stood by our parking spot shaking their heads.

'*What the ...?*' Little Charlie broke into a jog.

Something had happened to the vehicle – the couple's vehicle. They'd spent the last forty-eight hours channel-hopping and had loaded their Range Rover to the roof with booze and fags, not realising someone was watching them from the clifftop.

The Scouse gang understood greed would lure the pair on board the last catamaran of the day, effectively incarcerating them at sea. As the service departed Dover, the crooks had smashed the 4x4's window and looted a grands' worth of easy pickings, knowing the husband and wife couldn't exactly report the theft to the police.

Charlie's stepdad owed us big time for avoiding this occupational hazard – not that we would receive a bonus or even a thank you. Back at the B&B, we crammed three hundred bottles of Famous Grouse and sixty thousand Benson and Hedges into the Cabriolet, leaving barely enough room for ourselves in the heavily overloaded car.

A nervous Charlie set off west, sticking to the speed limit and repeatedly glancing in the rear-view mirror. Knowing the others would soon fall asleep, I rode shotgun to keep him awake and take over the driving if necessary. Leaving London's hectic M25 orbital, we picked up the quieter A303 dual carriageway to avoid motorway cops and CCTV cameras. Soon we were cruising through Wiltshire's open autumn countryside.

'*Fuck!*' Charlie's mouth fell open and he began glancing down. 'What's up?' I asked.

'It's the steering...' He jiggled the wheel. 'It's gone all *heavy.*'

'Pull over, you fucking spanner. We've got a *puncture!*'

With the driving skills of a handcuffed crab, Charlie rammed the car onto the verge, bringing us to a skidding stop somewhere near Stonehenge. There were colourful words as the sleep-deprived crew clambered out.

'What do I *do?*' Charlie looked as if he would burst into tears. He whipped out his mobile and stared at the keypad. 'Shall I call the AA?'

'Calm down.' I smiled. 'We'll change the wheel.'

'*B-b-but* I don't know *how!*' Gangster C's bottom lip wobbled.

'Yeah, coz you're a nob.' I popped the boot and began passing out the duty free bags. 'Put them in the field.' I nodded at a five-bar gate, beyond which lay corn stubble. 'In case the law turns up.'

Surprise-surprise, who should come around the corner as the last bag disappeared behind the hedge but a police patrolman in a high-performance chase car.

Five prayers snaked towards Heaven ...

A blip of a siren and on came the naughty lights – God wasn't home.

The copper pulled up behind the cabriolet in his fluorescent-striped crook catcher, its electric-blue strobe dancing around the hedgerows and bathing us in doom. 'Got a problem, folks?' he asked in a soft southern burr.

'Puncture, officer. Just changing the wheel,' I replied, before Dents or Charlie said something stupid – basically anything.

'And where you heading to?' he continued, his comical accent undermining the diamond-white patrol car's intimidating presence.

Rather than risk the next question being, 'And where have you come from?' I pre-empted with, 'We drove up from Plymouth,

Sergeant, to see the sunrise over Stonehenge.'

'But you're travelling in the wrong direction?' He eyed our ragtag brigade with dubiosity.

'One of my racehorses went lame,' said a quick-thinking Jemma, dropping a 'class' hint to put the officer on the back foot. 'I need to get back to Devon to liaise with the vet.'

'Right-o,' said the copper. 'But Oy'll call the breakdown service and get you towed off this busy road.'

Five hearts stopped. Why couldn't he just accept we were druids on an equine emergency and fuck off. Now we were in danger of him spotting the gear – or of us returning later to find a pissed-up farmer blowing smoke rings while celebrating a bumper crop.

The well-meaning policeman walked back over. 'Truck's on its way, so mind you keep back from the road until they arroyve.' He jumped into his mechanical fascist and sped off.

Five hearts went into overdrive. Big Charlie and I changed the wheel quicker than a Formula One pit crew, while the others shoved the bags back in the boot. Jemma, Dents and Big Charlie dived into the cabriolet's compact rear and took the punctured wheel on their laps. Little Chaz and I hopped in and, relief all round, we screeched off in the direction of home.

In Plymouth, Charlie drove straight to Shotgun's lock-up to unload the gear. 'Do you want dropping at yours, Chris?' he asked.

'Oh, I can take him. It's on my way,' said Jemma.

I felt the tingle that comes over you when you're about to have some privacy for the first time with someone you fancy. I don't think I was the only one because back at my place our rum and coffees went untouched.

Jemma and I met up once or twice a week, enjoying easy chats over a cuppa at mine or driving into the countryside to go for a walk. Jemma wanted me to visit her cottage on Dartmoor and ride the horses, but as she was still technically married to a guy who lived in the property, accepting the offer felt wrong.

'But we're *separated!*' Jemma would insist with a chuckle, saying it wouldn't be a problem as he worked up country during the week anyway. When I finally acquiesced, it was a relief to see that behind the rose-clad idyll's whitewashed walls the two of them really did lead separate lives.

On future occasions, while Jemma attended to the stables, I'd wander down to the field and stroke Moonstone, my favourite horse. After gaining the gorgeous golden-brown mare's trust with a long hug, I'd hop astride her bareback and we'd go galloping through the forest.

Jemma was super pretty and wonderful company. She didn't care if I took drugs. She simply cared for *me*. 'I love you for who you are,' she would say. 'I'll even divorce my husband.'

The Advert

In the months leading up to Christmas, three baccy runs a week provided human company, ninety quid and a little excitement. Life continued to improve, but the irony of my fortnightly 'speed' binge meant it wasn't going anywhere fast. I still intended to travel to all the exotic destinations I'd marked on my original seventies illuminating globe *and* tick off the adventures on my bucket list, but these ambitions smouldered on the backburner in my never-say-never mind. For the time being, I was simply content to be out of that flea-infested ditch, steady on my feet and adjusting to my happier headspace.

Now, when I *sat* in clean new clothes – as opposed to *lying* in a filthy old sleeping bag – on my smartly covered sofa, I no longer doped myself up with the cretinous drivel debasing my TV screen these last eighteen months. Supermarket Sweep brushed off, Judge Judy banged to rights and Jerry Springer sprung. However, Detective Columbo would forever have the right to peel a hardboiled egg in my front room. 'Just one more question, sir ...'

Instead, I enjoyed meaningful documentaries, anything about history, science, culture, nature and the great outdoors. I'd had my forty days in the wilderness – certainly forty solitary nights – and now it was time to remount the horse and ride towards the light. There was so much to learn about our incredible planet, its memorable people, far-out places and unreal events, that binging on mindless mainstream garbage seemed a crime.

After watching a program about Australia's Great Barrier Reef, I added scuba diving on this spectacular natural wonder to my growing catalogue of goals. I immersed myself in chronicles of legendary exploration such as Scott, Shackleton and Amundsen's forays into Antarctica, looking forward to the day I would explore this vast white continent myself. I even went as far as splashing out the massive sum of £1.50 on a video, *Point Break,* to rekindle my membership at the nearby rental shop.

In the film, Keanu Reeves stars as Utah, an FBI agent tasked with infiltrating a gang of bank robbers known as the Ex-Presidents. Patrick Swayze plays Bodhi, the gang's charismatic leader. 'Other guys snort for it, jab a vein for it, but all you gotta do is jump,' Bodhi informs a reticent Utah, handing him a parachute as the Ex-Presidents clamber aboard a sputtering Cessna on a ragged airstrip in the sticks.

My eyes were glued to the screen, adrenaline pumping as the band of bohemian thrill-seekers bundled themselves into the raging slipstream at fifteen thousand feet to commence a mad freefall into a shimmering blue lake in California's burnt-orange desert. No doubt about it, skydiving was on my bucket list, *one hundred* percent.

And on the subject of flea-infested ditches, I think I'd worked out what these bloody alien mites were – *skin!* Seriously, when your body's in hyperdrive on amphetamine your nails grow at three times the usual rate, so it's logical to assume your skin is shedding likewise. Not only does this rapid exfoliation cause the hideous yet seemingly unexplainable itches, but the skin follicles, which when dug out in clumps look like alien foetuses, particularly when you're hallucinating after days without sleep, end up *everywhere* – including your tobacco, hence the fizzling puffs flying through the air. If only the medical community had been made aware of this ...

A downside to my newfound understanding was society's *mis*understanding of drugs, moreover their relationship to addiction. I had no regrets about hitting rock bottom, which isn't to say I didn't feel sadness. Getting so ill that I shinned along a flimsy wire between two tower blocks was an awful state of affairs, as was having to leave Hong Kong.

However, drugs were not the root of my problems. Substance use cannot *cause* addiction any more than driving a car can *make* you have a speeding ticket. In truth, unresolved childhood trauma was the driver behind my challenges. It's a mental health imbalance and completely unrelated to a pill or potion or a plant that grows in the dirt.

But thanks to a disingenuous government and their sensationalist media – not to mention recovery programs promoting guilt, stigma and helplessness – the public are presented with a skewed and scaremongering picture of drugs. You can get addicted to food, sex, alcohol, medication, pornography, gambling, shopping, exercise, video games, television, adrenaline, even sun, and suffer *hugely,* and no one gives a shit. Throw in the D-word and everyone starts banging saucepans and shoving garlic in their ears.

Millions of people in the United Kingdom take Class A drugs every weekend without any major issue, but for a minority this artificial sense of wellbeing develops into an unhealthy behaviour pattern. Any social or teaching professional worth their salt could have looked at my unstable upbringing and predicted I was a candidate for addiction – as is done on a points-based red-flag system in Australia. So why had no one *warned* me of this? Why was there zero substance-misuse education – *life* education – in school? Why was society's dialogue on drugs always black, white and intimidating?

That said, I wasn't complaining. I hadn't had a *breakdown* but a *breakthrough.* This was a rite of passage I'd needed to transition in order to understand myself and curtail some seriously crooked thinking. The shame of it was few people had supported me in my darkest hour and yet everyone seemed to have something condescending to contribute now I'd emerged the other side.

Well, they could all get lost. I was not only grateful for my experiences but a far more rounded person because of them. I might be sticking my life back together, but it was better than being a briefcase-carrying clone driving an expensive tin can deeper into the spiritual void.

In between my fortnightly drug binges, I had a lot of time to ponder the mechanics of life. It got to the point where I could no longer talk to Ben about my observations. My brother simply couldn't appreciate how getting a grip on political agendas, global affairs and human conditioning helped me frame my own situation and continue building an informed platform to maintain equilibrium. 'You *think* too much!' he would snap. 'You've got *too* much time on your hands.'

How could I explain I *had* to think a lot because I'd been on the bullet train to Cremation City? As the record showed, there was something deeply wrong in my head and only I could fix it.

This wasn't just some Hong Kong hiccup, either. Looking back, I realised my escapist habits first surfaced at ten years old, when I would rush home from school for a coffee. By twelve, I was drinking my old man's potent home brew and smoking cigarettes. Aged sixteen, I had a soul-destroying addiction to fruit machines and my first toke of weed. So, controlled by a destructive pattern of behaviour fostered over eighteen years, I had no choice but to rejig my understanding of the world if I wanted to remain in it.

When I next visited Benny and Mike, we settled down with our oven-cooked fish and chips and microwaved mushy peas to watch the *Six O'Clock News*. The headline report came from Sudan, where civil war and a failure of the international community had resulted in a massive famine.

The camera operator zoomed in on a man lying naked in the dirt, unable to walk another step towards a nearby aid station. Although only thirty, he looked seventy, his thin brown skin appearing vacuum-packed around limbs as thin as broom handles. The bright whites of his eyes and teeth protruding from a shrunken face made him seem like a grotesque racial caricature.

An emaciated mother clutched a skeletal baby, too weak to brush the flies from her dying offspring's weepy eyes. It wasn't just dire, shocking and a stain on humanity, it was so *real,* as if the television didn't exist and you were standing amongst the horror playing out on that harsh arid landscape yourself.

As I took in the baby's scrawny arms, tiny hands and huge

terrified eyes, features so characteristically *human,* a wave of emotion crashed down on my shattered nerves. I'd never felt such empathy. Why was this world so unfair, especially to those least deserving of such hardship? How could we sit here shovelling junk food into our comfortable western grids while atrocities such as this were unfolding?

But there was something else. Those poor Africans crawling out of the desert, that man, that woman, that child, they were formed from the exact same earth as I was. They had conscious thinking minds like mine.

I wasn't trying to be clever or new age or any of that jazz. I simply realised, right at that moment, we're a human family. We share one spinning ball. We experience the same bodies, traits, senses, feelings and aspirations, no matter where we live. We're not the oh-so-special self-interested individuals, zooming in incredibly important directions on our custom-painted Segways, our elitist masters would have us believe.

What I mean is, when I looked at that baby in an advanced state of malnutrition, flies buzzing in and out of its mouth, I saw *me* and every other human being on the planet.

Jenson had promised to call from Exeter Prison but three months on still hadn't. This made what happened next something of a surprise.

I was in the front room watching the Hollywood adaptation of Henri Charrière's bestselling memoir, *Papillion,* chronicling the innocent man's death-defying escapes from the former French penal colony in the South American jungle. I'd recently read the book and had made up my mind to go down to French Guiana at some point to visit the infamous Devil's Island myself. As I reflected on the logistics of such a trip, the phone rang.

'Hi, Chris, it's Margret. Jenson's mum.'

Oh dear …

From her upbeat tone, I could tell Jens hadn't told her about his package holiday.

'Is he home?' she continued.

'Margret, I'm afraid Jenson's in prison.'

'*Oh* ... my word.'

Credit where it's due, his mother kept her cool. After the initial shock, 'What happened?' she asked.

'He got caught in a nightclub with a small amount of amphetamine.' I didn't mention the dealing or his dropping out of uni.

The irony came two days later when she and her husband drove down from Shropshire to collect his possessions. Jenson's dad wouldn't speak or make eye contact. I could only assume he thought I was responsible for his son's downfall – as opposed to putting the lad up free of charge and getting him a job. No wonder Jenson ended up a rebel without a 'course'.

'Chris ...' Margret leant towards me from the sofa.

I worried what was coming.

'Jenson said he dropped out of university ... to *sell* drugs.'

I wasn't sure if this was a question.

'*Please* ...' Her eyes begged. 'Tell us he never took any himself?'

Fuck me! How deluded can you get? These pair of Joneses weren't bothered their son was in prison for dealing what they deemed 'poison' to other people's kids, only that he might have taken the stuff himself!

Jenson sat in Exeter Prison as Simon shot out of it – straight around to mine ... *after* an all-night coke, speed and hash binge.

It's funny how you recognise other people's poor choices but not your own. Simon was waltzing down the same path that had led to his incarceration, without any insight into his actions or awareness people had moved on.

The rave era had ended – the Criminal Justice and Public Order Act blotted out that ray of community cohesive sunshine. The dance clubs had closed or become spiritually weakened hybrids seeking to accommodate the aimless agenda of dissociated binge drinkers.

The government had restricted the sale of the chemicals required to make decent amphetamine, and the demand for safrole, the key ingredient in ecstasy, had seen the *Cinnamomum parthenoxylon* tree in South-East Asia harvested almost out of existence. Manufacturers of these 'statistically' safe drugs now had to rely on crappy synthesised and potentially dangerous elements, which produced a plastic high akin to nibbling your mum's cooking chocolate and thinking, *What the fuck is this shit?*

And the sensuous and alluring house music which had changed the lives of us dancing people, the most conscience-raising anthems ever produced – Hoddle and Waddle's 'Diamond Lights' and Chaz and Dave's 'Snooker Loopy' excepted – had shifted so far from its soulful Chicago roots that it was now just repetitive din.

The fun was over ... but *not* for Simon, who stood on my doorstep feeling completely out of sorts in brand-new sports gear bought by his doting mum. 'I'm Reebok Man ...' He shrugged, yanking off his beanie to give me a hug.

I put the kettle on forgetting there was a bottle of rum in the cupboard. Mind you, Siborg rarely drank beer let alone spirits. Unlike me, with this exciting drinking-at-home malarkey, he was still firmly in the Class A zone.

'So how was it inside?'

'All *fairly* mundane until a couple of days ago ...' Simon began rolling a joint.

This linguistic positioning, a mix of innocuousness and suspense, was typical of my bro. It meant Arthur Anecdote was locked and loaded and coming my way.

'There's this Chinese guy in the cell next to me, yeah?'

'Right ...' I stirred the tea.

'After lights out, he only goes and ties up his cellmate and proceeds to *rape* him all night.'

'Oh dear.' I nodded at the front room.

'Then he takes up a Bic razor and cuts the lad, *hundreds* of times, all the way down his back.'

'As you do.'

'Yeah, but get this. Come seven in the morning, when the screw unlocks the cell door, the Chinese bloke unties matey boy – who promptly legs it naked and covered in blood to the governor's office – and makes a cup of *tea!*'

Simon's prison tales were certainly shocking but not as much as his parole conditions. He'd agreed to reside at his mother's address, which made sense, and attend Plymouth Drug Service for counselling. What I couldn't get my head around, though, was the top-whack prescription of Dexedrine they had put him on.

'But you've had a year *off* that shit!' I felt angry on his behalf. 'Can't they support you in a better way? Like therapy and stuff.'

'I had no choice, Chrissy.'

'And do you think dexys will *help* you keep off the gear?'

Simon had a needle fixation and a huge tolerance to the drug, and so the answer was a no-brainer. I wanted to hear his response, though. Not to be mean or disrespectful, but to gauge where we both were on our respective journeys. You don't get balance back in your life by not being able to spot a drug-seeking mindset – yours or others'. Simon would be exchanging those piss-weak midnight runners for super-strong amphetamine on the black market next week.

'I'll probably score some base for old time's sake,' he replied, 'but I'll keep control this time.'

'Oh really?' I smiled.

'Chrissy!' Simon snapped. *'You're* as addicted as *I* am!'

'No, mate, you don't get it. I'm *never* gonna say "never" to the occasional hit, but I don't want to chase that life anymore.'

Now it was my turn to receive the 'Yeah right!' look, but I didn't mind. My actions would speak for me and show the way to a brighter future for both of us.

Ben and Mike flew to Thailand for the fortnight leading up to Christmas. I was dead chuffed for them, having visited the Land of Smiles myself and knowing the mind-twisting adventure lying in wait. Benny was expanding his horizons – and lending me his car.

Simon called to ask if I could drop him to his mother's cottage on Dartmoor. I should have known it wouldn't be that simple. Simon – at least in his own mind – had perfected the art of casually securing a lift and then hitting you with an itinerary to make Travis Bickle proud.

Ignoring the local news advice not to venture out unless absolutely necessary, I chucked my duvet, Arctic base layers and a thermos of tea on the back seat of Ben's Metro and set off through thick falling snow. The gritted roads inside the city limits were relatively free of hassle, but chauffeuring Simon to dealers' gaffs all over town and waiting in car parks for callbacks and drop-offs that never materialised was not.

I didn't ask the real reason we were burning petrol and chasing wild geese in a blizzard. Trapped in the endless fuck around of addiction, Simon would never be honest with me. All his promises of 'keeping control' and 'getting a job' had gone south faster than a homesick penguin. The prescription of dextroamphetamine deemed a harm-prevention measure by Plymouth's dubious drug service was already funding his growing base habit. A thousand used syringes under the spare bed in his mother's ivy-clad home testified to that.

There are two activities that seriously retard a person's maturation into adulthood. One is addiction, because while using substances to escape reality you don't learn how to negotiate everyday human emotions and relationships. The other is spending time in institutions. I was having to spot such flaws in my own character and could certainly see them in Siborg. However, him thinking he was smarter than the average bear (which he was) *and* every other bear didn't help matters, especially when he tried to pull the fur over my all-seeing eyes.

'I've got hash, but "we" need some speed,' he said – as if I couldn't see through this manipulative posturing. In Simon's substance-dependent mind, he assumed that I too *had* to be a slave to amphetamine and was therefore at his beck and call. He was unable to consider I might simply be a loving mate attempting to keep the bridge of friendship open.

We left Plymouth three hours later with the snow falling ever heavier. In the suburb of Plympton, Simon asked me to pull into a petrol station for supplies. I parked on the forecourt and followed him into the shop to rewarm. While Simon bought tobacco, rolling papers and ... *cupcakes,* I picked up a free newspaper and began to browse.

> *Development instructors required to work in sub-Saharan Africa. Training provided. Write to Den Reisende Hogskole, 2866 Lillehammer, Norway, or call 00 47 612 164444 for an information pack.*

I pictured those poor kids dying of starvation in Sudan. Okay, so I obviously wasn't about to go gallivanting around the globe helping people – not while getting over a major drug problem – but I could see myself hurling sacks of grain off a flatbed truck in the dust and heat of the African plain. And not only that but the 'training provided' part appealed to me, so I chucked the paper on the back seat of the car.

When Simon had completed his mini-market sweep, we ventured forth into slippery white madness, soon swapping Plympton's flat snowploughed tarmac for hilly lanes buried beneath freshly fallen flakes. It was great fun rallying my brother's car around, but as we got further into the Dartmoor highlands the chances of reaching the cottage diminished.

As the wheel spinning increased, so did Simon's desperation. He argued against turning the car around, before it got well and truly stuck, insisting we press on like Captain Scott and his ill-fated expedition. I wasn't sure what the urgency was but could guarantee it had something to do with drugs.

Through perseverance and guile, I got the car to within a mile of our destination, but a final monster hill stood between us and a cup of cocoa, mince pies and the Johnny Mathis Christmas album.

'Mate, we're gonna have to turn back.'

'*No ...!*' Simon slapped the dashboard.

'Okay, I've got an idea.'

I spun the Metro around, let some more air out of the tyres and asked Simon to hop out. Then leaning out of the window to see the road behind, while revving the engine like Schumacher on pole, I shouted for him to push hard on the bonnet. The car rocketed backwards up the steep incline, its front-end slip-sliding between the hedgerows.

'*That's it,* mate, *push-push-push!*' I yelled over my shoulder.

'*Come on,* Simon! *Bloody push!*

'*Halfway,* bro, give it *all* you've got!'

'*Little* bit more!'

'*Almost* there!'

'*Don't* stop now!'

'*Yes! Yes! Yes!*

'Well done, Sim –'

He lay face down in the snow at the bottom of the hill, arms still stretched out in front.

When we finally arrived at the cottage there was a note from Simon's lovely mum, Caroline, saying she was staying at a friend's for the night. This came as a relief, for although we got on well I always felt guilty taking drugs with her son.

While I rekindled the fire in the front room, Simon disappeared upstairs. Upon his return, 'Here!' he said, lobbing a loaded syringe at me. 'It's speed and E, but mainly E as I never scored any base.'

This was an unexpected bonus and good timing too because with the snow continuing to fall I wasn't going anywhere soon.

After a night of smoking hash and listening to music at Simon's preferred maximum volume, we sat at the kitchen table getting deeper into conversation – not a good idea as when drugs wear thin so do tempers. I wanted so much for my old mate – more than he wanted for himself at this stage in his journey – but when I tried to put this into words, he took offence.

'*Chris!*' Simon glowered. 'What makes *you* think you can get me to give up the drugs, when my *school* failed, my *mother* failed, the *doctors* failed, the *social workers* failed, the *drugs workers* failed and so did *prison?*'

'You *don't* get it, Simon!' I slapped my palm on the table. 'I'm *not* saying give up the drugs, but don't *willingly* invest every fucking part of yourself in them.'

Jeeze this was exasperating! For all of Simon's intelligence, he was unable to rein in his schoolboy pride and see this *wasn't* a lecture. At the very least, he could contribute to a constructive discussion, perhaps learning by osmosis while supporting the lifestyle changes *I* was trying to make.

The problem was we were at different stages on the circuitous and repetitive voyage of recovery, courtesy of a complex web of factors and the way our minds made sense of them. Simon's self-centred and overly sensitive behaviour was typical of someone in the 'precontemplative' phase of change, the place I'd been in Hong Kong when it hadn't even occurred to me ice was a problem. To rejoin the human race, I'd needed to crash so hard that the only acceptable course of action was to address my substance use.

I was learning to appreciate the here-and-now, depersonalising the past and reframing the future to make the present a more habitable abode. By opening up to fresh ideas and listening to my inner voice, I'd allowed my core being to go through a metamorphosis, during which the blinkers to perception had dropped away. I saw life for what it was now and not how greed, class, superstition, misplaced loyalty, blind following, redundant tradition, cowardice, fear, celebrity and phoney-baloney etiquette constructed it to appear.

Core human attributes of empathy, forgiveness, non-judgementalism, appreciation and gratitude were no longer vague tokenistic constructs buried in my wallet until *BBC Children in Need* rolled around. Now they flooded my pneuma, enriching my thoughts, directing my actions and aligning my understanding to true north, ultimately creating a more meaningful experience for the *real* me.

Although this might sound like hippy-dippy shit, I was by no means the next Buddha nor did I want to be. I knew nothing about philosophy or psychology and couldn't put any of my metaphysical learning into words, let alone academic ones. Suffice to say, it was as if I'd tuned the crystal in my head to a higher frequency and tweaked my antenna to produce a clearer picture. Nothing huge, not like I was having visions or about to cure some lepers, but compared to the blinding fog in which addiction had walked me into the gutter, it was monumental and there was no going back.

Under the thumb of his inner demons, Simon had yet to work any of this Recovery 101 stuff out. Until he found a release from the stranglehold of negative thought patterns and gave his inner critic a good kick in the bollocks, my dear mate had no hope of developing the inner peace needed to cut down on the drugs.

'What, like *you've* got balance back in *your* life?' Simon scoffed and got up to make coffee. 'You're a fucking *drug addict*, Chris. You're sat here *on* drugs, for fuck's sake!'

'You don't get it, mate.' I wished he didn't see this as a competition. 'I don't want to be addicted anymore. I don't want to spend every day high on drugs or in a mess when I can't get hold of them. I don't want to pick holes in my skin and live in chaos. I *like* having food in my cupboards. I *like* having people around me – friends that take drugs for fun and not because they have to. I *like* wearing decent clothes.'

It was all too much for Simon. His face darkened, frustration set his jaw and menace emanated from his pupils. He grabbed the ashtray, *'Urrh!'* and went to smash it over my head.

Maintaining eye contact, I didn't flinch. I knew if I projected even a slight lack of conviction, I'd end up on a hospital ward with Humpty Dumpty. The ashtray stopped an inch from my skull.

'Listen,' I said calmly. 'I'm over this shit. And if I say I'm going to do something, I always fucking do it.'

The Interview

I stood in the Intercity 125's filthy restroom, dressed in my expensive pinstriped Italian suit, button-down Ralph Lauren dress shirt and silk tie. Leaning back on the melamine sink unit, I had a foot pressed against the stainless-steel toilet bowl to keep me upright. This way, I didn't have to sit on the piss-soaked plastic horseshoe while attempting to jab my arm with a syringe. I'd stuck to my one gram a fortnight limit but had brought the treat forward a couple of days because I needed to be on form for an event in London.

I'd finally stopped procrastinating and rung *Den Reisende What'sItMcCalled* in Norway, the place recruiting development instructors for aid projects in Africa. I spoke to a Czech girl named Iveta and she gave me a rundown on the six-month training program and her own volunteering experience in Namibia. Iveta explained that the organisation's international title was the One World University and invited me to attend an information meeting here in the UK.

'Paddington, Paddington, the next station stop,' came over the Tannoy, so I packed the syringe away in a sunglasses case and left the train to grab a tube to Tottenham – the home of quality football and most of Istanbul.

The address turned out to be a charity clothes shop in a prefabricated concrete arcade. In the window, a large decal featured a world globe with the words 'Humana People to People' encircling it. A One World University flyer stuck to the glass confirmed it was the meeting place.

I spoke to a woman at the counter and she directed me past a carousel of dead men's cardigans and a rack of sturdy black shoes with ample heels and into a dingy stairway. At the top of the flight, a long corridor led to some sort of staffroom cum storage area. Through the open door, I glimpsed several other information seekers lounging on plastic chairs, most dressed to impress in jeans and a T-shirt.

By the time the group's radar picked me up, I'd crammed the suit jacket and tie into my Eric Jansen briefbag and untucked the shirt. Had the passageway been three feet longer, I could have lost my shoes and socks and gone for the 'If you can remember Woodstock ...' look and probably fitted in even better.

Feeling a little less like Patrick Bateman on prom night, I greeted the slouching bunch with a smile. 'Hi.'

'Right on,' said a guy in a faded denim jacket, whose craggy grid and shaggy golden mane made him the double of Rick Parfitt from Status Quo. He added a fist pump for good measure – rock 'n' *roll,* baby!

I took a seat between a chap with lank dyed-black hair, fifty-hole Docs and piercings, and a late-middle-aged woman who likely owned lots of cats.

After a time, I began to worry I might be in the wrong room. Perhaps this was a recruitment drive for the charity shop or a mandatory employment event organised by the job centre. I tried not to fidget but the speed had put my sleepless self on edge. Sweat ran down my back and the battle of appearing 'normal' had begun.

'Hejsan!'

We turned to see a young woman with chestnut hair, freckles and smart square-framed glasses. Wearing a red roll-neck sweater, she looked like Velma from *Scooby-Doo.* Oozing the sort of enthusiasm only oozed by people who work for an organisation that doesn't pay a salary, she plonked herself in a chair and grinned. 'So, my name is Veronica and as you have probably guessed, I'm *Swedish.'*

Veronica remained blissfully unaware that to the average Brit *'hejsan'* could be any number of languages, including Klingon, and that most people in the room were now picturing Heidi, chocolate bars and cuckoo clocks.

After handing out information packs, the smiling Swede explained Humana People to People was a Danish NGO and the umbrella organisation for a long-established portfolio of humanitarian efforts in Africa. Along with charity shops throughout Europe and Scandinavia, they owned the One World University, or 'school' as she referred to it, in Norway and another in Denmark.

Having participated in the volunteer program herself, Veronica now ran the recruitment drive for the Norwegian campus, whose next intake would train to work in Angola, a former Portuguese colony emerging from years of bloody conflict. She gave us a keen overview of Humana's projects, which included street-children schools, agricultural initiatives, AIDS and HIV awareness campaigns and teacher-training establishments.

As a member of a ten-person team, you spent six months at your chosen school studying the different aspects of rural development work and learning your destination country's national language. In addition to the academic curriculum, we would participate in a range of summer and winter sports, take turns to cook for eighty staff and volunteers, clean and maintain the school and travel around Scandinavia street-fundraising for our chosen assignment.

Then came the exciting part when you flew to Africa to spend a further half-year working in a remote village, living amongst raggedly dressed locals and sleeping in forty-degree heat under a mosquito net and an umbrella of stars.

It sounded a wonderful opportunity, perfectly suited to my personality and skills. I felt excited and energised as I had when poring over recruitment brochures for the Royal Marines or witnessing Quorum International's business plan for the first time. I *had* to do this. I *had* to fly to Norway and train with these amazing people from a rainbow of nations. I *had* to invest my services in the dust and heat of war-torn Africa.

The Angola course began in five months and I wanted to be on it. My mind began to address the logistical practicalities such as earning some cash, renting the house out and donating the Supersport to a classic-car museum. To prevent the enormity of these tasks detracting me from my goal, I visualised the African sun tanning my skin as the latrine I dug for starving orphans grew deeper.

As for fluency in Portuguese, despite having visited Lisbon on my aircraft carrier I knew zilch about the language. Wasn't it similar to Spanish? No matter, I'd learn to speak like a native, the tribal tongues too. *Wow,* this was exciting!

'You'll get subsistence pay equivalent to the local rate when you're in Africa and your education is *free!*' Veronica grinned, flashing her perfect Scandinavian *lax* axes. 'You *only* pay for food and accommodation at the school.'

Oh ... This was a surprise.

'How much is *that?*' asked Rick Parfitt, looking doubtful his royalties would cover it.

'Two thousand, two hundred and thirty pounds.' Our host didn't bat an eyelid.

The collective mood in the room dipped.

My own enthusiasm slowed to a canter. I didn't begrudge paying the money, but this unexpected hurdle was rather a large one given my current circumstances.

'*But* there are scholarships available.' Veronica attempted to rescue the situation.

I reckon all of the other attendees would have left at this point had it not been for British politeness. The cat woman asked a token question, something about the school in 'Norrovia', and Marylyn Manson jumped the gun by putting his headphones on ... and then remembering we weren't at school and this wasn't the bell, took them off again.

Eric Jansen once said if you want to get where someone else is in life then buy them lunch. So as Veronica began packing her bag, I introduced myself and invited her for a McDonald's.

'Are you sure?' She pulled her head back in surprise. 'Shouldn't *I* be buying *you* food?'

'You're a guest in my country.' I smiled. 'So I'll get this.'

As her flight wasn't until the evening, I'd effectively extended the 'Any questions?' part of the meeting for as long as it took to get mine answered. I couldn't wait to learn more about life and work in the bush.

Veronica obviously had targets to meet but she wasn't pushy and seemed genuinely invested in Humana's mission. When I asked about Africa, she told me her team had helped to run an agricultural college on a cashew nut plantation in Mozambique. She said the day began at dawn, when everyone rose with the already scorching sun, and went on to describe the highs and lows of training novice farmers, the majority of whom had never seen a white face before. In the evening, having slapped on mosquito repellent to avoid contracting malaria, the team would sit outside their hut, gazing at distant campfires and listening to tribal drums.

'It gets *toh-tally* dark at six o'clock,' Veronica continued in her delightful Swedish lilt. 'And often the electricity is, how do you say, *sluta?*'

'Cut off?'

'Yes.'

'What do you do, then?' I grinned. 'Crack a few beers?'

'Oh *no!*' Veronica's head jerked back, a chip stopping midway to her mouth. 'I meant to say in the meeting, there is *no* drinking or drugs allowed. We get many people recovering from addiction problems, so the rule is to protect them.'

'Good idea.'

A year without drink and drugs didn't concern me. Veronica had sold me on volunteer work – volunteer work had sold me on volunteer work – and my loyal heart was already prepared to uphold Humana's values. The stumbling block was the £2,230. I gave up trying to force down a quarter-pounder and asked, 'What about the scholarships you mentioned?'

'They're really for people from Eastern Europe. We get a lot of volunteers from Czech, Poland and Hungary, and they simply don't have the opportunity to earn very much.'

Disappointing but fair.

'But you can apply anyway,' she continued.

'Nah, it's okay. I'll get the money. Which is the best school?'

'It depends on whether you're a city person or an outdoors type.'

'How come?'

'The Norwegian school is an old wooden ski lodge on top of a mountain. In summer, you can fish or kayak on an enormous lake and good swimmers go out around a little island. There is moose and deer and even bears. In winter, we have to clear snow from the road with a tractor, but there is often *so* much we get cut off for days. We have a swimming pool and sauna, but being Swedish I like to ski. We have ski-touring all around the area –'

'*Cross-country* skiing?'

'Yes, in Swedish, *längdskidåkning.* Do you know it?'

'Yeah – from the military.'

'Så …' Veronica beamed. 'Du måste komma till Norge.'

'Sorry?'

'I say, you must come to Norway. You are going to *love* it!'

Job Centred

I fully intended to study in Norway in August and qualify as an international development instructor to work in Angola – not that I knew much about the country. What I did know about was life. Moreover, the inconvenient habit it has of getting in the way of itself.

Entering summer, the country was in the grip of World Cup fever, with Baddiel, Skinner and the Lightning Seeds' '3 Lions 98' blaring from every speaker *in* the country. Football fever reached a pitch as Glen Hoddle's England beat championship favourites – *erhum* – Columbia. Anderton scored, as did skipper Beckham, who ran the show from midfield... alongside a successful underwear campaign for Calvin Klein.

My small circle of friends had expanded to include Lucas, Ash and Mal. Lucas was my teenage mod buddy, the guy I'd smoked the contents of our mothers' herb racks with in a juvenile attempt to get high. It was his family who'd taken me in off the street when I became homeless at fifteen. Having bumped into Ben recently, Lucas had got my number and invited me over. He rented an old town house with Ash, a former soldier, and Mal, who was in my year at school.

On Christmas morning, Benny touched down from his fortnight in Phuket, but Mike had perforated an eardrum scuba diving and couldn't fly until it healed. Wanting to spend time with my bro on this special family day, I'd cooked Christmas dinner, substituting chicken for turkey to save my pennies for Africa. However, when Ben stepped through the door, eating a roast meal was the last thing on his mind. His head spun faster than the girl in *The Exorcist.*

'I met someone,' he panted.

Welcome to Thailand! I smiled.

'I'm jacking in my job and moving over there.'

I was dead chuffed for my brother and knew he meant it. How was I going to get out of the country, though? August was only two months away and the community cocoon that fed and sheltered me during my time of need was fast becoming an invisible prison. My house alone posed a plethora of issues. No letting agency would take it on unless I gave it a complete makeover and replaced the appliances. Then, after everything met the required standards, the garden needed sorting out. I was looking at a thousand pounds or more on top of the school fees for Norway.

A letter dropped through the door. I could tell by the address on the back of the brown envelope it was from the Department of Social Security. Something told me to expect bad news.

> *Dear Mr Thrall,*
> *Thank you for informing us of your employment with South West Crane Hire.*
> *The conditions of your income support allowance clearly state you must obtain written permission from this office before engaging in work, paid or otherwise, even if it falls below the 16 hours per week threshold.*
> *As such, your benefits have been stopped and you must pay back all the money received since the date you commenced work, as you stated in your correspondence.*
> *Should you disagree with this decision, you are entitled to appeal in writing…*

What the hell? South West Crane Hire sacked me *six* months ago – and the DSS had only just replied to my letter! Who the *fuck* waits half a year to begin a job? Surely, they would want people on benefits to get back into work as soon as the opportunity arose.

I did the maths. *Bastards!* Over a *thousand* pounds – all the money saved from the tobacco runs. The ugly red tape of seemingly insurmountable bureaucracy now stood between a more-than-willing me and my dream of helping starving kids in Africa – *and* I had the rigmarole of getting my benefits reinstated.

I immediately sat down to write an earnest appeal detailing my battle with addiction and the fight to win my life back. I included a copy of the solicitors' letter stating I was suffering from severe psychiatric illness and unlikely to recover. Anyone reading such a heartfelt plea, anyone with a *single* strand of human DNA, would retract the ridiculous penalty forthwith.

Not surprisingly, no such person worked in the Ministry of Hate's austere bowels, certainly not the lobotomised prole who red-stamped my request for clemency before dropping it into the Chute of Broken Dreams.

> *Progress is Punishment ...*
> *Punishment is progression ...*

When I appealed the decision, the same grey-suited no-lifes adjudicated at my hearing. Three of them – two male bots and a female droid – sat on authentically calloused backsides, staring through rheumy eyes – and all just to tell me that *rules* were *rules* and there for a reason.

Wasn't that what the Nazis said at Nuremburg?

I faced similar disenfranchisement when filling in the claim form for unemployment benefit – all thirty-seven pages of it. How was I supposed to know what type of National Insurance contributions I'd made? What the hell was a P45 and how could I request one from my last employer when my last employer was pissed off with me?

Staring at the bulk of paperwork invoked the feelings of helplessness I'd experienced while sitting school exams, when I would put my name at the top of the paper and gaze out of the window for two hours. Why wasn't there a simple tick-box format?

a) Would you consider part-time work?
□ Yes □ No □ Do I have to?

b) Do you hold a current British driving licence?

☐ Yes ☐ No ☐ Disco Dave can get me a decent fake

c) Do you get fucked up on drugs and shouldn't really operate a teaspoon let alone heavy machinery?
☐ Yes ☐ No ☐ Stopping for a bong

d) Good weed?
☐ Asleep ☐ Munching on peanut butter ☐ Sorry, what was the question?

In the end, I got so *bloody* upset. I banged a fist down on my writer's desk and bussed to the Job Centre to ask for help.

'So you need an interpreter?' asked the woman on reception.

'No, I'm English.' I frowned.

'But you can't *read* English?'

'I can read English, but not *that* English.'

'Ah, you're visually impaired. We have a phone number –'

'But I'm *not* blind.'

'I *never* used that word!' She folded her arms in outrage.

'No, I mean I'm not ... *visually* impaired. I'm just having trouble understanding the form.'

'So you *do* need an interpreter?'

Ahhhhhhhhhh!

I tried not to get angry – although being an illiterate blind immigrant, I had every reason to be. But *visually impaired?* How did she think I got there – flying *fucking* carpet?

'No, I *don't* need an interpreter. I've been off work *extremely* ill and I'm having trouble filling in the form.'

'So would you class yourself as disabled?'

'*Sort* of ...' I played the mental health card. 'I've never actually registered, though.'

'Then we can't help you.' She shoved the paperwork back across the desk. 'Try the Citizens Advice Bureau.'

I breathed a long sigh of frustration, until there was nothing left under my bomber jacket but a unemployed DNA sample. In the time this had taken, she could have helped me answer the five or so questions I'd marked with asterisks on the application form. This whole signing-on business was going to be a nightmare.

Rather than waste a journey, I decided to check the job vacancies, but perusing the racks of postcards only increased my feelings of inadequacy. I had none of the necessary qualifications – unless I wanted to try and sell windows to people who lived in houses that already had them.

One card raised a glimmer of hope.

> *Barman or woman in Minkerton Chavvy. Preferably familiar with serving in a busy village pub, but training can be provided.*

The five-mile cycle from Carroll Road would be a slight drawback, but the thought of getting a job and not having to complete that merciless benefit form outweighed it. I noted the reference number and queued to see an employment advisor.

The Strutting Cock

I sat in my suit in the lounge of the Strutting Cock, surrounded by more horseshoes than the infield at Aintree. The Chemical Brothers' 'Block Rockin Beats' played on the jukebox, a reminder of the exciting and uplifting nature of bar work.

Dick, the landlord, was late thirties. He was also a former Royal Marine but looked more Jack the Lad in his Timberlands, Burberry shirt and Armani jeans. He gave me the job – as is bootneck protocol in Civvy Street – but that's where our brotherly bond ended.

He was on my back from the start, telling me to 'Fuck off!' when I asked which way the knives and forks went for the Sunday lunchtime settings. Being ambidextrous meant I'd never had cause to internalise this particular point of etiquette.

On another occasion, I messed up a customer's lager, unable to achieve the all-important frothy head. Instead of simply telling me to nudge the pump lever *backwards,* which puts a burst of fizz into the drink, Dick Face raised theatrical eyes, elbowed me aside and poured the pint himself.

When he disappeared out the back, a white-haired no-nonsense farmer-type leaned over the bar. 'Chris, mate, Dick's a fucking *wanker.* Us lot only drink in here because it was our local long before 'e arrived.'

I appreciated the old boy's support and decided, there and then, to go above and beyond for the punters, knowing my efforts would be appreciated and prove my worth.

Jemma turned up at Carroll Road unannounced to solve my transport issue. 'Get in!' she ordered, and then drove me into deepest darkest Cornwall to pick up a red Nissan run-around.

Mondays to Thursdays I worked the dayshift. I'd pull up in the pub car park at 10am wearing a white shirt and polished boots, stub out a rollie and make my way to the lounge. Having arrived before me to open up, Dick would then leave for the cash-and-carry in his Range Rover.

At this juncture, I'd open up a bar of my own – a cocktail one – necking a shot of whichever liqueur took my fancy.

Baileys – *Check!*

Tia Maria – *Roger!*

Bols Crème de Bananes – *Rude not to!*

Each day, a sickly sweet treat went down the hatch courtesy of Dick the Prick, the resulting alcohol buzz mellowing me into the dayshift. After this, I'd eat my fill of bar snacks, treats I'd gone without for three years.

Twiglets – *Oh, go on!*

Salt and vinegar crisps – *Yes, please, sir!*

Cheese Flavoured Moments – *You cheeky monster!*

After a swift half of lager, I'd restock the mixers, by which time Dick's wife, Lorna, would arrive in her convertible BMW to tend to the accounts. With her big hair, beauty salon polish and soft Essex accent, Lorna was something of a trophy.

Dick was a trophy too – the kind you win if you shoot a panda.

When the pub was empty, Lorna would pull up a barstool and chat. She was so stunning it was hard not to feel a little intimidated in her presence. But there was something more because when Lorna stared into my eyes with her crystal-blue ones, I felt pretty sure she had a crush on me.

I knew pub landlords were a tight bunch, but Dick took this to a whole new level. He never bought any of his regulars a drink and only treated the bar staff to half a pint after closing on a Saturday. You could see why many of the Cock's long-standing clientele now patronised Minkerton's 'other' pub.

I employed a different approach as it was obvious regular punters sought three things – alcohol, companionship and belonging. Therefore, if you topped up their beer *on* the house and took the time to chat, you provided all three. It wasn't about giving drinks away for nothing. It was about recognising loyal customers, appreciating their business and building a sense of community.

One hero gave me grief from the start, Fat Terry, a local builder. Fat Terry – his beer brothers' epithet and not me being cruel – failed to grasp the concept pubs have to take on new staff occasionally. He viewed it as a personal affront when an unfamiliar face appeared on his ale patch. Seriously, you'd think he was Boudicca facing down the Roman Empire – as opposed to a chubby xenophobic bricklayer with a chip on his shoulder.

Standing in the bar, surrounded by his mates, Terry would make overly loud snipes, such as how crap I'd pulled his pint, how I was 'so much slower than the last one' and how 'she was a useless effing cow anyway'. Other times, "Ere, *Dick,* show him your *dick!'* he would shout just out of the landlord's earshot before guffawing with the lads.

His derision was often at the expense of the boss and his numerous affairs, this particular one referring to my predecessor's rapid departure. According to the customers, Dick had crept up behind the girl as she stocked the bar one morning. Flopping out his purple crusader, 'Want some of this, love?' he'd asked – and it appeared she did not.

Since walking out, there and then, she'd become 'the one Dick tried to dick' or 'the one that wouldn't let Dick stick his dick in her'. No member of staff stuck around long enough for the punters to remember their actual names.

One busy evening, Fat Terry entered the lounge to the sound of Aqua's 'Barbie Girl' blaring from the jukebox. I smiled. It's hard to look cool with a Euro-trashy dance hit popularized by ten-year-olds as your walk-on.

Wearing an England shirt large enough to cloak the whole team, 'What you 'aving, boys?' he shouted, but approaching the bar, patting his pockets, the compo cowboy went bright red.

It was obvious he'd left his wallet at home, so I waved a discreet hand and pulled the five pints regardless. Terry gripped the bar's mahogany handrail, flustered and mumbling an unnecessary explanation.

When Tel made a beeline for me the following evening, brandishing a crisp twenty-pound note, I raised another surreptitious hand. Dirty Dick could afford it. He drove a Range Rover.

From that moment on, I could do no wrong in Fat Terry's eyes. 'Best barmen we've 'ad in here!' he'd shout across the pub. 'That tight cunt, Dick, should give 'im a pay rise!'

And it wasn't only big-bellied brickies who appreciated my efforts. Before long, I was social worker to half the village. You can apply a barperson's rule of thumb to daytime drinkers. If they're not scratching at the crossword while nursing a pint of bitter, or stopping in for a lunchtime bite, then they likely have some issues.

What with my recent stumble out of the umbra, I felt duty bound to lend a sympathetic ear and offer encouragement and advice, classic bartender style as portrayed in American films. The pearls I dished out weren't rocket science but usually a suggestion to step outside the box and view life's problems from an alternative angle.

Kev Moody, a carpenter, was a case in point. A devoted father to two young boys, he was off work with depression following a recent divorce. Kev was unhappy his wife had got the house and moved a fella in within a month, but the real seat of his unease was the negative way he framed these events – and having a peer group who reinforced rather than challenged his doom-filled outlook wasn't helping.

'So, Kev.' I topped up his Kronenbourg. 'What's most important in your life?'

'Me kids,' he muttered.

'And what do kids need more than anything?'

'Love?' He shrugged.

'Sure, but I reckon stability comes first. So your missus –'

'*Ex*-missus.'

'Your *ex*-missus ain't doing them any favours by going out with the first bloke she meets *and* letting him move in.'

'He's already moved out – *twice.*' Kev scowled.

'Exactly. So you can hold your head up because you're not behaving irresponsibly. You're putting the boys' needs first.'

'Yeah ...' Kev's eyes lit up. 'No one's put it like that before.'

'And as for the house, it's just a pile of bricks. Nothing worth getting upset over.'

'It's not, Chris ...' He shook his head thoughtfully. 'Thanks, mate.'

When the bar was busy, I kept ahead of the drinks orders by totting up prices and calculating customers' change in my head. I got so fast at this I had to wait for the cash register to catch up.

'Dick!' I shouted through to the kitchen on Silly Steak Night. 'Here a minute.'

The till roll had run out, leaving the printer head making an unhealthy clicking sound. With customers demanding drinks, now wasn't the right time to figure out how to change it and risk suffering the boss's foul temper.

Dick pulled the roll of transactions from the machine and, without so much as a glance, dumped it in the waste bin.

Ahhh ...! I could only assume the till roll was there to prevent the printer vibrating itself to pieces *or* for referring to should a customer raise a query about their bill. The pub obviously didn't require it for accounting purposes. This made things a lot easier because typing the price of each and every drink on the fiddly worn-out keypad, along with the amount of money handed over by the customer, was slowing me down. If the till roll ended up in the bin anyway, I could stick with the mental arithmetic and no longer worry about the odd error in my typing. I didn't think anything more of it ...

Sparked

I'd been behind the bar of the Strutting Cock two months and had managed to time my fortnightly speed binges so they didn't affect my job ... *much*. Duane was now in prison, so every other Friday after work I stopped by the Wizard's place with my minimum-wage packet. I would stay up all night painting the mural and go into the pub still buzzing on Saturday, then crash out until my quiet shift on Monday evening.

Now that I owned a car my skip-diving forays had moved further afield – to the rear of Plymouth's Travel Tavern, four miles away. Hotels chuck out all manner of goodies to occupy the obsessive-compulsive mind of a fidgety speed user, from mint-condition mattresses to coffee makers and trouser presses. On this occasion, I secured a load of pristine pine-wood slats, having kung-fu kicked them out of discarded put-you-up beds, and a half-moon-shaped bedside light. I packed my bounty into the boot of the Nissan and drove home listening to 'The Drugs Don't Work', a pertinent reminder if ever there was one.

The following Friday, the pub didn't need me, so I picked up my money and stopped by the Wizard's place. Back home, after cooking up a hit, I cut the brightly coloured battle-crying face of a yakuza warrior from a Manga comic book and papered it onto the semi-circular shade of the bedside light from the Travel Tavern. For safety, I replaced the bulb with a lower-powered one and covered the picture with a sheet of overhead-projector transparency to further protect it from the heat.

With the curtains drawn, I flicked the lighting appliance's inline switch. The result was delightful, one of the best things I'd built, a smart arty Manga lamp that projected a uniquely Asian feel into the room.

Being an end-of-terrace property, the house had a round feature window set into the attic's gable-end brickwork. I contemplated sticking a bat-shaped stencil over the swirl-patterned glass and shining a spotlight through it to recreate Gotham City's famous distress signal, the one used to summon the services of the caped crusader. Surprise-surprise, I became side tracked with my mural and never followed the idea through.

On Saturday morning, I was labouring away using the wooden slats I'd salvaged to create a parquet-flooring arrangement in my kitchen's tiny dining area. The bell rang and I opened the door to Jane, my neighbour, standing there grinning.

'Chris, that was *so* funny last night!' She chuckled.

'What was?' I sensed déjà vu.

'Up in your loft,' she continued. 'The Batman light shining out of the window. Me and the girls were getting in the cab to go down town and it had us *creased* up!'

Well, this was a spinner. I swear I hadn't got around to going up in the roof, let alone sticking a bat-shaped logo on the window and shining a spotlight out of it.

I went back to the flooring job and was fitting a sawn-to-size slat into my ingenious concentric-squares pattern when the phone rang. 'Chris, it's Dick. I know you're working tonight but is there any chance you can come in tomorrow as well?'

I should have told him a definite 'No', as the hectic Sunday lunchtime shift was insanity in a can, but being a loyal nobhead, I said, 'Yeah, sure, mate.'

Before leaving for the Saturday night shift, I made an inane pledge to go straight to bed when I got home and save the rest of the speed for Sunday lunchtime – a pick-me-up before work because I would damn well need it. As it panned out, the devil on my shoulder insisted I stay awake for a second night in a row and inject every last grain of base in the bag.

By late morning, I was in a super-unsophisticated state, so much so I probably qualified for a full-time carer. I had to force myself away from adding the Statue of Liberty to the mural and take a shower and iron a fresh shirt for the pub.

When I arrived at the Strutting Cock, anxiety rode me like a porcupine on a mule. My eyelids twitched, I yawned incessantly and sweat ran down my back. I took a deep breath and walked inside wishing I could be anywhere else on the planet.

'Hi, Dick!' I fired a cheery bluff across the crowded lounge and without waiting for a reply went directly to the cellar to fill a crate with mixers. I managed to eke this evasion exercise out for fifteen minutes before a shout of, 'Chris, getting *fucking* busy up here!' rang out. I wiped my brow with a bar towel, adjusted my shirt and went to join Cheerful Charlie behind the bar.

As with every pub in the country, the place was packed with Sunday socialites chatting loudly and knocking back drinks under a cloud of cigarette smoke. Along with the Cock's regulars, the Carvery Club was in en masse and under strict orders from our chef to hide a second slice of beef, pork or turkey from Dickhead's penny-pinching gaze, most opting to smother their portion privilege with a generous ladle of gravy.

The pub's football team had dared to make an appearance, although no one would deny them the opportunity of drowning their sorrows in light of last season's performance. Standing in front of a bar must have been hard for the striker – what with his two left feet itching to punt a ball five metres over it.

And God must have cast out the Minkerton Methodist Massif, who'd rocked up on their mobility scooters and were busy slinging gin and tonic at the church's temperance roots. I prayed these devil dodgers wouldn't lead the football team into temptation, perhaps initiating a naked-drinking session or snorting horseradish off the goalie's nipples.

The drinks orders threatened to swamp the bar, only in my sleep-deprived state I couldn't remember them. 'Sorry, bud,' I said to one chap a third time. 'What was it again?'

'Three pints of John Smith's, a rum and Coke with a slice of lemon and no ice, a vodka and orange with ice but no lemon, and a packet of cheese and onion.'

'Right-right, sorry.' I turned to face the optics, trying to remember what the fuck he'd just said. I was acutely embarrassed *about* my acute embarrassment, which was in itself... *acutely* embarrassing. I felt like someone who had been wired on hard drugs for three days *and* that everyone in the pub knew it.

When, exasperated, I had to ask the gentleman a fourth time, Fat Terry rode in on a white cement mixer. 'That's some *'angover* you've got!' He chuckled and threw in a knowing wink.

'Sh*yeah!*' I feigned a grin.

'Chris 'ad a few beers last night,' Fat Terry told my customer and then took me through the order, drink by drink, so I couldn't mess it up. The shift was out-and-out torture and how Dick didn't sack me I don't know.

I stood behind the bar chatting to the daytime drinkers as Elton's ill-thought-out tribute to Princess Diana, 'Candle in the Wind 1997', played on the jukebox. I'd made this place my second home. The punters loved me and my interpersonal touch was clearly an asset to the business – unlike its greedy proprietor. I always made sure to remember people's names and take time to chat. I continued topping up the regulars' drinks, costing the pub nothing because since I'd started working there the number of patrons had swelled.

Dick popped his head into the bar. 'Chris, can I have a word out the back?'

'Sure, mate.'

He leant against the huge gas range in the kitchen, clutching two slips of till roll between his fingers. 'I think you've been pilfering.'

'What?'

'The takings haven't tallied. Last week we were six quid down. This week we're fourteen pound up.'

I neglected to point out that if the takings were *up,* then I stood accused of putting money *in* the till. I briefly considered explaining what had happened, that I thought the till roll got chucked in the bin and therefore hadn't put much effort into my tillmanship, but I knew this wasn't about the money. As Dick said, 'I'm gonna have to let you go,' the stupid thing was I understood the guy better than he did himself – *and* I fucking liked him.

When I went out through the lounge, Fat Terry patted me on the back. *"Ere's* our boy!' He beamed. 'Everything alright, Chris?'

'No, mate, it's not. Dick just sparked me for stealing.'

As a look of disbelief rippled along the row of drinkers, Terry jumped off his barstool. 'Why doesn't that *wanker* tell you the real reason!' he shouted through to the kitchen. 'It's because 'is missus fancies *you* chronic and she don't fancy *'im!'*

Thanks, Terry. I clicked the pub door shut, smiled, and drove to the Wizard's place to pick up a potion.

Firewalker

I can't say I was happy to get the sack, but on the other hand I'd developed a degree of resilience. I was a guy who'd worked a dozen jobs since leaving the marines less than three years ago and lost almost all of them – and I still respected myself as much as ever, if not more. I wouldn't be getting a massive downer on because I'd failed to factor till rolls into society's seemingly pointless equation. As my old dad always said, there was nothing wrong with me, and one or two issues on the job front were not going to define my whole existence.

Over the next few months, I sidestepped the regular employment scenario and went on as many baccy runs as possible to earn the money for Norway. During this time, a court found the twenty-four-year-old office worker guilty of Josie's murder and having received death threats at HMP Exeter he was now serving a life sentence in the Scrubs.

Neil Diamond got in touch to say his parents had bought him a ticket to Hong Kong and if I put sixty quid in his bank account he would post some crystal meth to me in a hollowed-out candle. I did … and never heard from him again.

One afternoon, I answered the door to find a middle-aged woman beaming at me.

'You must be *Chris.*'

'Yes, that's me.' I smiled.

'I'm Daniel's nan.'

It took me a moment to realise she meant the Danny who had smashed my window – although I doubt his nan knew about this. Since doing so, he often knocked on the door and we'd developed a special bond.

'Oh *right!*' I shook her hand.

'He stays with me at weekends – to give his mum a break.' Her theatrical pained expression painted the bigger picture. 'And he never *stops* talking about you.'

'Only the good stuff.' I chuckled, slightly embarrassed.

'It's only ever good, Chris.' She squeezed my arm and gave me a heartfelt look. 'His mum and I just wanted to say thank you.'

I continued seeing Jemma but had begun to put some distance between us. She was wonderful company and extremely loving but still legally married, which made me feel grubby and underhanded. I knew she and her husband lived individual lives under the same roof – I'd seen the separate bedrooms – but I couldn't reconcile myself with the situation and didn't want to.

Then Charlie called to ask me why Jemma's husband had phoned him to enquire who 'this bloke Chris' was. I attempted to skirt the issue, but Charlie wasn't stupid. 'Look, mate,' he said. 'I don't have a problem with you and Jem, but you've got to understand her chap is a *fucking* psycho. He followed her last fellah home and baseball-batted the fuck out of him. He was in hospital for a week.'

I don't know how Jemma's estranged husband found out about me – and even knew my address – but having to hide a pickaxe handle by the front door didn't exactly ease my qualms. I appreciated her loving me for who I was and not giving a damn about the drugs, but while down town celebrating Chunks' fortieth birthday we had a sincere chat and agreed it best to move forward as friends.

Chunks' niece, Jeanette, was also at the party. Tipsy to say the least, she ambushed me as I exited the gents, locking her arms around my neck and unleashing a straight-from-the-heart torrent of flattery. I was so taken aback by her unbridled adoration it didn't occur to me to ask where Carlito was – probably trying to buy a packet of cigarettes from the jukebox or a Bacardi and Coke from the DJ.

In town a few days later, I passed a billboard advertising Cadbury milk chocolate bars. A strip of text pasted along the bottom of the hoarding caught my eye. It was a request for men to join the books of an escort agency. Easy money came to mind as I pictured my maverick self as Richard Gere in *American Gigolo,* but there was something more ...

Whereas before I'd crashed down to Earth on my drug-smacked arse, when I would have viewed such a position as seedy and the clientele desperate, I felt differently now. Everyone had a right to happiness and respect and what with my newly nurtured empathy, I was sure I could be the man to bring a smile into a woman's life. I posted off a passport photograph and the thirty quid registration fee and waited for my first appointment ...

My Africa plan came up in conversation the next time I went around to Lucas, Ash and Mal's place to smoke joints and play *Tekken.* I tended to shy away from the video game scene, unimpressed with the over-the-top passion with which these guys fought their phoney onscreen battles. To me, it was a boring substitute for real adventure – the Northern Ireland Conflict was a proper fight – and would far rather we drank beer and escaped into a good film.

These boys weren't into drinking like I was, though. I got through a four pack of lager every night now, referred to in recovery circles as sidestepping into another addiction. I knew it wasn't good behaviour but loved the buzz beer gave me. Besides, waking up with a slight hangover and then cracking on with my day as opposed to losing a week to hunger, exhaustion and depression on a speed comedown was a no-brainer. Beer definitely seemed the lesser of two evils.

Lucas was a good guy only he had an Aspergic-like tendency to blurt out whatever was on his mind. 'Why don't you *stop* going on about Africa!' He tutted and shook his head. 'You're *never* gonna leave Plymouth.'

I felt upset my friend had so little belief in me, but I didn't say anything. I'd recently spoken on the telephone with Veronica in Norway and we'd agreed to delay my start date by six months. I would now join a team in February and train to work in

Mozambique. I'd also contacted my local British Legion and an understanding retired Royal Marine helped me write out an application for a career-development grant. He said up to a thousand pounds could be available. What with the four hundred quid I had saved from my tobacco runs, things looked promising. I didn't respond to Lucas's baseless accusation. Actions speak louder than words, plus I had something big planned ...

A light evening breeze blew off the English Channel and along the picturesque estuary, the driftwood fire's embers shimmering thorough orange, yellow, green, grey, white and black. I stood yawning and twitching on a sand and silt strip, the high-tide mark on the Cornish bank of the River Tamar. A bed of tall reeds stretched thirty metres inland and treacherous black sludge led down to the receding waterway's lazy brown flow. I could feel the amphetamine leaving my body and a comedown settling in its place.

Once again, I was following Eric Jansen's advice. He said, when faced with a challenge you *must* take action, because action *creates* action. Eric had come home one day to find a repossession notice pinned to the door of his house. Fed up with burying his head in the sand, he kicked off his shoes and ran ten miles along the beach. Three years later, while piloting his private helicopter the self-made multimillionaire realised he was flying over the very skyscraper he'd been working in as a janitor when his life had crashed.

Another skill Eric taught us at his seminar was firewalking and more importantly the theory and mental preparation behind it. By conditioning your mind to conduct a seemingly impossible act *at* will, in this instance padding barefoot across red-hot coals, you can then meet similarly stressful day-to-day encounters head on without fear of failure.

I'd always accepted I had an issue with drugs and had never been in denial about my addiction – the depths to which I had sunk, maybe. Yet throughout this challenging and often painful period of discovery and growth, I had maintained my self-belief. If, like Lucas, people had begun to doubt my integrity then it was time to step up to the plate and smash a fucking fist through it. I could justify spending two and a half years banging up drugs in a hellhole if it meant learning who I was and the direction my life should take. Now that I had these answers, I could procrastinate no longer. I needed to follow Eric's instructions and show people what I was capable of, dispelling some of the myths around addiction in the process.

I'd driven to the Royal Navy's 'relocated' China Fleet Club, which sat on the Cornish bank of the River Tamar. The Ministry of Defence had sold the original Hong Kong premises in the build up to the handover and reinvested the profit closer to home. Leaving my car in the posh leisure club's landscaped parking area, I'd skirted their impressive driving range to get to the estuary, scrambling down a vertical bank of mud and exposed tree roots to reach the shoreline itself. A raft of tinder-dry driftwood provided the perfect fuel with which to build a two-foot-high and ten-foot-long pyre. Two hours later and I now stood shoeless looking out over a three-inch-deep carpet of glowing red embers.

This had better bloody work, Chrissy!

It was one thing to conduct such a feat with two thousand willing participants during a life-changing seminar, yet quite another coming down off drugs while alone on a deserted riverbank at dusk.

So long as I do everything Eric taught us, I rationalised, *I'll walk calmly over this red-hot rug without getting a single blister.*

No one knows why you don't end up in A&E following a firewalk. There are a few hypothesises, none of which involve running like fuck or applying special cream to your feet. All I knew was that *if* I put myself into a trance, I'd be fine.

I began to meditate, arms relaxed by my sides, staring dead ahead while taking deep breaths. I emptied my mind of clutter, until the sound of engines carrying across the water from the Tamar Bridge faded away, leaving the vehicle's headlights zipping like fireflies through the dark periphery of my vision.

'*Come* on! *Come* on! *Come* on!' I shouted into the magical half-light, shattering the tranquillity to psych myself up. Despite an audience of one, this was my crowning moment, a chance to demonstrate I had life firmly in my grasp.

'*Come* on! *Come* on! *Come* on!' I built to crescendo.

'*Whaaaah!*' I smashed a fist into my chest and stepped with purpose and unwavering self-belief onto the unforgiving embers.

'*Cool* moss! *Cool* moss! *Cool* moss!' I shouted, thus hoodwinking the pain receptors in my brain.

Walking at a sedate pace, I felt totally serene. Universal energy pulsed through my every molecule ... *I feel everything ... I am everything ... I can do anything!*

Before I knew it, I was wiping my feet on the clump of wet seaweed I'd placed at the end of the amber walkway so any hot ashes sticking to my feet wouldn't burn me when I exited the trance.

Well done, mate! I punched the air like a cup winner, completing the walk another five times, until the dying coals told me my work was done.

For someone ridiculed, rejected, pigeonholed and abandoned this wasn't about barefooting it across fire. It was so much more. I'd put money where my mouth is and proved that Chris Thrall had walked out of the wilderness and that he *still* had my six.

Back at Carroll Road, I cracked a beer and necked it, immediately opening another and rolling a spliff. Tucked down the side of the sofa was a large white envelope containing information detailing my upcoming educational experience at the One World University. I hadn't looked through any of it before, but now I soaked up every word and found it fascinating.

This wasn't your run-of-the-mill learn-by-numbers academia, the kind of functionalist suggestion implanted into the middle classes, with a certificate upon completion for not rocking the boat by daring to think freely. It went much deeper. We would learn to view the planet as an ecosystem and critique our position and responsibility within it.

Each day began with a communal meat-free breakfast followed by an hour of cleaning and maintaining the aging lodge. After this came a group assembly and lecture, a team Portuguese lesson, a school sports session, a vegetarian lunch, classroom time, afternoon tea and cakes, an individual learning period, dinner and then an evening program – for example, watching a film, music and singing, tobogganing, a sauna party or conducting a debate on an emerging global theory, philosophy or trend.

A sophisticated computer package outlined the objectives of the core curriculum and offered a range of group and individual tasks with points attached to each, three thousand being the required amount to graduate as a development instructor and climb aboard a plane bound for Africa. So you could read a groundbreaking text like *Gaia* or instructions for avoiding malaria and then complete an assessment on the computer to earn ten points. As a team, you might decide to ski thirty kilometres or sleep in a snow cave and earn a hundred points.

I stared in near disbelief at photographs of the school in its picture-postcard setting, nestling on top of one of the mountains that had hosted the 1994 Winter Olympics. Surrounded by dense pine forest, home to the moose, ptarmigan and bears Veronica had mentioned, the enormous lake shimmered emerald-green in the summer. In winter, tree branches sagged under a weight of snow, a soft white blanket laying all around. I looked forward to giving it my all in the organisation's very own Winter Olympics, during which we would compete against workers from Africa and students from Denmark and a newly opened school in the United States.

All of the students and teachers left the mountain to street fundraise for three two-week periods and spent a week in Denmark performing a play or opera in yet another inter-school competition. Other than this, the only student travelling up and down the mountain – to conduct a weekly food shop or deliver participants to and from Lillehammer railway station – was the designated driver, a British student, as under Norwegian law our full UK licences permitted us to operate a minibus. Along with overseeing the sports sessions, I knew which job I'd be volunteering for!

The program discussed the challenges students faced. For some it was the academic work, others selling £3,000 worth of postcards to strangers on a Scandinavian street. Many individuals had never taken part in a sport as an adult and most needed teaching how to cross-country ski. The odd numpty even got homesick!

I couldn't care less about these issues. Perusing the literature, taking in new words, phrases and concepts – many arising from something called 'Marxism' – I was *hooked*. The course was so much more than learning how to dig latrines and I couldn't wait to start.

Then, despite the alcohol buzz, my mood took a downturn as the thought of saving the school fees and fixing up my house lodged heavily in my mind. I massaged my forehead with a thumb and finger, rolled another spiff and cracked a third beer. It was tempting to focus on the negative, but Eric Jansen would have kicked me in the clappers and told me to man up. What would he suggest? He'd say, 'Action creates action.'

What action could I take, though? I would bank the thousand pounds from the British Legion and I had a little more to come from the tobacco runs. But how could I make up the shortfall?

Then it came to me ... *a world-record firewalk!*

That's what I would do!

I jumped to my feet, body alive, mind gripped by direction and certainty. *Yes!*

I'd find a place to set up my fire and then invite the public and ask them to make a donation to support my work in Africa. It seemed the answer to my prayers, so I got on the phone to Chunkity Chestnuts

'I'm in, Kristofan!' he bellowed. 'I'll be the event organiser and put the *full* weight of my promotion company behind it.'

All I needed now was a venue. My brother suggested Saltash Yacht Club because stoner Pat's father, Alan, was the commodore there. I called the venue and introduced myself and my mad plan.

An affable chap, Alan oozed enthusiasm, offering me the club's riverfront car park without hesitation. So that parents could bring their kids and to leave people's weekend free, Benny and I decided to hold the spectacular on 7pm the following Wednesday.

On the morning of the big day, Chingly Chunkenhammer turned up at mine clutching a green PVC banner scrounged from a pub landlord. 'Don't worry,' he assured me. 'I used to be a sign writer,' so I left him daubing 'Firewalk for Africa' in white gloss and spent several hours driving around the local area, collecting scrap wood and delivering it to the site.

Upon my return, 'How we getting on, mate?' I shouted over the garden wall.

'*Firing,* Kristobell. It's a *walk* in the park!' He chuckled at his clever wordplay. 'Do you dig?'

'I dig, mate. I'll look out for you on *Countdown.*'

I popped my head out the backdoor, expecting to see the finished item, but when I saw his progress my jaw dropped. '*What?*'

'What?' He held out innocent arms.

'Firewall 4 *Africa.* 'I slammed my keys down on the sideboard. 'Fucking hell, Chunks. We're not providing them with Internet security!'

'It's called antivirus ...' he mumbled.

'And where the hell is *AfricaO?*' I demanded, the name of the continent having a big splodge at the end of it.

'I wrote Afri*cans* by mistake.' His bottom lip tremored. 'But because you'll be feeding starving kids over there in Mogadishu, I covered it with a symbol.'

'Go on ...'

'A hamburger.'

After agreeing to meet Chunkfest at the yacht club around sixish, I repainted the slogan on the back of the banner. Then I stuffed twenty tin cans with rags soaked in a mixture of petrol and diesel. Come evening, I would place these improvised torches on either side of the firewalk, their wicked flames licking the dark to add further drama to the thirty-foot dare.

Down at the yacht club, I'd just finished stacking the wood when Chunks rocked up in the Pink Panther, Chelle in the front seat and the *full* weight of his promotion company squabbling in the back – Leroy, Kodiak, Benz, Hawk and Jack. 'Boys, get Uncle Christolow the wood we brought from the shed!' the media tycoon ordered.

I had to smile. In homage to my daring stunt, Chunks had wrapped a rising-sun bandana around his head, the mark of the kamikaze. You'd think he was risking his *own* life – or feet!

The clan went to the back of the Volvo and fetched a smashed-up bedside table, enough wood for them to donate a kindling-size piece each – the two youngest having to squabble over their bit. Give the Chungster credit, though, he had contacted the local radio station, Plymouth Sound, who'd broadcast news of the firewalk to the nation ... hence the three giggling teenagers that had gathered. He'd also arranged for the *Evening Herald* to take photographs and *Spotlight,* the local TV news, to film the event.

A car horn blared, shattering the waterside peace. I looked up to see the first of the yachties arriving for their Pimm's and lemonade.

'Excuse me!' the elderly seafarer shouted from the window of a Porsche, his bulbous whiskey nose matching a burgundy cravat. 'I'm trying to bloody *park* here!'

'Sir, we're holding a charity firewalk to raise money for children in Africa.' I kept it simple. 'If you'd be kind enough to leave the car outside.'

'What the *dickens* are you on about? Bloody *Africa!* I'm a *member* here for heaven's sake!'

'Sorry, but if you could park elsewhere, sir. Just for tonight.' I fought to keep my temper.

'Park *elsewhere?* We'll bloody see about that. *I* know the *commodore!'*

I smiled.

He left his Porsche in the middle of the gravel-strewn car park and stormed into the clubhouse to see Alan. Three minutes later, he stormed back out and parked elsewhere.

We went through similar temper-tantrums another five times, each accompanied by threats of 'Do *you* know who *I* am?' and 'We'll *see* about *this!*'

Chunks, not a man used to dealing with reality let alone upper-class thugs, grew increasingly edgy. 'How about we move it somewhere else?' His eyes pleaded.

'Like where?' I shrugged.

He scanned around for a spot to get these psycho sailors off our backs, his gaze fixing on the River Tamar. 'There!' he beamed. 'We'll do the world's first firewalk on water.'

'Mate, I'm not fucking Jesus!'

'We'll build a raft.'

'*No!*'

I felt let down he'd even considered such a thing. These snobby upstarts didn't intimidate me. Kids were starving in Africa – it was on the pretentious farts' precious BBC news. How could they sleep at night having tried to sabotage my efforts just so they could park their sportsters ten metres closer to the clubhouse?

To put the issue to bed, I torched the thirty-foot-long pyre and, handing them a bucket, asked the boys to approach the growing crowd for donations.

By the time the fire burned down to a pile of smouldering embers, the spectators had surged to over two hundred and the great British chant of 'Why are we waiting?' went up, adding to the suspense. I fetched a boogie box from the car and played house music at full volume. Then I raked the red-hot base into an even runway and set the cans of fuel-soaked rags on fire, marvelling at how spectacular the stunt set looked as dusk settled.

I kicked off my shoes and socks and changed into a sports vest and shorts – to dramatise the fact I was about to roll. On the booming dance track, a gorgeous-sounding black woman began singing about the world coming together as one, and as her appropriate message hyped the crowd still further, I experienced a moment of intense pride. There was *nothing* wrong with me.

The newspaper photographers arrived, as did my mother, brother and Mike. I stationed Benny next to a wet piece of carpet at the end of the runway, with strict instructions to make sure I wiped my feet before snapping out of the trance.

This was it. A glowing two-foot-wide pathway stood between me and my dream of helping those orphans in Mozambique. There was nothing more to do except walk, and I was ready.

I absorbed the dance music and the roar of the crowd, converting the energy into pure adrenaline. I stared up at the majestic bridge, focusing in the now, knowing my life would change forever as I earned my passage to Africa and made a mark in history.

With the exception of the soulful dance track, everything went silent. It was just me, my fixation on the burning mat and complete confidence in my ability. No one had ever walked barefoot over *thirty* feet of hot coals before, and I was about to become the first.

Go! Go! Go! Go! Go!

Allowing the crowd's encouragement to breach my controlled world, I felt invincible, invigorated and strong. *'Whoaaar!'* I smashed a fist into my chest and walked.

Although in trance, I sensed the soles of my feet contacting the ferocious embers, yet it felt as benign as bimbling along the beach. *Cool moss! Cool moss! Cool moss!* I bellowed, knowing I was halfway and it was going well.

Before I knew it, *'Wipe your feet!'* my brother screamed, clutching me as tears poured down his face.

I wiped my size 7s, snapped out of the spell and we hugged some more.

The crowd went wild.

I'd done it.

I was one step closer to Africa.

Motorbiking

For the benefit of my audience, I conducted the stunt three more times, delighting the newspaper guys, who snapped away eagerly. Unable to believe I hadn't burnt myself, they even photographed the soles of my feet. Back at Ben and Mike's house, we downed a large glass of Sang Tip, a sugary Thai whiskey, and shared a spliff. I felt like a million pounds and a *little* bit of a hero. I'd put my money where my mouth was *and* raised a good few quid.

A cheque for a thousand pounds arrived from the Royal British Legion and another from SSAFA, the Soldiers, Sailors, Airman and Families Association, for one hundred. Charlie's stepdad now paid sixty quid for each baccy run, and my bank account had £1800 in it. A few more weeks and I would have the money to pay the One World University and start fixing up the house.

Chugely Chuglebugler rang. 'Christmas Crackers, me old bean, have you seen the paper today? You got a *whole* page!'

'Really?'

'Really McFeeley. They've come up with a clever headline that – swit-*swoooooh* zzzz chisbizts'n tintz-tizt *ding!* – even beats my literary genius.'

I chuckled as I visualised the Changlemaster spewing his far-out Chunk-speak, a combination of random whistles like some elusive endangered bird, plus nonsensical words, clicks and chirps like a Tourette's sufferer attacked by a swarm of bees.

'Go on.' I crossed my fingers, hoping it wasn't cringeworthy.

'*Sole* Char, *Sole* Good!'

You had to laugh.

'They took a couple of cracking photos too.'

I walked to the corner shop and bought a copy of the *Evening Herald*. With a degree of trepidation, I thumbed through it on the way home, delighted to come across a quarter-page colour photograph of me striding confidently across the intimidating orange strip. Now that I'd cut back on the speed and recovered some muscle tone, I looked quite the athlete in my Adidas vest and shorts. Due to me being in trance, my steel-blue eyes pierced the darkening sky, projecting the image of someone on a mission.

Had the Department of Social Security not penalised me for rehabilitating myself from chronic ill health – without the help of professionals, support groups or God – I would be winging my way to Scandinavia right now to train as an international development instructor, preparing to help those even worse off than the mind-controlled civil servants with their grey personalities, sloping shoulders and foul coffee breath.

Yet, government red tape wasn't the only resistance I encountered. When I told Dad my plan to work with street children in Mozambique, he shook a puzzled head. 'Can't you get a *normal* job?' he replied, as if I'd announced my intention to become a serial killer.

For my mate Dan, viewing from the officers mess's crystal-cut windows, it was about the lack of career progression and financial recompense. '*Why* volunteer work?' he demanded, sounding clearly frustrated over the phone. 'Listen, I know people in the City who work for the big NGOs, yeah? I can get you a job with the Red Cross on thirty grand a year.'

Both Dan and my dad didn't get it. I *had* to go to Africa *and* offer my services for free or this whole recovery deal wouldn't work. Professing to help starving kids while leaching thirty thousand pounds from the very funds donated to support them would be an insult to us both.

In line with my developing philosophy that action creates action, the telephone rang. 'Hi, Chris. It's Katie. We met at the Wallington House rave.'

'*Hey* Katie!' I remembered her immediately. A while back, Chunks and I had gone to a wicked dance party thrown by the lord of our local manor. As the sun came up, Katie and I sat on cushions in the chill-out room, reassuring a chap who'd snorted way too much disco dust that he wasn't about to explode. She'd got my number from the newspaper article.

'Listen, I've got an idea how to raise some money,' she continued. 'Why don't you pop over to mine?'

Slightly older than me, Katie lived not far away in Lantern Park. She was cooking tea for her two teenage boys when I arrived. Smart and polite lads, it was clear to see they doted on their loving mum. 'I volunteer in Oxfam, Chris,' she said. 'If I borrow a collection tin, we can go around the Dance Academy on Saturday night and collect a few quid?'

It was a great idea.

Our evening went well and the party crowd were more than generous when reaching into their pockets, purses and wallets. Katie had kindly palmed me a pinger beforehand, which hit the spot as we moved around the chill-out areas showing clubbers the *Evening Herald* article. Seeing people's reactions, I was suddenly able to appreciate my efforts and experience a modest sense of pride.

By the end of the night, the charity shaker was full of notes and coins. We estimated about three hundred quid, meaning I could now transfer £2,230 to the One World University. Katie had the keys for the collection tin at home, so we agreed she would keep the cash safe until Monday.

A major motivation for overcoming addiction is the total fuck-around the lifestyle entails and the constant compromising of your moral standards. While accumulating demons in your head and skeletons in the closet, you meet a fuckload of nobheads *and* often have to prostitute yourself to them. I trusted Katie entirely, but her caring persona attracted sketchy hangers-on and common sense told me mixing drugs with business could turn sour.

On the Monday, 'Chris ...' Katie began.

Someone had stolen my money.

A letter arrived from the Halifax demanding I pay my mortgage arrears. While off my head in Hong Kong, I thought the bank had repossessed Carroll Road, but as it turned out my old man had covered some of the payments and got the letting agency on the case. I made an appointment with the bank's city centre branch, put on a suit and drove down there.

'Have you considered repossession, Mister Thrall?' asked the personal advisor, a straight-talking woman who seemed affable enough.

I hadn't.

'A lot of people find it a huge relief when they're in arrears,' she continued.

Just the word 'relief' sold me on the idea. *Why own a house if it only brings you aggro?* I rationalised, saying I would go away and think about it before handing over the keys.

'Nah!' My magical friend gave a vehement shake of his head. 'Tell them to freeze the interest and pay the bastards when you can, Chris.'

'Will that work?'

Sitting in the Wizard's garden shed – the Wizardess wouldn't let him smoke in the house – I took a drag of his spliff and checked the little Ziploc bag was safely in my sock.

'Mate, there's no law against owing money. They're just trying to fuck you over to protect their investment. What you owe is *nothing* compared to some people.'

It was excellent advice and another reminder of how the system makes no allowances for mental health illness. I felt a little disappointed the woman in the Halifax had tried to take advantage of me, as she didn't seem the type. I spoke to the bank, who informed me they had already frozen the debt and agreed to let me pay it off after my volunteer work.

I continued the tobacco runs with Charlie and Dents and paid the school in Norway, but then the Nissan's engine blew up. Luckily my actions continued to create action and the day before my twenty-ninth birthday I had a phone call from my mum saying she wanted me to visit her and Dave in Cornwall and would come and pick me up.

On the driveway of their modest house an immaculately restored vintage Suzuki 125cc motorcycle rested proudly on its stand. 'We heard you needed transport,' said my mum, 'and David saw this in Colin Flashman's window. We've taxed and MOTd it for you.'

My gentle giant of a stepfather stood astride the magnificent little machine, making it look a mere toy as he kicked it into life. *Nimm-nim-nim-nimmmm!* the metallic-blue beauty reacted like an angry wasp.

I felt made up – and not only with this thrilling mode of transport – as this was my mum's way of supporting my newfound direction.

David appeared from under the garage door with a helmet and gloves. 'Borrow these as long as you like.' He beamed.

I gave my mum a hug – a first for our family and another positive to come out of addiction – and hopped on the blue bullet to head for home.

I arrived back from Belgium early the next Saturday with my usual bottle of rum and five packs of baccy. I'd bought a carton of Lambert and Butler for Katie, having agreed to meet her in a dance club in Torquay that evening. The venue was a former monastery, complete with stained-glass windows, a pulpit and bell tower. Its tongue-in-cheek owner had gone full-sacrilege to come up with the fiendishly cryptic name ... *The* Monastery. I looked forward to the twenty-mile journey on my new motorbike, not a powerful beast but a great fun ride.

Unfortunately, rain bucketed down adding further misery to the afternoon's horrific events. In defiance of Northern Ireland's Good Friday Agreement, a splinter group claiming to be the 'Real' IRA had detonated one of the biggest bombs in the history of the troubles. In the market town of Omagh, it killed twenty people and injured hundreds more, a woman pregnant with twins being among the dead.

I packed Katie's cigarettes and a change of clothes into a daypack and strapped it to the pillion seat with a bungee cord. Then I fired up all one hundred and twenty-five of my cubic centimetres and shot off up the A38, the flimsy Millets waterproofs I wore on the outside of my body belying the heart of a speed racer within.

The wind kicked up and rain came at me sideways. Despite wearing a sturdy leather jacket under the waterproofs – one Mike had kindly lent me – I was soaked to the skin in seconds. Every minute or so, a car or truck blasted past, frightening the life out of me, yet unperturbed I pressed on ten miles to the Torquay turnoff. It was a huge relief to leave the dangerous dual carriageway and take a sheltered back road into the seaside town.

Although unnecessary, I decided to check the daypack was safe, pulling to a stop and glancing over my shoulder.

What?

There was nothing, not even the bungee.

My heart pounded. It was probably the next worse experience to turning around and finding your pillion passenger gone. I felt sick at the loss *and* the shear inconvenience of having to ride all the way back to Plymouth to begin searching for the bag, with no guarantee I would find it.

My new jeans, shirt and skate shoes and the two hundred ciggies for Katie *gone,* along with the daypack itself. There was no point continuing on to the club. I was wet through, and besides, I couldn't say goodbye to my belongings that easily.

The problem was the central reservation's metal crash barrier because it blocked my view of the opposite carriageway as I motored back to Plymouth. To get around this, I got the bike into fifth gear in the outside lane and stood on tiptoes on the foot pegs, scouring the oncoming lanes for any dark lump that might be the khaki bag.

Luckily for me, approaching midnight the traffic had eased off. Unluckily, I rode the ten miles home and still couldn't find my stuff. Rather than stop at Carroll Road, I went around to my brother's. Benny was in Phuket for a fortnight, seeing his girlfriend and looking for a job. He'd left me the keys for his Metro in case of an emergency – although I doubt he'd envisaged one such as this. I reversed out of the drive and floored it towards the A38.

Not holding out much hope, I combed the road using the figure-of-eight pattern taught to us in the fieldcraft phase of commando training. Christ knows how I hoped to find my bag, but with the bit between my teeth I continued forth into the storm.

A mile out of the city, a small white stick in the carriageway caught my eye. It looked immediately out of place on the glistening black tarmac. As I drew near, the Metro's headlights picked up another one ... then another ... and another ... until the whole roadway was covered in little white sticks – of the cigarette variety.

One of my skate shoes sat in the outside lane, so I slammed on the brakes and skidded to a stop on the hard shoulder. Leaving the hazard lights flashing, I ran over and grabbed the wayward footwear, delighted to now have enough of the right attire should my left leg ever want to take up skateboarding.

The loose cigarettes were sodden, but my spirit soared like Eddie the Eagle when I spotted a whole packet ... crashing like Icarus as I realised the flap had been ripped off along with all the filters.

My backpack had been subjected to the same injustice. I spied the odd canvas strap, clip and buckle, leading me to the other shoe. Then I waited, heart in mouth, as yet another juggernaut gave my possessions a good trampling. Finally, after running fifty yards up the highway I had all my belongings, but the result wasn't brilliant.

I'll give the Monastery a miss tonight, I thought and drove home.

Dover or Bust

At 3.05am, we exited the Channel Tunnel and Charlie drove us up the ramp towards the platform's exit gates. Denton and a slightly older chap named Kempy were the other runners in the car. Charlie's BMW was being serviced, so Shotgun had lent us the Cabriolet again, which although new felt a banger in comparison.

So far we'd been lucky with our smuggling runs, managing to avoid customs' searches, but the authorities were clamping down on the illegal trade and several gangs had been pulled. Drawing upon his Borstal education, Shotgun came up with an algorithm he reckoned the bigger criminals employed to protect their investment. Rather than go lighter on the tax-free tobacco, you smuggled even more, thus increasing overall profit and minimising the loss should the authorities confiscate a consignment.

But what about ending up in jail? I wondered, figuring X was missing from Shotgun Freddy's equation.

Heading out of the port, we silently congratulated ourselves on the extra-large bounty, so complacent it never occurred to us the shit might hit the fan.

Blue lights erupted ...

Sirens wailed ...

Cop cars swooped ...

The shit had hit the fan.

'Fuck!' Charlie stomped on the accelerator.

A patrol car cut across our path.

Charlie jumped on the brakes and began punching the steering wheel. *'Fuck! Fuck! Fuck!'*

'Charlie, calm the *fuck* down, man!' I shouted.

'My stepdad's gonna fucking *kill* us!'

'I'll kill you if you don't shut up,' I replied.

'Oh *fuck ...*' sighed Kempy, who'd recently served ten months inside after the cops caught him unloading a rental truck full of bootleg baccy. 'Looks like I'm back in the nick.'

I cursed our readiness to comply with Shotgun's greedy agenda, carrying double the amount of product for a measly sixty quid. Africa suddenly seemed a long way away. I could imagine Veronica's disappointment when I told her I wouldn't be attending the school due to unforeseen circumstances – namely being bummed in the shower by a bloke with the prefix 'Nails'.

A police officer climbed out of the nearest patrol car and swaggered over. 'Gentlemen, follow that customs vehicle and don't try anything stupid.'

'What, like scratching our nose with an elbow?' Dents piss-took in his funny Janner drawl.

'Fuck off, Jethro.' The officer scowled and walked back to his copmobile.

As the customs vehicle led us to an enormous operations shed, we were silent, each wishing this wasn't happening. Then Charlie began flapping about Shotgun's tobacco again – to a salvo of, 'Shut the *fuck* up, Chas!' Inside the shed a customs officer in a dark-blue jumpsuit indicated Charlie park in one of several rows of dubious-looking motors, the large number of white Toyota minivans being the obvious clue as to their owners' crimes.

'Right,' said the officer, lowering his head to look through the window, 'if you lot can shift yourselves over there and leave everything where it is.' He nodded to a plastic bench arrangement running along the nearest wall.

'What about this?' I held up an EastEnders carrier bag containing my five packs of baccy and bottle of rum.

'Nice try.' He gave me a wry smile.

We watched in agony – actually, we watched Charlie in agony – as two customs guys removed the black bags of Golden Virginia and Cutter's Choice from the Escort's boot.

One of the men looked at Charlie and held up a bin liner. 'Mate, how many?'

'Ton in each,' Chas replied, saving the officers the job of counting by confirming what they already knew – that serious runners fill the bags with a hundred packets to make distribution easier.

'Cheers for that.' The chap scribbled a calculation on the back of his hand in biro.

By the time they'd finished gathering potential evidence, the sun was coming up, filling the dismal shed with rays of false hope. The searchers sealed everything inside blue plastic tubs, labelled these heavy duty containers and stowed them in the car.

'They've put it *back!'* said Dents, thinking we'd got away with it for personal use.

'Nah.' I hated to point out the obvious. 'The other cars are full of tubs too.'

A customs officer approached. 'Right, who's the driver?'

Charlie raised his hand.

'Okay, if you come with me *and...* ' – he scanned along the bench for a second interrogatee – *'you.'*

Something about my face meant I always got picked for a shit sandwich but never the England team.

Charlie and I followed him to a portacabin set against the far wall of the enormous metal structure. It was a far cry from the cop-shop-and-cuffs I'd been expecting, but customs were going to try and force a confession out of us and the thought of a night in an actual police station made me go firm on my response – *deny everything!*

Inside the portacabin were two doors, Charlie ushered through one, me the other. In my room, a man in a white shirt with gold insignia sat behind a desk. He invited me to a chair and after preliminaries, said, 'So if you admit to smuggling, we'll call this a day. You can go home until the court case.'

'Smuggling!' My facial expression highlighted the absurdity of this allegation ... that we both knew was true.

'You've got one thousand five hundred packets of tobacco. How come?'

'I like smoking.'

'According to your passport, you've been across the channel

thirty-eight times in six months. How do you explain this?'

'I don't have to.'

As my eyes wandered around the cramped office, the guy interviewing Charlie entered and whispered in his boss's ear.

The two of them threw me sly glances.

'Right, your friend's told us everything,' the head honcho announced.

'Okay, that's good.' I made to get up.

'So you're standing by this being for personal use?'

'Yes, sir.'

If I stuck to our official story – which I knew Charlie would – they couldn't prosecute us for smuggling due to the loophole in the law. Namely, there *was* no law, not around how many packets you could import for personal use.

When Chas and I reunited, we gave each other the *Did you say anything?* look and shook our heads, but the head honcho had one last trick up his pristine white sleeve.

'So we'll make this simple. If you're saying all this tobacco' – he pointed at the car – 'is for personal use, then you can drive away now, *but* you'll all have to come back and face smuggling charges. The other option is to leave everything here and we'll take no further action.'

'Including the car?' Charlie asked sheepishly.

'Including the car.'

I looked at Charlie. He looked at Dents and Kempy. We began walking towards the shed door.

The customs guys weren't stupid. They obviously had an officer parked at the EastEnders warehouse recording British number plates. And which petty criminal would take on the might of the law and expect to win? The head honcho knew, given the option, we would dump the car.

As we headed into Dover to hop on a bus bound for London, I could see the strain on Charlie's face as he anticipated Shotgun's reaction. I could also see the tobacco running and the easy money it provided was over.

Man Down

'Chris, you're *never* gonna go to Africa!' Daryl shook her head the moment I mentioned my plan.

I'd met Daryl and Kev a couple of years ago at one of Simon's parties but had kept my distance in recent times, what with speed for companionship. Kev was a market trader and Daryl a stay-at-home mum to their four gorgeous kids. I thought the world of them, particularly Daryl, who was one of life's solid characters.

I was upset Daryl didn't believe me about Africa. In her defence, she'd grown up in Plymouth's toughest borough and knew addiction only too well. Having lost several friends and relatives to drug overdoses, Daryl had heard all the grand promises and phoney resolutions before. I wouldn't bullshit people, though. If I said I was going to do something, I would.

Rather than show my hurt, 'How about a pizza?' I suggested, figuring it would go well with the cans of Holsten Pils the ever-generous Kev had in the fridge. My trusty little motorbike was parked in the street and I sought any excuse to hop on it.

'Yeah, go for it,' said Daryl. 'Do you need any money?'

'Nah.' I shouted down the garden path. 'I got this.'

I scanned up and down the road ...

Fuckers!

The motorbike was gone.

I walked back inside. 'Bike's been nicked.' I shrugged.

'Fuck off, Chris!' Daryl chuckled.

'No, it has.'

Kev stared at me, grinning like an inbred while waiting for the punchline.

There wasn't one.

The police phoned me back in the morning to say they'd found the Suzuki smashed to bits in a field. According to them, there was nothing worth recovering, so I never saw my vintage racer again.

Good to his word, my bro jacked in his job at the metal workshop and bought a one-way ticket to the Land of Smiles. On his previous visit, he'd secured a role as a stage rigger at Phuket Phantasy, a popular theme park, and so was all set for a new life in the sun.

Following an evening spent drinking Thai whiskey and smoking hash, Ben, Mike, Charlie and I crashed out one by one. I was expecting Ben to wake us up when Charlie drove him to Bretonside Bus Station at 5am to board a coach for Heathrow. The problem was no one heard the alarm – if there ever was one.

Opening my eyes in a drunken stupor, I glanced at the G-Shock. *'Guys,* you're *three* hours late!'

'Oh … *shit!'* Benny leapt off the couch and began flapping like a chicken with its armpits on fire.

'Fuck the bus. I'll drive you to London,' Charlie offered without hesitation. 'Can someone hop in with us?'

Both Mike and I insisted on going.

Ben's flight left Heathrow at 11am. Taking his checking-in time into consideration left us a little over two hours to drive two hundred and twenty miles. We didn't even have time for a cuppa. Ben grabbed his bag and we piled into Charlie's BMW and roared off.

Fortunately, the roads were quiet and Charlie was able to cruise at 130mph in the outside lane. We even had time for coffee before Benny went through to the departure lounge.

'Gonna miss you, mate.' I gave him a long hug.

'You too, brother.'

And that was it. Ben lived in Thailand.

Charlie, whose loyal gesture I would never forget, drove home at a somewhat more sedate speed. I sat in silence in the sports car's cramped rear. When we pulled into Mike's road, Chas drove past the house and stopped five doors down.

'What ya doing, you fucking bellend?' Mike stared at him, aghast.

'Parking the car!' Charlie defended himself. 'What do you think I'm doing?'

'It's the *wrong* fucking house!' Mike shot me a look.

'*Charlie!*' I snapped. 'Have you got your contact lenses in?'

'Nah, I left 'em at home.'

'So you just drove us to London and back and you can't even spot a house five fucking metres away?'

'I got you there, didn't I?'

True.

'Chris, do you wanna come in for a bit?' said Mike, noticing my dip in mood.

'If you don't mind, mate,' I replied, unable to face going back to my desolate pad.

As I slumped on Mike's couch, the enormity of the situation came crushing down. I couldn't believe my little brother, the chap I loved more than anyone else in the world, had left for good. My head dropped into my hands. 'I'm going to miss him ...' was all I could manage before the floodgates opened.

Mike went to the fridge, grabbed two of the leftover beers and pressed one into my hand. 'You'll be okay, Chris,' he said. 'Just think how far you've come.'

Leaving on a Jet Plane

My brother had surpassed me in the adventure stakes and now it was my turn to go walkabout. The February 1st deadline loomed and I didn't want to let Veronica down by delaying another six months, especially with people questioning my worth.

With mixed feelings, I took up a brush dipped in emulsion and stared at my mural. My designs proved I wasn't the failure the education system had made me out to be and it was a shame to see them go. 'Onwards and upwards, Chrissy!' I grinned and began slapping paint on the bionic spider.

Decorating the house had been my sticking point with respect to leaving the country. I'd done my best with limited funds, borrowing a carpet-cleaning machine and employing more initiative than cash to complete the rest of the superficial makeover. Using ink cartridges from colouring pens, I tinted some cans of magnolia paint recovered from a skip and now the bathroom walls resembled a shade that could pass as 'Lavender Blush' and the bedrooms 'Botswana Blue'.

Seeing me unable to progress, certainly not to the standard a letting agency required, my dear mum stepped in. *'Go* to Norway,' she ordered, promising to find me a lodger.

Simon hadn't done too well with the drugs since leaving prison. In a last ditch attempt to help my mate before leaving the country, I set up a firewalk on Dartmoor. Simon charged across the red-hot coals with total belief and not a trace of fear.

The problem was my brother from another mother had unresolved childhood trauma and a deeply shattered sense of self-worth. Simon once told me he had tracked down his absent father. After my bro had introduced himself, his old man said, *'What* are you doing turning up here?' and slammed the door.

Naturally, I wanted the best for my mate, but it was Catch 22. While masking your issues with drugs, you don't develop the skills needed to move on from addiction. Plus, you're not accruing social capital, such as employment history, wide-ranging life experience, regular income, stable accommodation, positive friends and so forth, which reward your efforts and motivate you to sustain change.

I spent my final forty-eight hours in the UK injecting speed and getting my gear together. I laid every item of clothing and equipment needed to survive a Norwegian winter *and* a tropical African summer in kit-muster fashion on the bed. As I listened to Macy Gray's 'I Try' for the umpteenth time, the confusion of sleep deprivation kicked in. I *couldn't* fuck this up. My bus and flight ticket were non-refundable and the school was expecting me.

A strange jittery sensation descended on my head and torso. I hadn't felt like this before, at least not in the security of my own home. I felt *extremely* nervous, as if something bad might happen. I began to doubt myself and worry about the road ahead.

This is stupid ...!

I wasn't afraid of a poxy trip to Norway or of new experiences, so why was I feeling edgy?

Yet again, I checked through the gear in as methodical manner as possible given my current headspace – winter hat, gloves, jacket, T-shirts, thermals, socks and boxers, swimming shorts, jeans, snow trousers, tracksuit bottoms, trainers, cross-country ski boots, flip-flops, sleeping bag, camera and film, binoculars, towel and wash bag, sunscreen, sunglasses, mosquito net and repellent, fishing tackle, snorkelling gear, sheath knife – until I felt certain I had every eventuality covered.

I cooked up a hit from the last bag of speed I would consume for god knows how long. With the school's rule about no drugs and alcohol was I going to miss getting high? *Hah!* I wouldn't even think about it. I was going on an adventure, meeting each day *full* on. I would take a couple of syringes worth of gear for the bus journey and a blim of hash for my night at Stansted Airport. Then that was it for the foreseeable future as far as substances went.

The thought of getting rid of the drug paraphernalia increased my edginess. I worried I might leave a syringe lying around for my parents to find. There was also airport police, sniffer dogs and customs to negotiate. What if some fucking K-9 GD-2 shoes caught a whiff of hash on my clothing and barked the place down? This wouldn't put me off taking the remaining gear to London, though, as I was still addicted to a certain degree and didn't have that option.

I loosened the drawstring on my bergen, pulled open the neck and scanned the piles of clothes and kit. *This is really it!*

I was about to place a fleece Mum had kindly made me into the backpack when the doorbell rang. It was Emily. 'So you're leaving?' she asked, and then sensing my anxiety, 'Are you okay?'

'I feel weird. Like really on edge.'

'Come here.' She gave me a huge hug. 'It's anxiety, Chris, but you'll be fine, honestly.'

Her words were comforting and somehow I knew everything would come good.

'Chris, I need to say something to you.' Emily stared into my eyes, her own ones welling up.

'What is it, hun?'

'I wanted to thank you for what you've done for my son. Alan loves you more than his own dad and I won't *ever* forget it.'

We embraced in silence and it felt warm and wonderful. I was pleased to have helped, but I loved that kid too. He was my mate and no one owed me anything.

I had a similarly humbling experience when I said goodbye to my neighbours. They all wished me well, particularly Jane's boyfriend. *'Chris!'* he screamed, dragging me into the house and shoving a beer in my hand. *'Don't* go to Africa. Our Kayleigh thinks the *world* of you, man!'

I left the house the next day intending to lock the front door and never look back. Having climbed into the straps of my bergen, daypack front and centre, I was about to slam the door when an anorak approached clutching a clipboard.

'Excuse me, sir,' said the man. 'I'm from the TV licencing company. Are you the owner of the property?'

'Unfortunately for me, I am, and *God* be damned, it's been the *curse* of Satan.'

'I'm sorry?' The guy frowned, demonic wrath being a difficult subject to negotiate.

'Look!' I swung my rucksack around. *'Can't* you see those heinous beasts have forced me onto the street?'

'So ... *who's* living here now?'

'Termites, sir!'

'I'm sorry?'

'Millions of the cretinous swine. Made quite a nest for themselves, they have – or should I say, *labyrinth.* Eaten me out of house and home. *No,* make that *eaten* my home!'

'Oh ... I see.' Trembling, he eyed the property as sweat flooded his Hush Puppies. 'So *no one's* going to be living here?'

'Not unless you include David Attenborough and a BBC film crew.'

The guy kept looking for a tick box on his pad. I don't think eating-disordered insects needed a TV licence. He tilted his head to look at my backpack. *'Erh ...?'*

'Homeless.' I shrugged. 'From now on it's the open road for me. Nothing but the *sun* in my ears, the *stars* in my hair, the *wind* in my toes ...'

'Well –'

'Catching what I grill, *grilling* what I catch, *eating* it over an open fire ...'

'Yes, I see –'

'Wherever I lay my head will be my home ...'

He was gone.

As the Ryanair flight trundled onto the apron at Stansted, I relaxed back in my seat. Having injected the last syringe of amphetamine twelve hours ago, I felt tired but unbelievably happy. I gazed out of the tiny window, watching the sun rise over Essex, a million and one memories floating through my mind.

Throughout the darkest of times, for *three* years, I'd remained proud of who I was and never lost my self-belief. When reality finally dawned, I'd reflected on my life choices, made the appropriate adjustments and stuck to the plan. Even at my lowest point, I'd been able to look in the mirror and respect the person staring back. I may not be out of the woods, but *nothing* phased me. This evening, I would be on top of a rugged Norwegian mountain, studying to help those less fortunate in Mozambique. I would be the epitome of what Team means, hitting the ground running and working hard to excel at every task put in front of me.

My future would never sink as low as that squalid pit in which I'd gone mad in Wan Chai. Return to Hong Kong? *Nah.* I would never forget the Fragrant Harbour and still felt determined to get to the bottom of the Foreign Triad business, but Hong Kong was simply another of life's rich experiences, and one experience would never define who I was. There were plenty more to come, my bucket list would see to that.

The master of my destiny was steering the good ship *Christopher* once more. I thought back to Old Man Lee reading my twenty-five-year-old palm in the *dai pai dong* restaurant that time. 'You have some *very* difficult years ahead,' he'd warned me. 'But when you reach thirty years old, you will be the *happiest* man you know!'

I would celebrate my thirtieth birthday while working with amazing human beings in a dream job, supporting vulnerable street children under Mother Africa's beautiful sky.

As the wheels of the plane left the runway and flight FR32 soared into the airspace above London, tears poured down my face.

You did it, Chrissy ... You did it, mate.

There was *nothing* wrong with me.

In Memory

'Vince' Lee Hok Keung
Simon Preece
Barbara Wright
David Wright

Acknowledgements

A huge thank you to my *Eating Smoke* readers who urged me to write a follow-up. To a dedicated delta team of Mike 'Rosco' Ross (RIP), Steve Glazebrook, Sian Forsythe, Marc Spender, Mel Eggleton, Kenneth Fossaluzza, Nikki Davenport, Dani Von Der Fecht, Pat Burke and Claire Nance for your feedback on the manuscript. Likewise, to my Jenny for her professional input around substance misuse and addiction and support telling this story, and to my three-year-old, Harry, for challenging me to a 'Fight?' when I should be writing

Chris Thrall

Chris Thrall was born in South-East London. A former Royal Marines Commando, he served in the Northern Ireland Conflict and trained in parachuting and Arctic warfare and survival. In 2011, Chris wrote the bestselling memoir *Eating Smoke,* detailing his descent into crystal meth psychosis while working as a nightclub doorman for the Hong Kong triads. A qualified pilot, skydiver and keen snowboarder, Chris has explored over eighty countries across seven continents, including backpacking through all of North, South and Central America. In 2018, he ran the length of Britain, an ultramarathon a day for #999miles, unsupported and carrying a 14kg backpack, to highlight the issue of veterans suicide. Chris has firewalked over red-hot coals to raise money to work with street children in Mozambique. He has driven aid workers to India and back by coach and scuba-dived in the Antarctic Polar Circle. In 2001, the Finnish Nation awarded Chris their Second Level Commendation on the grounds of human generosity. He has a degree in youth work and is a life coach and addiction specialist. Chris lives with his partner and son in the UK and plans to continue adventuring and charity work.

christhrall.com
facebook.com/christhrallauthor
twitter.com/christhrall
instagram.com/chris.thrall
youtube.com/christhrall

Subscribe to Chris's newsletter and receive updates, videos, motivational tips and complimentary books:
christhrall.com/mailing-list

Books by Chris Thrall

NON-FICTION

Eating Smoke: One Man's Descent into Crystal Meth Psychosis in Hong Kong's Triad Heartland

Forty Nights

How to Write a Memoir (**FREE** – link on newsletter)

FICTION

The Hans Larsson series

The Drift (**FREE** – link on newsletter)

The Trade

Services by Chris Thrall

Motivational Speaking

Life Coaching

Writing Guidance and Mentoring

Sessions to suit YOU via phone or video calls

Please visit christhrall.com for further information or email info@christhrall.com to arrange a FREE consultation